Spiritual Emotions

Spiritual Emotions

A PSYCHOLOGY OF CHRISTIAN VIRTUES

Robert C. Roberts

WILLIAM B. EERDMANS PUBLISHING COMPANY
GRAND RAPIDS, MICHIGAN / CAMBRIDGE, U.K.

Published 2007 by
Wm. B. Eerdmans Publishing Co.
2140 Oak Industrial Drive N.E., Grand Rapids, Michigan 49505 /
P.O. Box 163, Cambridge CB3 9PU U.K.

Printed in the United States of America

12 11 10 09 08 07   7 6 5 4 3 2 1

Library of Congress Cataloging-in-Publication Data

Roberts, Robert Campbell, 1942-
    Spiritual emotions: a psychology of Christian virtues / Robert C. Roberts.
        p.   cm.
    Includes bibliographical references.
    ISBN 978-0-8028-2740-1 (pbk.: alk. paper)
    1. Emotions — Religious aspects — Christianity.   I. Title.

    BV4597.3.R63   2007
    248.2 — dc22

                                        2007009304

www.eerdmans.com

Contents

Preface

This book is a descendant of *Spirituality and Human Emotion* (Wm. B. Eerdmans Publishing Co., 1982). Five of the chapters are touched-up versions of chapters from the earlier book; the other seven are new additions. Since the publication of the earlier book, the emotions have become a hot topic in a number of academic disciplines: philosophy, psychology, anthropology, neuroscience, and history. In each of those disciplines, some work has been devoted to religious emotions as a part of the academic study of religion. More than a century ago Friedrich Schleiermacher, Rudolf Otto, and William James gave religious emotions treatments of very different kinds from that of the present work, and even earlier Jonathan Edwards offered a theological account of Christian emotions that still stands as a classic. But in recent theology the emotions still have not been given a thorough treatment. This book is perhaps a beginning for a renewal of theological and pastoral inquiry into the emotions. The basic view of emotions on which the present book trades is explained in greater depth and in more detailed interaction with the scholarly literature in my book *Emotions: An Essay in Aid of Moral Psychology* (Cambridge University Press, 2003).

Chapter 7 was originally published as "The Logic and Lyric of Contrition" in *Theology Today* 50 (1993): 193-207. Chapter 3 is a revision of "Tolstoy and Freud on Our Need for God" in *Should God Get Tenure? Essays on Religion and Higher Education* edited by David Gill (Wm. B. Eerdmans Publishing Company, 1997). I thank the Wm. B. Eerdmans Publishing Company and the editors of *Theology Today* for permission to use these materials. Unless otherwise indicated, Bible quotations are from the New International Version (Grand Rapids: Zondervan, 1973).

I thank Richard Olmsted, Neal Plantinga, and Linda Zagzebski for comments that improved Chapter 7, and Ellen Charry for a comment that improved Chapter 2. Richard and Neal both also influenced the earlier book in some ways that remain in the present one. Elizabeth Vanderkooy Roberts has given me helpful suggestions, and I dedicate this book to her, in gratitude for her love.

PART ONE

A Christian Psychology of Emotion

CHAPTER ONE

Emotions and Christian Teaching

CHURCH SHOPPING

In 1984 Elizabeth and I, with our three young children, moved to a new town and began looking for a congregation of Christians among whom to worship and work. Elizabeth had grown up in the Christian Reformed Church, an ethnically Dutch denomination of a Reformed character, and I in the United Presbyterian Church. We had been Presbyterians in our former town in Kentucky, so we visited a local Presbyterian congregation. In the new place, unlike the one we had come from, were a couple of Christian Reformed congregations, so we included them in our shopping tour. One of the congregations was almost a caricature of the Christian Reformed Church: worship, it seemed, consisted in *being explained-to*. The congregation sat passively while the Ten Commandments were read, with a bit of explanation; a passage from the Heidelberg Catechism was read and explained; some passages of scripture were read, and the sermon was an explanation of them. I don't want to give the impression that the service consisted *entirely* of explanations, because we did sing some hymns (we even stood up to do so). But before each of them, the pastor gave a short explanation of the hymn-text. As a philosophy teacher, I go to lectures (and give them myself) rather frequently, and was a little disheartened by the prospect of making Sunday morning just another day of the week.

If I remember right, it was just after that super-CRC experience that our new next-door neighbors invited us to worship with their Episcopal congregation. Being as denominationally promiscuous as most Protestants these days, we were game. That church was in some respects Anglo-Catholic and in others Evangelical and Charismatic. The congregation received little explanation of texts, though theologically rich texts abounded: four scripture lessons, wonderful prayers of thanksgiving and confession, the Nicene Creed, and the liturgy, which is a rehearsal of the whole history of salvation. The sermons might have been a source of instruction, but they were short and not very definite. The congregation moved their bodies a lot in participation: kneeling for prayers, crossing themselves, processing in and out, bowing before the altar, walking to the rail to receive the body and blood of the Lord, reaching out to take the food and drink; and the more charismatically inclined would raise their arms in adoration and sometimes softly mutter affirmations. The clergy were fully vested in the colors of the church year season. As the months went by we discovered that the worship space was sometimes filled with the smell of incense, and with more time the new choirmaster introduced Latin motets and the music was Very Good.

And so we became Episcopalians. A few blocks from our house was a Baptist church that I visited sometime later. I told a deacon I was a visitor, and he welcomed me and showed me where to sit. This service was as "liturgical" as the Episcopal one, but in a quite different way. Little of the "liturgy" was written down (no prayer book was in evidence), though it did seem to be standardized, after a fashion. Texts were far less evident than in the other two churches. After a while the choir, which was about half the congregation, came in dancing and singing, and this processional seemed to light a fire in the rest of the congregation. Some of them yelled encouragement to the choir, some joined in the singing, and some stood up and sort of swayed in place, to the music. The preacher preached far, far longer than the Episcopal priest did, and more definitely: he told the people how to live. In the midst of the sermon, people would wail or sing out prayers. When the excited preacher said something especially impressive, members of the congregation would yell encouragement to him, or thank God for what he had just said, and this seemed to make him more excited still. Every cinder block in the walls seemed to ring with spiritual intensity of joy, thanksgiving, contrition, and hope.

An issue raised by all three of these worship styles is how to integrate Christianity into the lives of believers — how to facilitate people's becoming more spiritual. All three congregations are descendants of the apostles, and each has its own special way of incorporating the apostolic tradition into the lives of the particular people who make up the congregations. In the Christian Reformed congregation, the main approach seems to be instruction: getting the individual believer to know what he or she believes, to be detailed and articulate in his grasp of the church's teaching. The teaching must be embedded in individual believers, not just "out there" in the tradition, in the prayerbook, or in the Bible; each individual member is to know and understand it as well as possible.

In the Episcopal experience the engendering of spirituality in the service seems to come primarily from reading — from the Bible and the Book of Common Prayer — in the context of a sensory dramatization. The apostolic tradition is there in all its glory — in the books. Far more of that tradition is voiced — that is, read from the book — on any given Sunday morning than in the Baptist service I attended. But of explanation there is very little. Often the sermon is not exploited as a forum for careful doctrinal instruction, and relatively little effort is expended to make individual believers understand what they believe. In some congregations, though not the one we joined, Christian teaching is, as *teaching,* an outright embarrassment, a stumbling block of foolishness: the doctrines are not to be believed, but somehow their "spirit" is to be experienced through the liturgy. How, then, does the apostolic tradition make its way into individual lives? Palpable drama, complete with stage-setting, incorporates it. The believer embodies the tradition in his gestures, by immersion in the sounds and smells, the beauty of the sanctuary, the woodwork, the windows, the vestments; the trappings of ancient tradition evoke a kind of historical nostalgia. Here, spirituality is chiefly by sensation or mood rather than emotion. Or one might say, the emotion I experience is not exactly *my* emotion, but the *Church's* (where "the Church" is the historical institution as a whole). One is almost tempted to call this spirituality by theater.

By contrast, in the Baptist church I visited, the mode of spiritual incorporation seems to be straightforwardly emotion. They teach that Jesus Christ is the Lord and Savior (without too much theological detail), and get excited about it. They weep for their sins and rejoice in their salvation.

In this book I want to think with you about the role of emotion in Christian spirituality, and I shall argue that it is an essential medium in which Christian teachings get incorporated into the life of the individual believer. I will not be advocating any particular denomination or worship style as best at fostering the spiritual emotions in Christians; clearly, this can happen in any of the denominations, and can fail to happen in any of them (including the "emotional" ones). I hope that through reflecting about what emotions are, how they are formed, and the nature of particular spiritual emotions such as joy, contrition, hope, gratitude, compassion, and peace, we can all become more faithful Christians and better nurturers of those whose lives we influence.

THREE RECENT REVOLUTIONS

In the past twenty-five or thirty years, three revolutions have shaken the fields of psychology and ethics. First, ethics has turned psychological. For the nineteenth and most of the twentieth centuries, ethics was about rules for action. It was about duties and permissions and prohibitions, and philosophers sat around their seminar tables asking what the basis of the ethical rules was. Then in 1958 the Christian philosopher Elizabeth Anscombe published one of the most influential philosophy papers of the twentieth century, "Modern Moral Philosophy," in which she pointed out that the only legitimate basis for the ought-rules was God. She pointed out that the idea of a command without a commander didn't make sense, and that the only commander with general authority over all human beings was God. But very few philosophers in those days believed in God. So in asking for the basis of the ethical rules, they were asking a question for which they had excluded beforehand the only reasonable answer. For them, the whole busy discussion of ethics as action-rules was a dead end. She proposed that, instead of thinking about action-rules, ethicists should think about the virtues in the way ancient philosophers such as Plato and Aristotle did — human traits like justice, generosity, truthfulness, and compassion, qualities that make a human person a good specimen of the human kind. That little seed took a while to germinate, but in 1981 Alasdair MacIntyre published *After Virtue,* one of the most famous philosophy books of the twentieth century, calling for a return to the virtues as a way of ending the interminable ethical disagreements that plague people in modern societies. MacIntyre's book began a renaissance of thinking about the virtues. But virtues are traits of character, and traits of character are a subject for psychology. So ethics has taken a psychological turn, and philosophers now regularly engage in a discipline they call "moral psychology," which is reflection about ethical traits, ethical motivation, ethical emotions, and ethical understanding and judgment.

A second and complementary revolution is that psychology has turned ethical. Professional psychology (therapeutic and experimental psychology) used to pride itself on being "value-free," ethically neutral. And yet psychology of all kinds, whether it be clinical psychology, neuroscience, or personality theory, always operates with some notion of what is "normal" or "healthy," and the farther one moves away from purely physical functioning, the more controversial the ideas of "normal" and "healthy" become. That is, these notions become less a matter of pure science, and more a matter of worldview — more like ethics, especially if one thinks of ethics as a study of the virtues. The clinician wants to help people function *well* (or better); the neuroscientist has to have some idea of the *proper* functioning of the brain; the personality theorist necessarily distinguishes *good* (mature, healthy) traits from bad (dysfunctional, developmentally challenged) ones. The notion of a virtue, which has come to dominate ethics, is precisely the notion of a trait-aspect of a *properly* functioning (good, healthy) person. As psychologists got free from the positivist myth of value-free inquiry, they came to recognize more and more clearly that they practice a normative discipline — that they are, in a way, philosophers of life, philosophers of the person, and thus ethicists in something like the sense in which virtue-ethicists are ethicists. Martin Seligman, a past president of the American Psychological Association, has spearheaded a movement of "positive psychology," which is all about character strengths and virtues, unlike the "negative psychology" that is all about pathologies and dysfunctions. He and a colleague have published a large manual, *Character Strengths and Virtues: A Handbook and Classification,* which they present as the positive counterpart of the famous *Diagnostic and Statistical Manual* (DSM) of the American Psychiatric Association.

The third revolution is that both psychology and ethics have turned emotional. In about the same period in which the previous two revolutions were being fomented, emotions have become a subject of intense investigation in several fields. Anthropologists turned their attention to the emotions of exotic cultures (Rosaldo, 1980, Lutz, 1988), some neuroscientists became emotion specialists (Damasio, 1994, LeDoux, 1998; Newberg and D'Aquili, 2001), as did psychologists (Frijda, 1986; Oatley, 1992; Lazarus, 1991), historians (Corrigan, 2002; Pinch, 1996; Spacks, 1995; Dixon, 2003), and philosophers (Solomon, 1976, 2003; Nussbaum, 1994, 2001; Griffiths, 1997; Roberts, 2003). Several philosophers of emotion, including me, have been interested in emotion in large part because of its connection with ethics: it is a central topic in moral psychology. Out of these many discussions have come a variety of proposals as to what kind of thing an emotion is, and the proposals invariably reflect the particular interests and commitments of the discipline making the proposal.

Anthropologists tend to think that emotions are culturally constructed modes of social interaction and control. For example, fear might be a way of showing others that you are an unthreatening, gentle person (Lutz, 1988). Neuroscientists tend to think emotions are neurological processes: for example, fear might be electro-chemical occurrences in the central nucleus of the amygdala, brought on by activity in the visual and auditory thalamus and cortex and in turn causing reactions in the peripheral nervous system, and thus muscular tensing, circulatory changes, skin changes, etc. (LeDoux, 1998). Some psychologists think of emotions as consciousness of bodily sensation associated with emotional behavior (see the famous theory of William James, 1950, and of his disciple Antonio Damasio, 1994); thus fear might be the sensation of your heart beating in response to seeing an approaching grizzly bear. Evolutionary psychologists tend to conceive emotions as strategies of evolutionary adaptation (Griffiths, 1997; LeDoux, 1998); for example, fear is a protective adaptation to habitats with predators. In a similar vein, one psychologist (Frijda, 1986) conceives emotions as action-tendencies; for example, fear is a tendency to emit danger-avoiding behavior. Philosophers such as Robert Solomon (1976) and Martha Nussbaum (2001), harking back to the ancient Stoics, have proposed that emotions are judgments; for example, fear is a judgment that a significant danger is in the vicinity.

A CHRISTIAN UNDERSTANDING OF EMOTION

This book is about spirituality and human emotion. As such, it is a book about Christian ethics or psychology, and its thesis is that that Baptist church I visited is on the right track about how to get the Christian teachings embedded in the individual's life. Christian virtues are, in large part, a matter of being disposed to a properly Christian joy, contrition, gratitude, hope, compassion, and peace. The spiritual Christian is the mature Christian, and the mature Christian is one who feels these emotions in the Christian way. She is "emotionally mature," because the Christian teachings have shaped her heart, and thus disposed her to behavior characteristic of the kingdom of God.

If we look in the New Testament for a concept analogous to our modern concept of an emotion, we come up empty-handed. None of the words that might initially be thought to work this way — for example, *pathos* or *epithumia* — is in fact a counterpart concept. So we will have to look at what the New Testament says about the things *we* would be inclined to call emotions — joy, gratitude, anger, fear, hope, peace — and then craft a concept that suits these things. In the New Testament, the mental states that we call emotions appear to have the following properties:

1. They are very important. To have the right kind of joy, gratitude, hope, peace, and compassion is the mark of the sanctified, converted, transformed individual. Emotions as felt and expressed at any given moment are indications of one's ongoing dispositional spiritual state.

2. Episodes of emotion can be commanded. Paul can command thanksgiving (I Thessalonians 5:18), not just as a verbal performance, say, as a heartfelt attitude and say: "Rejoice in the Lord always. I will say it again: Rejoice!" (Philippians 4:4).

3. Emotions can be shaped, or determined in their internal nature, by the concepts and narrative of grace. The emotions that are normative for Christian spirituality are theological, teaching-based.

A Christian psychology of emotion will therefore need to be consistent with these features, and preferably to show how emotions can have these features. I shall now sketch a concept of emotion that seems to accommodate and explain them.

THE SPIRITUAL IMPORTANCE OF EMOTIONS

Among the virtues that make up the mature Christian character, some go by the names of emotions: gratitude, hope, peace, joy, contrition, and compassion. Other virtues, such as patience, perseverance, courage, and self-control are pretty clearly not emotions (perhaps they could be called "strengths"); and love (whether of God or neighbor) is a special case (for a discussion, see my *Emotions,* pp. 284-97). Humility is a still different kind of virtue, and seems to be a disposition *not* to experience certain emotions, such as envy and invidious pride (see Chapter 5 for more on this). But the emotion-virtues, as we may call them, are central among the Christian personality characteristics that St. Paul calls "fruit of the Holy Spirit," and I will focus on them in this book.

I invite the reader to meditate with me on the emotions, in the interest of spiritual growth — yours and mine. Thinking about the spiritual emotions can help us become more spiritual in our emotional life. But is my hope that reflection will foster spiritual growth consistent with the idea of the fruit of the Holy Spirit? If these emotions occur simply as a result of God's direct action — when God takes possession of an individual's personality — it seems that nothing can be done to foster them: they are supernatural, and if we covet them, we just have to wait, hoping that God will act.

In the New Testament, the Holy Spirit normally works in connection with the preaching of the good news about God's redemption of sinners through the life, death, and resurrection of Jesus of Nazareth. This good news has a double role: it is the *news* that God has reconciled the world to himself (that is, information about what God has accomplished in Christ), and at the same time an *instrument* by which that reconciliation is worked out, in some small and anticipatory way, in the communities and individuals who give ear to it. That reconciliation works itself out in people becoming obedient, grateful, hopeful, at peace with themselves and God and their neighbor, and being filled with joy in the Lord and love for their brothers and sisters. So great is the role of preaching and hearing the gospel in bringing about this transformation, that we could call these traits "fruit of the gospel." But if we did, they would be no less fruit of the Spirit of God. For the work of reconciliation in which they participate is God's work in his people.

But if the fruit of the Holy Spirit is connected in this way with the gospel — if this is the way the Spirit bears his fruit — then reflection takes on a clear importance. First, the gospel, as news, can be thought about, meditated on; indeed, it is hard to see how it can be planted in people so as to bear its fruit if it is not thought about. We will be doing such thinking in the course of this book. But beyond a plain meditation on the gospel, the individual who wants a deeper spirituality may find it helpful to become clearer about what emotions are and how they function in our lives. The emotions that make up the Christian life are not inscrutable psychological phenomena mysteriously caused by God, as inaccessible to our understanding as the origin of the universe. They are, after all, emotions, and since they are, reflection about the nature of emotion may lead to a kind of self-knowledge that can be applied, in various ways, to the task of becoming a more spiritual Christian.

EMOTIONS AS CONCERN-BASED CONSTRUALS

If emotions like joy, hope, gratitude, and compassion are to be fruit of the Holy Spirit, they need to be something spiritual. To suppose, as some emotion specialists do, that emotions are electro-chemical states of the brain and other parts of the central nervous system does not do justice to their spiritual character. The same can be said of the proposal that emotions consist, most centrally, in awareness of various states of the subject's body. Emotions are often states of action-readiness, as Nico Frijda holds — for example, genuine compassion is a readiness to help a sufferer — but to make that the defining mark of emotions also seems not to do justice to the importance the Bible ascribes to them. To Christians they seem more like attitudes toward things, ways a person's heart is oriented toward something. The Christian psychologist has no stake in denying that emotions have neurological correlates, or that they often involve bodily sensations or issue in actions; but none of these features can be the central or basic character of emotions, according to a Christian psychology.

I have proposed that emotions are concern-based construals (Roberts, 2003), and I regard this proposal as an example of Christian psychology. To say that emotions are concern-based construals is to say that they are states in which the subject grasps, with a kind of perceptual immediacy, a significance of his or her situation. Emotions are interpretive in a broad and loose sense: two subjects with equally acute powers of sense perception and intellection may see the same situation in very different ways, experiencing widely different emotions in response to it. As interpretive perceptions, emotions can be right or wrong about the situation, true or false of it. And they are motivational. As concern-based, they are affected by what the subject cares about, what is important to him or her; and many emotions tend to move their subjects to action in a way that is suggested by the concern that is basic to the emotion, along with the particular way of construing the situation that the emotion involves.

Let me illustrate these basic points with a simple example. Consider Hank the gardener and his response to the weatherwoman's prediction of hail. He is apprehensive. Why? Well, he's got new tomato plants out, and construes them as endangered. But this answer is incomplete; Hank's having tomato plants out will explain his apprehensiveness only if he cares about the welfare of those plants. If he were not a conscientious gardener and just did his job because he was paid, perhaps he wouldn't give a flip what happens to the plants. In that case Hank wouldn't be apprehensive about the approaching storm — at least not on account of the tomatoes. His apprehensiveness is grounded in his concern for his plants. If the storm passes, so will his apprehensiveness — most likely into a quiet, joyful sense of relief. And this emotion is grounded in the same concern as the other, namely Hank's concern for his tomato plants. And if Hank's apprehensiveness remains, the concern behind it is likely to give rise to action: Hank will probably do what he can to protect his plants against the hail.

So Hank's concern is an emotion-disposition. It is not itself an emotion, but instead a disposition to a variety of emotions. What, then, determines *which* emotion arises in Hank's heart? It is how Hank construes the circumstances that impinge on his concern. If the weatherwoman predicts hail, Hank sees his tomato plants as threatened, and his emotion is apprehensiveness, fear, anxiety, or some such thing. If the storm passes, then he construes his plants as safe after all, and he has a sense of relief; his heart is glad. If he thinks his plants are being knowingly damaged by a responsible agent (if, say, the teenager next door tears across the tomato patch on his motorbike), his emotion will most likely be anger. If he wakes up on a frosty morning and finds that during the night his neighbor, seeing the danger to Hank's plants, has beneficently covered them while Hank slumbered in oblivion, Hank's emotion may well be gratitude. And so forth. So an emotion is a way of "seeing" things, when this "seeing" is grounded in a concern; and a concern is a disposition to have a range of emotions. For convenience I employ the language of vision, speaking of ways of "seeing" things, but not all construals are visual. I can construe a person's spoken words as an insult or a compliment, construe the dampness I feel in my baby's pants as the milk she recently sat in, construe the smell of smoke in the house as harmless, etc.

How does this apply to Christian spirituality? Just as Hank would have no emotional response at all to the news of the approaching storm if he didn't care about anything on which that news impinges, so a person will not respond to the news of the gospel with joy, peace, gratitude, and hope, if she doesn't have the concerns on which this news impinges, and also the wherewithal to see the situations of her life in terms of this news. The gospel message provides people with a distinctive way of construing the world: the maker of the universe is your personal loving Father and has redeemed you from sin and death in the life and death and resurrection of his Son Jesus. You are a child of God, destined along with many brothers and sisters to remain under his protection forever and to be transformed into something unspeakably lovely. Because these others are also his children, you are expected to treat them gently, to help them when they are in need, and in general to respect and love them as fellow heirs of your Father's kingdom. If a person doesn't feel a hunger for the righteousness and eternal life proclaimed and promised in the Christian message, then it is not surprising that the gospel falls on deaf ears. Blessed are those who hunger and thirst for righteousness, for to them (and them alone) the gospel of Jesus is the satisfaction of peace and joy. Because this concern is an absolute prerequisite to the bearing of spiritual fruit, I devote a large portion of this book (Chapters 3-6) to clarifying what kind of life and consciousness is most likely to give rise to such fruit.

Consider the joy that the apostles felt after being arrested, imprisoned, and beaten for telling the good news about Jesus (Acts 5:41). Arrest, imprisonment, and beating are not typical occasions for joy among human beings. Most people, when such things happen to them, perceive the situation as unfortunate and are likely to feel distressed, angry, fearful, or sad; but the apostles respond with joy because they see themselves as having been "counted worthy of suffering disgrace for the Name" of Jesus. Given that they were persecuted for their forthright witness to Jesus, the persecution seems to them to be a very good thing. This is because they love Jesus, want to imitate him and to associate themselves with his ministry. Thus a situation that would be repugnant to people with a different interpretive scheme and/or different concerns is for them an occasion for rejoicing. The apostles' concern-based perception is an important spiritual state because it is a manifestation of their concern for the kingdom of God, their affection for the Lord, and their understanding of themselves and their situation in terms of the gospel.

It is plausible to assume that, if the apostles had been hooked up to some brain-scanning device at the time that they experienced this holy joy, the device would have registered neurological processes characteristic of joy. And it is also plausible that, if the apostles had turned their attention to their bodily states at that moment, they would have noticed some perturbation in their midsections, an excitement in their limbs, or something of the sort. But it is very implausible to think that when Luke saw fit to mention the apostles' emotion in this passage of the Book of Acts, he was interested primarily in these bodily processes. Instead, he was interested in how the apostles were seeing the world, how they understood their situation, and how they were motivated.

CHAPTER TWO

Emotions and Christian Character

EMOTIONS AS EXPRESSIONS OF CHARACTER

I have suggested that emotions have a lot of moral importance; they are spiritual and indicate the character of the one who experiences them. Reflecting on them can help us to grow spiritually. But some will object that, on the contrary, emotions are shallow, unstable, and untruthful. Instead of being something you can foster through mature reflection, they seem slated, like superstition and bad logic, to disappear from a person's life as he becomes more reflective. The Stoics thought that if you really understood yourself and the universe you live in, you wouldn't have any emotions at all, except perhaps for a quiet satisfaction in the fact that you no longer have any emotions. According to them, emotions are a fruit of shortsightedness.

Earlier I expressed a sort of provisional approval of the Baptists whose worship service I visited, as having found a biblical way to integrate Christian teachings in members' lives. But a person taking the Stoic line might point out that the members of that congregation seem to be responding to very immediate environmental stimuli — the music, the melodramatic inflections of the preacher, and one another's whoops and hollers and gesticulations. They are not responding to a well thought-out, objective, general view of the world — so it seems unlikely that the emotions experienced in the service really express anything very deep about these Christians' lives. According to the Stoic way of thinking, we see here, not a spiritual expression of character, but a phenomenon that psychologists sometimes call "emotional contagion," a sort of crowd-frenzy that is quite irrational.

When we describe someone as "an emotional type," we do not intend to give a compliment. We mean he is not quite in possession of himself; he is rather chaotically subject to vicissitudes, whether of his environment or of his hormones (or both). He is weak, immature, hollow, shallow, flabby, not "together." Trivial successes and modest beauties, which would distract a more mature person only momentarily, are to him a gale of ecstasy that "blows him away." He gets upset easily, on occasions that would count as a crisis only by a stretch of the melodramatic imagination. He is especially vulnerable to situations of emotional contagion.

This is not a pretty picture, and it has led many to be suspicious of emotions in general, and to think that personal maturity is largely a matter of suppressing, if not eradicating, the emotions. But only a little common observation is needed to see that this picture cannot be generalized to all whose lives exhibit strong emotion. The capacity to be affected emotionally is not a characteristic only of weak people but also of very strong ones. Winston Churchill, Mother Teresa, and the apostle Paul were all strong people of deep feeling. I have noted that emotion is founded on concerns. It is the fact, among other things, that they are driven by some passion or other — whether it be love of country, concern for intellectual and moral integrity, or the love of God — that makes concerned people such strong, integrated persons. But their passion is also the basis for a wide repertoire of emotions.

And now another objection looms. All emotions — at least all the ones that interest us here — are, according to me, based on concerns. But if so, does it not follow that all persons who have emotions are persons of character? And if some people's emotions are shallow and thus not based on character, it seems to follow that not all emotions are based on concerns. Maybe the shallow ones are just reflex-like responses to environmental stimuli, a bit like the startle-response to a sudden, loud noise. You do not need to be concerned in one way or another to jump when a rifle is discharged nearby; it's just an automatic physical response. Maybe the Baptist worship service is just a set of stimuli, and the emotions are reflexes that indicate nothing about the Baptists' character.

I admit that some emotions are rather reflex-like. For example, we are initially "hard-wired" to shrink back in fear when we perceive ourselves close to an unprotected precipice. But even this is not much like the startle-response. The natural fear of heights involves construing ourselves as in an unprotected situation and seems, plausibly, to be based on an instinctive concern for self-preservation. But the emotions of the characteristically "emotional" person are even less reflex-like than the fear of heights. The person who gets inordinately excited about finding five dollars on the street is seeing himself as the object of extraordinarily good fortune, based on a concern for good fortune and a certain conception of good fortune. Compare him with the person who rejoiced intensely at the election of Nelson Mandela to the presidency of South Africa, out of a concern for justice and the well-being of that country. That rejoicing traded on a very different and more mature understanding of good fortune. The boy who falls in love with every pretty girl who smiles at him is similarly experiencing concern-based construals, but he is characterless compared with the man who has loved the same woman with deep devotion for thirty years. The mature man may not be totally insensitive to the charms of some pretty women who show him their attention, but these concern-based construals are controlled by and subordinated to the central concerns of his life — his love for his wife and his commitment to the good and to commitment. All standard emotions are concern-based construals, but people's personalities are differentially organized, and the understanding that informs the emotions can be more or less adequate. The concerns of more mature people are ordered in a hierarchy according to their value, their comportment with the real relative importance of things. And where spontaneous emotion does not exemplify the proper order of a person's cares, the person of character has the "strengths" of courage, perseverance, self-control, and the sense of duty by which to make corrections, to compensate for residual disorder in his concerns. In the kind of "emotional" person we have been considering, this order, both spontaneous and controlled, in the emotional life, is weak and incomplete.

The "emotional person" I described earlier is weak not because he has emotions, but because he has such poor ones, or such a limited repertoire. The concerns his emotions go back to are themselves momentary, primitive, immature, badly ordered. He lacks personal integration and depth not because he feels strongly, but because his feelings are erratic and chaotic, or because he feels strongly about the wrong things, or because he lacks something that ought to be present in addition to his strong feelings, something we might call presence of mind, self-possession, or self-control. And such self-possession may itself be largely a matter of having certain stable and worthy master concerns, such as the concern for integrity, for the commonwealth, for some life project, or for the kingdom of God. Most people feel fear when they are endangered, but some fall apart and become unable to act intelligently, while others keep their cool. What might the difference between these types of people be? One kind of difference is this: fear disconcerts some people because they lack a sufficiently strong countervailing concern. For example, part of Socrates' ability to face death with equanimity was that he feared something else (namely the betrayal of his moral self) even more. And a parent may master his fear and go into a burning house largely because he fears something else more than the danger to himself — the death of his children. In such cases the concern for moral integrity or the concern for one's children (which are emotion-dispositions) plays a role in holding the person together.

EMOTIONS, PASSIONS, AND TEACHINGS

I have said that emotions are construals that are based on concerns. The orienting, integrating kind of concern that I have been attributing to Socrates, Churchill, Mother Teresa, and Paul, and to the man who has loved the same woman for thirty years, I now want to call a *passion*. A passion is a concern that can give a person's life a center, can integrate and focus the personality and give a person "character." A passion, then, is a kind of concern, but not every concern is a passion. The word 'passion' has a variety of uses in modern English, and I am trading on just one of these. We sometimes speak of a person as "flying into a passion" if he is overcome by a strong emotion. We sometimes say, too, that a person "has a lot of passion," meaning that he does everything with gusto. Passion in this sense is largely a genetic endowment, a matter of chemistry. But I am not using the word in either of these two senses. I use it to refer neither to emotions nor to a general spiritedness of personality, but to a person's long-term, *characteristic* interests, concerns, and preoccupations. Thus in the present sense of the word, a person can have a passion for antique automobiles, for justice, for historical scholarship, for the well-being of poor people, for photography, biking, intellectual honesty, or any number of things. A passion in this sense is a concern that defines one's psychological identity.

Hank the gardener does not have a passion for his tomato plants. He might have a passion for gardening, and even for tomato plants in general, but it would be strange if he had a passion for those particular plants that he's watching this year. He is concerned about them, but his concern is not a passion. Why not? The reason is that his concern for them does not determine sufficiently long stretches of his emotional and active life. He cannot be concerned year in and year out about *those* plants, in the way that he can be about his children, or biking, or intellectual honesty. That is, his concern for those tomato plants may characterize Hank for a few weeks, but it does not characterize him as a person. It is not a character trait.

By contrast, Socrates' concern for intellectual integrity, the caring for honesty and virtue that led him daily into the marketplace to converse with others and try to get them to care more for virtue than for money and fame and preserving their lives — this concern is surely a passion. It forms the deepest regions of Socrates' psychological identity. It determines how he daily sees the world and conducts himself, but more than that, it gives him a kind of consistency and equanimity in the face of events that would bring others to despair. This point signals an ambiguity in our use of the word 'character.' In two different ways we praise people for having character: a morally neutral way, and a morally pointed way. Thus a man's long and steady devotion to money making constitutes his character in a generic sense, and while we may not praise the love of money making as such, we can see something valuable in the steadiness. But when we say that some-body has character in a second sense, we praise him in a more robust way. We are not just saying that he has some passion or other, but that his pas-sion makes him into an excellent human being. It is what Søren Kierke-gaard calls an "essential passion" — one that defines not just some human being, but a *genuine* human being, one that is formed as human beings are supposed to be formed. Both essential and unessential passion give a person steadiness, reliability, a kind of transcendence of the ups and downs of im-mediate circumstances. Socrates and Mother Teresa have not just character, but moral character, because their passions are moral passions. Socrates' passion enables him to remain consistent in his unwillingness to speak any word that he believes untrue or to use any survival tactics that would fit poorly with his lifelong insistence on rational discussion and persuasion. Both essential and unessential passion are admirable in their own ways. One has only to read G. Gordon Liddy's autobiography, *Will,* to see that a person whose passion is a "will to power," rather than a moral passion, can be admirable for his character, without being morally admirable. Of course, if a person's passion is positively *im*moral, then while we may admire its steadiness, we should rather feel contempt and hatred for the passion itself.

At the end of the last chapter I said that Luke showed his spiritual un-derstanding of emotions by being interested, not in the bodily perturba-tions and neurological processes of the apostles when they rejoiced in their sufferings for Jesus, but in the way the apostles were seeing their situation and in what they cared about. Luke was also interested in how thoroughly the apostles had integrated this understanding and motivation into their character; he was interested in its depth of ingression into their personality, so to speak. Emotions are episodic states. They come and go, lasting sometimes just for a second or two and sometimes for more extended periods. They are not themselves traits of character. They can, however, be *indications* or expressions of more permanent features of persons. In Acts 5:41, Luke seems to suggest that the apostles were excellent exemplars of Christian character. In Romans 5 the apostle Paul says this:

> Therefore, since we are justified by faith, we have peace with God through our Lord Jesus Christ. Through him we have obtained access to this grace in which we stand, and we rejoice in our hope of sharing the glory of God. More than that, we rejoice in our sufferings, knowing that suffering produces endurance, and endurance produces character, and character produces hope, and hope does not disappoint us, because God's love has been poured into our hearts through the Holy Spirit which has been given to us. (vv. 1-5, RSV)

Real spiritual hope is not a matter of feeling hopeful now and then, when circumstances are looking up, even if the thought that goes with that hope is that we are due to share the glory of God. It is not real, spiritual hope if, for example, you feel it only in church, with the help of the vaulted ceiling, the unctuous preaching of Easter, and the resounding chords of "Christ the Lord Is Risen Today." The hope needs to be a character trait, and a character trait has to be characterized by "endurance" (*hypomonē:* steadfastness) — by the ability to feel the emotion even in situations that don't seem very propitious for it. This feature of the apostles' spirituality was evident in their ability to rejoice even when, by worldly standards, things were going rather badly for them; they were not easily discouraged. And Paul suggests that Christians are (or should be) reflective enough about spiritual development to know that suffering produces endurance and endurance produces character, and thus to rejoice in their sufferings on that account as well.

A Christian psychology of emotion needs to be able to explain how emotions are expressions of character traits. This demand is rather distant from the concerns of the emotion theorists I mentioned in Chapter 1. Some do have ways of explaining emotion dispositions. For example,

LeDoux creates a fear-disposition in experimental rats through conditioning that establishes synaptic pathways. He repeatedly pairs a certain sound with an electric shock, thus inducing in the rat a disposition to respond with fear when it hears the sound (LeDoux, 1998). But conditioning is at best only part of the story for us who are interested in spiritual traits. Spiritual traits are dispositions to respond with joy or compassion, for example, in virtue of a spiritual *understanding* of things, not just in response to an environmental stimulus. Evolutionary theorists too have their way of explaining emotion dispositions. For example, the process of natural selection is supposed to have favored individuals that were afraid of predators and thus survived to pass their disposition on to future generations (Griffiths, 1997). But evolution explains only the traits of species, not the ones that distinguish more spiritual from less spiritual individuals. Finally, the thinkers who are closest to being concerned about genuine spiritual or moral traits (Solomon, 1976; Nussbaum, 2001) regard emotions as judgments; but they say little about judgment-*dispositions,* much less explain how we acquire them.

The understanding of emotions as concern-based construals makes it possible for the Christian psychologist/ethicist to make sense of the idea that emotions can be expressions of character traits: emotions are based on concerns, some concerns are passions, and passions are character traits, ongoing master concerns that deeply characterize a person. The apostles' joy about being counted worthy to suffer for the name of Jesus expressed their virtues of faith and love because faith and love are a passion for the Lord and his kingdom, and their joy was based on that passion. Peter, Paul, John, James, and the other apostles had a passion for the gospel of Jesus Christ, and any well-developed Christian will have a passion for the kingdom of God, a hunger and thirst for the righteousness of the kingdom. The emotions that are based on this concern and shaped by the good news of the gospel — joy, gratitude, hope, contrition, peace, compassion — are the fruit of the Holy Spirit and express Christian character.

What shall we say about the Stoic objection to the Baptists I visited? You will remember that the Stoic worries that the emotions so evident in the service do not express Christian character, but are just superficial episodes of excitement in response to the theatricality of the immediate environment, a winsome and genteel sort of crowd-frenzy. The Baptists seem on the right track because of the place they give emotion in the Christian life, as compared with the Christian Reformed congregation, which appeared to be experiencing only didactic "cognition," and some Episcopalians, who don't get much beyond a rich experience of visual, auditory, olfactory, and kinesthetic stimuli. But what about the Stoic worry? It is legitimate as a worry, but unless we are doctrinaire Stoics, this is only a worry, not an indictment. I do not know the Baptist congregation well enough to tell whether the emotions were just feelings, or expressions of the Christian virtues. It seems likely that this congregation, like most, would have members at various stages of Christian maturity. If so, then in some members, the emotions would just be episodes of stimulus-excitement, while in others they express traits of character. If the pastoral oversight of the congregation is wise, the pastor and elders will know this difference and instruct the congregation in it. Part of the program will be the kind of thing the Christian Reformed Church is so good at: careful instruction in the biblical message itself, so that the joy-construals and the hope-construals and the contrition-construals will have a genuine Christian character. And part of the program will be to encourage bodily ministries of mercy such as the apostles were practicing when they were thrown in jail and beaten up. Sunday theatrics and celebration are wonderful, but more essentially the church is God's school of character.

This last statement may raise a question about my whole procedure in these first two chapters. I have illustrated approaches to *spirituality* using examples of *worship* styles. Have I not confused worship with Christian education? One might think that the Christian Reformed congregation we visited is guilty of my confusion in spades, but the Episcopalians and the Baptists may not even be trying to do Christian education: they are engaged in worshiping the Lord, which is an entirely different matter.

The answer to this question lies in the nature of worship, which is not just doing things — singing, reading, bowing, walking around, raising one's arms, shouting. If it were, Christians who were too busy to worship could hire actors and dancers and singers to do it for them; these people would get the job done, and probably do it better than we, who sing off-key and stumble over the reading, who chew peppermints in church and drop things. But such hirelings would *not* get the job done, of course, even if they did it to dramatic perfection, because the point of worship is not *performance,* but *expression.* Worship is (ideally, in intention) an expression of our hearts, of our lives, of our character. It is communion with our God, and thus needs to come from our heart, just as perfectly as our communion with our lover. I wouldn't hire somebody to write a love letter to

Elizabeth, because it is essential to the act of writing the love letter that it come from the heart. Thus worship cannot be detached from spirituality; if it is merely a reveling in the sights and smells, the pastor's baritone voice and the excellent choir, the beauty of the worship space, and so forth, then it's *not* worship. If it is just momentary feelings that we have in response to the music, the wailing, the emphatic voice of the preacher, and the lady who fainted dead away three rows ahead of us, it's not worship. As an expression of our hearts, the worship has to be the same *kind* of activity that shapes our hearts in the first place. That is why worship style is relevant to Christian education and spirituality.

In the fourteenth chapter of his first letter to the Corinthians, the apostle Paul emphasizes the importance of conducting worship services in such a way that they build up the members of the church. Speaking in tongues, he says, is a good thing, but it is "pure worship," communion with God dissociated from building up the congregation spiritually, unless it is interpreted in plain language. For this reason, "prophecy" — a communication to the church of some truth from God — is more important than speaking in tongues, and when tongues are spoken in church, they should always be interpreted, that is, turned into a kind of prophecy or teaching.

EMOTIONS AS SUBJECT TO COMMAND

Emotions are literally *pass*ions in an older sense of the word — that is, undergoings, events that happen *to* us, rather than *act*ions that we perform — and many people think it follows from this fact that emotions *just* happen to us and that we have no mastery with respect to them. Yet people commonly say things like "be grateful for what you have" or "try not to be angry with her" or "get hold of yourself; don't despair!" The New Testament takes the side of common sense on this issue, and we find emotions being commanded. Jesus endorses the double commandment that you love God with all your heart and your neighbor as yourself (Matthew 22:37-39). The philosopher Immanuel Kant famously said that this commandment cannot be requiring that we *feel* a certain way towards God and our neighbor, but must mean that we should *act* lovingly towards him or her. The reference to your heart and mind and soul in the commandment suggest that a Kantian reading is not adequate, and that we are indeed being commanded to *feel* adoration for God and positive appreciation and well-wishing (as well as loving action) toward the neighbor. The apostle Paul is perhaps even more unequivocal in commanding emotion: "Rejoice in the Lord always; again I will say, Rejoice" (Philippians 4:4). A Christian ethics or psychology of emotion will need to make sense of this possibility.

The people with the view of emotion closest to the one I am proposing are those, like Robert Solomon and Martha Nussbaum, who say that emotions are judgments. In fact, a significant trigger of my view of emotions, which I developed in the late 1970s and early '80s, was Solomon's book, *The Passions*. Judgments are more spiritual than bodily perturbations and neurochemical processes; so the joy and hope and gratitude commended in the New Testament are *more* like judgments than they are like neurological processes or bodily perturbations. But what is a judgment, exactly? Judgments, I take it, are episodic beliefs, episodes in which a subject takes an assenting attitude (a "yes"-attitude) toward some thought or proposition or perception. By contrast, to say that emotions are concern-based construals is to say that emotions are more like perceptions and so involve some kind of experiential presentation to the subject. They make an impression on the subject. If you have the emotion of fear, you do not just *assent to the thought* that you are facing a threat; the situation *impresses* you as being threatening. It *presents* itself to you under that aspect. In this way, emotions are a bit like sense perceptions. After all, when you see something, something has to happen to you, namely that you have a visual experience of what you are seeing. Thus sense perception involves passivity, even if you actively initiate the perception — say, by intentionally looking for whatever you end up seeing. Judgments are different. Sometimes we judge with respect to a presentation, but often we don't.

Consider, for example, your judgment that an apple is red. Sometimes you do this while looking at an apple. You look at it, it impresses you as red, and you form the judgment *this apple is red*. Here you do assent to a perception, an impression of the apple as red. But you might also judge that the apple in the paper bag, an apple that you are not seeing at the moment, is red. (Your mother says, "What color are the apples?" and without looking at them or conjuring up a mental image of them, you say, "Red, Mom.") So you can judge with respect to something that is not being perceptually presented to you. But you can't perceive something that is not being perceptually presented to you. This, then, is the first difference between construals and judgments: construals necessarily involve having an impression of something being a certain way, while judgments do not. And I am saying that emotions are construals. They are a kind of impression.

Another difference is that construals, unlike judgments, do not necessarily involve assent. Consider a classic case in which assent and the content of an emotion come apart. You have a snake phobia, and you know you do. You also know in advance that the four-foot bull snake that is going to be presented to you is utterly harmless. You convince yourself of this by reading up on bull snakes and assuring yourself by careful investigation that the snake in question is a legitimate, card-carrying member of that harmless species. You ready yourself with full conviction that the snake that is about to be brought into the room is no threat to you. The snake is then brought in and presented to you. You freak out, break into a cold sweat, tense up all over, and want nothing more than to get out of that room. All the while, if asked whether you think the snake might harm you, you aver that it is completely harmless.

This case is analogous to cases of perceptual illusion in which the subject knows about the illusion. The highway continues to look wet to my eyes, even though I judge (believe) that the appearance is a mirage; I know the highway is as dry as it can get. The stick in the bucket of water looks bent, though I know from having inspected it a moment ago that it is perfectly straight. On the view of emotions that I am proposing, when I fear the snake while in full knowledge that it's harmless, I construe (perceive) the snake, based on my concern for safety, as a threat to me, while judging it not to be a threat. It *looks* like a threat to me, but I don't believe my emotion. This is very much like seeing the road ahead as wet, while not believing my eyes. In this regard, emotions differ from judgments. I can disbelieve my own perceptions without the perception changing; but if I disbelieve my own judgment, then the judgment has changed. So I propose that emotions are not judgments, but perception-like mental states that I call construals. Of course, this is not to deny that in many cases we do believe our emotions, just as we normally, though not always, believe our eyes.

Now, to see what construals have to do with the possibility of emotions being commanded, let us think a bit more about what a construal is. Classic cases of construal are the perceptions of those gestalt figures found in psychology books that can be seen one way — say, as a pretty young lady with a dainty nose looking away from you — or in another way — as a decidedly less pretty old lady with a very large nose, looking off to the side (see p. 25). It is important to note that impressions are not necesarily sense impres-

sions. When you see the figure in the one way, and then shift to the other
way of seeing it, the purely sensory data do not change; either way, your eyes
register the same configuration of black splotches on a white background.
But your way of taking or "seeing" those data makes all the difference in the
way you *experience* the drawing. The construal view of emotions proposes
that emotions are like that: they are perception-like ways of "taking" the situations in which we find ourselves. So when, in the situation of having been
arrested, imprisoned, and beaten for telling the good news about Jesus, the
apostles go on their way rejoicing, it is because they are construing their situation in terms of their relation to the living Jesus. Their punishment
strikes them as a very good and satisfying event. They are using the gospel
story and their place in it as a way of construing their punishment, much
the way the person who sees the old lady construes the drawing by using his
knowledge of what old women look like.

This flexibility of perception in the broader sense of construal makes it
possible, sometimes, to obey a command to feel an emotion. In the Acts
story, it appears that the apostles felt the joy quite spontaneously; but we
can imagine that some less mature disciples — in whom such high-level

spiritual joy was not such an engrained habit — felt rather depressed about their maltreatment at the hands of the authorities. Peter then might have said to such a disciple, "Rejoice! for you are imitating the Lord today!" Now the less mature disciple already knew that he was imitating the Lord, but he was feeling depressed. And Peter's command has the effect of getting him to recruit what he knows in the interest of a perception of his situation. He is like somebody who has it in his perceptual repertoire to see the figure as a young lady, but his default construal is to see the figure as an old lady. Then somebody commands him to see it as a young lady, and he recruits from his perceptual repertoire the wherewithal for this construal, and obeys the command.

The construal understanding of emotions offers a more natural explanation of their voluntary nature than the judgment view. The voluntariness of judgments is limited by the fact that they involve assent. Perhaps some people can shift at will between contrary judgments, but the more rational a person is, the less is he able to do this. Contrary construals meet no such limitation, since construals are not necessarily assented to, though the vividness of a construal is analogous to the conviction of a judgment, and can make contrary construal difficult. If one judges the gospel to be false, then one cannot, as a rational person, voluntarily judge the gospel to be true. But a person who judges the gospel to be false may perfectly well, with more or less difficulty, construe parts of his life in its terms — in a sort of "as-if" attitude.

The fact that a person can construe a situation in terms that he does not take to be true of it seems important for the development of Christian emotion-dispositions. A person who wants to become a Christian but does not yet believe might hear the gospel and willingly construe himself in terms of it. In doing so, he might feel Christian gratitude or joy or hope "experimentally." This might well be a stage on the way to genuine Christian conviction. If emotions were judgments, this sort of emotional experimentation would not be possible for rational people. The phenomenon of "as if" emotions is extremely common in human life. We feel emotions in response to stories that we take to be fictions: we fear that the heroine will drown, we are appalled at the nasty uncle, and so forth. And I am saying that someone might read the gospel narratives in the same way, experiencing some of the Christian emotions in this "as-if" mode, and this might be a stage in the process of the reader's becoming a believing Christian.

BEHAVIORAL CONTROL OF EMOTIONS

In *The Principles of Psychology* William James makes the following commonsense observation about how emotions can be controlled:

> Everyone knows how panic is increased by flight, and how the giving way to the symptoms of grief or anger increases those passions themselves. . . . In rage, it is notorious how we "work ourselves up" to a climax by repeated outbreaks of expression. . . . Whistling to keep up courage is no mere figure of speech. On the other hand, sit all day in a moping posture, sigh, and reply to everything with a dismal voice, and your melancholy lingers. (vol. II, pp. 462-63)

In other words, if you want to encourage an emotion, act in conformity with it, even if you don't initially feel like it; and if you want to discourage one, refuse to act in conformity with it, or better yet, act in conformity with a contrary emotion. This strategy does not always work, but often it does, and it works more often for people who practice the policy assiduously and self-consciously.

Conceiving emotions as construals helps us to understand why this way of controlling our emotions sometimes works, and also why it sometimes doesn't: when I *act* angry, it is much easier and more natural to *construe* the situation as one to which anger is the appropriate response. If I don't put my face in an angry expression, put an angry tone in my voice, and say angry things, I lack the kinesthetic "feedback" that helps to give me an impression of myself as offended and of the situation as containing an offense. If I act in ways positively contrary to anger — speak in a kindly voice, mention reasons for approving of the offender, and so forth — then I am giving myself feedback for emotions that are at odds with anger. The strategy doesn't always work, because the feedback I am giving myself only *disposes* or *influences* me not to construe the situation in an angry way; it does not guarantee that I will not construe it in that way.

Let us say I have explained a point to a student a number of times, and he has now come to my office complaining that he still doesn't understand. By this time I am inclined to see him as obnoxious, and as imposing unnecessarily on my time and energy. But I sit down with him beside me at my desk, and explain the point once more by making a diagram on a piece of scratch paper. He still does not (or will not) understand, and something in his voice seems to accuse me of making things too complicated. I am inclined to rebuke him sharply and send him away. But instead, applying James's advice, I lay my hand on his shoulder in a fatherly way and speak some gentle words of encouragement to him. The anger that was threatening to come over me dissipates. By contrast, if I control my behavior just enough to avert a complete social disaster, but then go home, draw a picture of my student's face on a pasteboard box and violently kick the box around my garage, complete with obscenities and much loud mention of my student's name, I will probably increase my anger at the student.

Gentleness therapy often dispels anger because becoming angry with someone necessarily involves construing him as obnoxious, offensive, or some such thing. It is much more difficult to experience someone as obnoxious if I have my hand resting affectionately on his shoulder and I am speaking gentle words of encouragement to him than if I am yelling and throwing him out of my office. It is not *always* effective because it is possible to construe someone as obnoxious while assuming the opposite posture towards him. Sometimes that initial construal just seems so right, and so natural and superior to every alternative, that no amount of dissonant behavior will change it. But our emotions are more often within our control than we tend to imagine.

Construals have just the mixture of passivity and voluntariness that emotions have. Sometimes, as in the case of the phobic person we imagined, people are stuck in certain ways of emotional response. This is like the person who can see the gestalt figure one way, but not the other. But people can be trained to see things in a different light; certainly the apostles' practice in Christianity had trained them to see persecution of themselves in a way that is unusual for humanity more generally. Once we have introduced a new way of construing situations into our repertoire, we have a new emotional freedom. We are like the person who has learned to see the gestalt figure either as a young woman or as an old woman. For such a person, the construals are more subject to voluntary control.

Earlier I said that emotions are literally passions, undergoings rather than doings; now I am saying that they are sometimes subject to voluntary control. You might think that I shouldn't have said both things. But the perceptual nature that I ascribe to emotions justifies doing so. We are inclined not to notice that ordinary sense perceptions are passions, since most of the time we can just open our eyes and see. But in seeing, something always has to happen *to* us, even though we can usually do something to facilitate this. Similarly, we can try to feel joy or anger or hope, but we will not do so until the experience *comes together;* and it doesn't always do so. So I am not saying that just any emotion is subject to just anybody's will under just any circumstances, but rather that some emotions are subject to some people's will under some circumstances. And this seems to be presupposed by the New Testament practice of commanding emotions.

C. S. Lewis somewhere advises that if you want to become a Christian, but find it currently impossible to believe what Christians believe, you may begin by acting like a Christian. No need to start with anything as heavy as belief. Just sing praises to God along with the Christians, imitate them in their posture toward suffering, join with them in their life of compassion and sacrifice. You will begin to construe the world as a Christian does, to experience Christianity from within. And who knows? That way of looking at things may eventually come to seem so superior to every other way, that you find, one day, that you believe.

EMOTIONS ARE SHAPED BY CONCEPTS AND NARRATIVES

The distinctiveness of Christian teaching and the concepts in which that teaching is couched determine the distinctiveness of everything else in Christianity — the art and architecture, the music and the institutions (hospitals, schools, the ecclesiastical structure itself), the activities and actions that Christians perform. Apart from the distinctiveness lent by the Christian teachings, all other distinctives are merely "accidental." This is especially apparent where mental life is intimately concerned. For example, as *behavior,* acts of compassion performed by a Christian might be indistinguishable from acts of compassion performed by Buddhists or ancient Greek pagans. The very same behavior of binding wounds, dispensing medicine, providing a comfortable place to lie, might be practiced by anyone. The distinctiveness of Christian compassion lies in how the Christian *conceives* himself, the sufferer, the suffering, and the larger universe in which he acts. (See Chapter 12 for particulars.) And this will be true of all emotions. Emotions can be distinctively Christian only if they can be shaped by Christian concepts and the Christian narrative. Distinctively Christian joy is joy in the Lord, gratitude is gratitude to God for his grace in Jesus Christ, hope is hope for the kingdom of God promised in the gospel, and so forth.

So a Christian psychology or ethics of emotions will have to conceive them in such a way that they can be shaped by concepts and narratives. Obviously a judgment theory of emotion satisfies this standard. Other theories seem less adaptable to this feature of emotions. Neurological accounts that limit themselves to conditioning as a strategy for emotional change and development preclude this style of explanation. Non-reductive neurological accounts that reckon with the linguistic parts of the brain are open at least to the possibility of narrative explanations of emotions, though they can offer fine-grained explanation of differences among particular emotions only by resorting to ordinary, non-neurological explanations of emotions, alongside the neurological ones. Theories that make bodily sensations the distinguishing feature of emotions do poorly with the narrative dimension, though recent versions of this theory mitigate the problem. Antonio Damasio (1994) adds a conceptual-narrative identifier to the bodily sensation that is supposed to be the essential center of the emotion itself: you know which emotion you are feeling in your gut reaction by knowing how you are seeing the situation that brought it on. According to Jesse Prinz (2004), emotions are states of the body, such as some combination of heart rate, skin conductance, body-part temperature, and so forth, that "track" various kinds of relations of the subject to his environment (danger, good prospects, sexual opportunity, etc.); thus emotions "represent" types of situations with respect to their value (negative or positive) for the subject, not in the way that a picture or proposition represents a situation, but in the way that a beep from one's fuzz buster represents a nearby police radar. While this view makes a pass at explaining the narrative structure of highly sophisticated emotions, its way of doing so seems awkward and not very true to experience.

The proposal that emotions are concern-based construals has been tailored expressly with this narrative and conceptual feature of the more spiritual emotions in mind. On this account, all of the distinctively Christian emotions incorporate elements of basic Christian doctrine, such as that God is the source of every perfect gift, that Christ died for our sins, that we are hopeless sinners apart from God's grace, that God has chosen us for eternal life in his kingdom, that every human sufferer is one to whom God offers his compassion, and so forth. Each of the Christian emotions is a construal of the subject's situation — both his immediate situation and the larger context of the world in which he finds himself — in these terms, based on the subject's concern for life and righteousness, for the kingdom of God, for his own happiness and the happiness of the world.

Emotions, then, are concern-based construals. Christian emotions will be ones that are based on a Christian passion — hungering and thirsting for righteousness, the yearning for eternal happiness, the longing for fellowship with God, the desire for his kingdom. In the next four chapters I will be exploring this passion in some depth. As Christian construals, spiritual emotions are a subject's perceptions of the situations of his or her life in terms of the Christian teachings about what the world is like, who we are, and what God has done for us. Christian character, as the set of dispositions to experience the Christian emotions, is not just proper passion, but also the well-engrained habit of seeing the world in Christian terms. In this, the Christian Reformed congregation that I described at the beginning of Chapter 1 was on the right track in its intense concern for proper doctrinal instruction. Without doctrinal clarity, the Christian's emotions will lack the sharp Christian outlines that I will try to describe in Chapters 7–12.

PART TWO

The Christian Passion

CHAPTER THREE

Two Modern Giants on Our Need for God

THE CHARACTER OF OUR NEED FOR GOD

The next four chapters are devoted to exploring the concern on which the various construals of God, the world, and oneself — the Christian emotions — are based. In the present chapter I will discuss the basic need, built into the human psyche, which, when it becomes conscious and mature, is the passion for God's kingdom. The idea is the familiar one that Saint Augustine expresses in the most famous passage from his writings:

> "Great art thou, O Lord, and greatly to be praised; great is thy power, and infinite is thy wisdom." And man desires to praise thee, for he is a part of thy creation; he bears his mortality about with him and carries the evidence of his sin and the proof that thou dost resist the proud. Still he desires to praise thee, this man who is only a small part of thy creation. Thou hast prompted him, that he should delight to praise thee, for thou has made us for thyself and restless is our heart until it comes to rest in thee. (*Confessions,* Book 1, Chapter 1)

Central to a Christian account of personality is the idea that the human heart needs God. In individuals the need may not be conscious, and so I speak of need rather than of desire. When Augustine prays that "man desires to praise Thee" or Kierkegaard says the self is in despair unless it "rests transparently in the power that established it" (*Sickness unto Death,* p. 49), they are not saying that each of us can, upon consulting the contents of our minds, find in ourselves a desire to praise God, or an emotion of despair that is obviously a frustrated state of our God-libido. Even if we are aware of wanting *something* that is not among the objects of our finite life, we may not know that we want God. We may be like the pubescent boy, underinstructed about sex, on whom it dawns that he wants *something,* and that it's in the general vicinity of girls, but without knowing more definitely what he wants. In any case, the Christian understanding of the psyche is that it is restless until it rests in God; it needs a positive and happy relationship with God as a condition of its being mature and healthy. In this, Christian psychology differs from virtually all theories of personality on offer today.

When a Christian psychologist like Augustine, Kierkegaard, Fyodor Dostoevsky, or Simone Weil alleges that the human heart desires God, the claim is *generic:* it is in the basic structure of the psyche to need connection with God, in much the same way as it is in the structure of the human body to need food, drink, a certain environmental temperature range, and sexual contact. It is true that some individuals have a poor appetite for some of these things; but that is usually taken as a sign that something is wrong with them. Or perhaps better, it is like the need for human contact and nurturing: people who do not get enough of this at a crucial stage of development do not mature properly; and if one has too little, or not the right kind, of it in adult life, one does not flourish (the failure to feel a need for human fellowship, which we see in some people, is itself a symptom of dysfunctional formation). To liken the need for God with these other needs is to say that it is not a product of human culture, such that people from one culture could be expected to have it, but not people from another culture. An anthropologist studying the Ilongot headhunters of the Philippine province of Nueva Viscaya will not be surprised to find they have no desire for computers; but she will be surprised if she finds that they never get hungry or have no sexual interests or no interests in friendly associations with other human beings — or no way of relating themselves to the transcendent.

This claim of genericness is compatible with noting that some cultures do a better job than others of expressing and eliciting the desire. For example, the Puritan culture in early America did a better job of it than the culture of Harvard's philosophy department in the 1960s. In this respect the need for God differs from the need to defecate. It can be far less obvious and urgent, is much easier to repress or ignore, and is more susceptible to cultural discouragement.

Like the sex-drive, the natural need for God may be contingent on maturation, and the consciousness of it may be contingent on an appropriate stimulus-situation. Augustine took quite a long and detoured path to find out that it was really God he wanted. The elapse of time may not so much clarify an already full-grown desire, as develop that desire to the point where God can clearly be its satisfaction. Often, people do not realize how much they need God until some situation of crisis or loss gives them perceptual clarity about the nature of their life. The experience of Leo Tolstoy that we will look at in a moment illustrates this possibility.

The psychological need for God that the Christian tradition ascribes to humans has several dimensions that correspond to generic features of our human life as they interact with features of God as he is conceived in the Christian tradition. First, part of our need for God is a need for something completely trustworthy to depend on, something that will provide absolute security; and God is trustworthy in a way that transcends anything that can be trusted in our finite, mortal life. Second, God loves us, and we need to be loved (that is, appreciated, accepted, valued, rejoiced in, solicited, admired) by One who knows us perfectly and whose love is absolutely worthy and completely trustworthy. Third, we are beings who live on "meaning" in the sense of life-purposes, some kind of directing orientation for our activities; and beyond all the finite orientations and purposes of our actions, we need one that is absolute. Clearly, all three of these interlocking and overlapping needs have finite counterparts, the satisfaction of which is quite important in itself — we need sources of security like present health and employment, a bank account and other property, etc.; family and friends who accept and appreciate us; and goals like earning a degree, writing a book, raising healthy children, and making a success of our business. But the Christian psychology says that in addition to the need for these finite forms of security, love, and meaning, we need a form of them that can come only from God.

Three tasks of the Christian psychologist are (1) to clarify what is meant by the claim that humans have a psychological need for God, (2) to consider the evidence for it, and (3) if possible partly to explain the need (bringing it into explanatory connection with other features of the psyche as observed and as understood in Christian terms). These tasks intertwine: as we consider the evidence, we become clearer what claim is being made and what possible explanations of this feature of the psyche suggest themselves; as we clarify the claim, we come to see better what would count as evidence for it and likewise are presented with some possible explanations. In the present section I have done a bit to clarify the claim, identifying features of the need for God by comparing it with other appetites and needs and dividing it into three aspects. In the next section I will focus on a certain kind of evidence —

broadly speaking, "clinical" — and my example will be a famous crisis in the life of Tolstoy and its resolution. I will then consider a standard way of dismissing this evidence, whose classic statement is found in Sigmund Freud's *The Future of an Illusion*. In the last section I will comment about the nature of any resolution of the "debate" between Freud and Tolstoy.

TOLSTOY'S CRISIS

As a child and young man Tolstoy strove for moral perfection, but early in his youth he realized that he did not believe the doctrines of the Orthodox Church. Through association with his upper class peers he was drawn into a vain, sensuous, and egoistical view and style of life. He succeeded at all he did, particularly his writing, but also at achieving physical strength, influence among his peers, and success with his estate. He accepted a nineteenth-century version of what we would call scientific positivism, the view that the physical sciences are the court of last appeal on questions of what is real. He adopted a typical nineteenth-century intellectual philosophy of the progressive perfectibility of humankind, and believed that he and his literary associates were the teachers of mankind. But, as he says, he had no idea *what* he was teaching, for really he had nothing to teach. And human progress, whether his own or humanity's, fell far short of satisfying his spiritual needs.

> I devoted myself to [my writing] as a means of improving my material position and of stifling in my soul all questions as to the meaning of my own life or life in general. (*A Confession*, p. 15; subsequent quotations are also from this book)

At about age 50,

> something very strange began to happen to me. At first I experienced moments of perplexity and arrest of life, as though I did not know what to do or how to live; and I felt lost and became dejected. But this passed, and I went on living as before. Then these moments of perplexity began to recur oftener and oftener, and always in the same form. They were always expressed by the questions: What is it for? What does it lead to? (p. 15)

Tolstoy says that these questions seemed childish, but when he "touched them and tried to solve them" he realized that they were the most momentous of life's questions and that he had no answer to them.

> Before occupying myself with my Samára estate, the education of my son, or the writing of a book, I had to know *why* I was doing it. As long as I did not know why, I could do nothing and could not live. Amid the thoughts of estate management which greatly occupied me at that time, the question would suddenly occur: "Well, you will have 6,000 *desyatínas* of land in Samára Government and 300 horses, and what then?" ... And I was quite disconcerted and did not know what to think. Or when considering plans for the education of my children, I would say to myself: "What for?" Or when considering how the peasants might become prosperous, I would suddenly say to myself: "But what does it matter to me?" Or when thinking of the fame my works would bring me, I would say to myself, "Very well; you will be more famous than Gógol or Púshkin or Shakespeare or Molière, or than all the writers in the world — and what of it?" And I could find no reply at all. The questions would not wait, they had to be answered at once, and if I did not answer them it was impossible to live. But there was no answer. (pp. 16-17)

Of course Tolstoy could have given the conventional, finite reasons for improving his estate, educating his son, and so forth. But his spiritual crisis consisted precisely in the fact that *such* reasons no longer struck him as adequate to give meaning to the activities in question, to supply the motivation needed to keep going. These finite reasons would make sense, it seemed to him, only if tethered to something larger, something eternal.

The evacuation of meaning from reasons not tied to something eternal was a consequence of having a vividly clear larger view of what his life consisted in and whither it tended.

> Today or to-morrow sickness and death will come (they had come already) to those I love or to me; nothing will remain but stench and worms. Sooner or later my affairs, whatever they may be, will be forgotten, and I shall not exist. Then why go on making any effort? ... How can man fail to see this? And how go on living? (pp. 19-20)

To live requires being "intoxicated with life," that is, confined to a short view of it. And yet even this short, intoxicated view is not merely finite, after the manner of animal consciousness; rather, the everyday human con-sciousness supplies a pseudo-infinite deceptive overlay that gives activities meaning. The adolescent sense of "immortality" differs from the time-consciousness of animals in that all activities are invested with a sense of in-finite future — and in the fact that that illusion can be dispelled by a more truthful insight. Drunkenness with alcohol was some relief, for it allowed Tolstoy to feel motivation by a sort of inertia of habit from a past in which his goals had made sense to him. But as soon as he was sober again, he would realize that such habit-motivation was a delusion. There was in fact "noth-ing to wish for. I could not even wish to know the truth, for I guessed of what it consisted. The truth was that life is meaningless" (p. 17).

Tolstoy stresses that his life was, by normal human standards, in no way pathological, deficient, or problematic. He was in vigorous middle age, still able to work both mind and body for long hours. He loved and was loved by the wife who had borne him vigorous, well-adjusted children. His estate was improving steadily; he was respected by acquaintances and relations, and famous as an author. "And in this situation I came to this — that I could not live, and, fearing death, had to employ cunning with myself to avoid taking my own life" (p. 19). Many atheists and agnostics find a great deal of meaning in their families, but without something eternal to tie them to, Tolstoy found his family, whom he loved, a source of intensified pain:

> 'Family' . . . said I to myself. But my family — wife and children — are also human. They are placed just as I am: they must either live in a lie or see the terrible truth. Why should they live? Why should I love them, guard them, bring them up, or watch them? That they may come to the despair that I feel, or else be stupid? Loving them, I cannot hide the truth from them: each step in knowledge leads them to the truth. And the truth is death. (p. 21)

The life of the creation of works of art and the contemplation of other peo-ple's works affords many people meaning, even in the absence of any eternal meaning. But, Tolstoy suggests, this is because people accept a concocted sense of the meaning of life that is created by a consensus that life makes sense and art mirrors that sense.

> But when I began to seek the meaning of life and felt the necessity of liv-ing my own life, that mirror became for me unnecessary, superfluous, ri-

diculous, or painful. I could no longer soothe myself with what I now saw in the mirror, namely, that my position was stupid and desperate. (p. 22)

Some who have felt the emptiness of life in the contemplation of the worms and collapse and oblivion in which all their interest and striving end have coped by resignation (see the discussion of Bertrand Russell at the beginning of Chapter 10). The despair derives from aspiring to what the universe cannot supply; so let us reduce our aspirations, measuring them to reality. This solution is the one to which Freud also urges us, and which he predicts will be naturally adopted as the human race comes to psychological maturity. Tolstoy rejects it as impossible for him.

> Had I simply understood that life had no meaning I could have borne it quietly, knowing that that was my lot. But I could not satisfy myself with that. Had I been like a man living in a wood from which he knows there is no exit, I could have lived; but I was like one lost in a wood who, horrified at having lost his way, rushes about wishing to find the road. (p. 22)

In other words, he could not shake the aspiration towards a transcendent positive meaning of his life. He found in himself what Kierkegaard calls "the passion of the infinite," which is characteristic of people who, unlike those whose spiritual sensibilities have been dulled, know "what it means to exist" (*Concluding Unscientific Postscript,* p. 249). To resign himself would be to shut out an insistent part of his being and thus to be dishonest. It would be to adopt, under ostensible honesty and resignation, the kind of self-deception that King Solomon more forthrightly commends: the person who indulges in pleasant activities "seldom reflects on the days of his life, because God keeps him occupied with gladness of heart" (Ecclesiastes 5:20). Furthermore, this part of his aspiring nature is something noble, and to deny it would be self-degrading.

Eventually, Tolstoy comes to see that his despair depends on accepting a certain conception of reason, whose principle (as we might put it) is that *reasoning is valid only insofar as it is limited to the finite.* One example of such reasoning is that of the natural sciences.

> ... in this sphere of knowledge the only answer to my question, "what is the meaning of my life?" was: ... "you are a transitory, casual cohesion of

particles. The mutual interactions and changes of these particles produce in you what you call your 'life.' That cohesion will last some time; afterwards the interaction of these particles will cease and what you call 'life' will cease, and so will all your questions. You are an accidentally united little lump of something. That little lump ferments. The little lump calls that fermenting its 'life.' The lump will disintegrate and there will be an end of the fermenting and of all the questions." So answers the clear side of science and cannot answer otherwise if it strictly follows its principles. (p. 31)

Another kind of example of "reason" is that of the philosophers. Schopenhauer, King Solomon, and the Buddha ask, "What is the meaning of a human life?" and each, in his own way, says there is no meaning and that suicide is the rational approach: in Schopenhauer, the death of the will; in the Buddha, the annihilation of the self; and in Solomon, a kind of oblivion of the nature of one's life generated by pleasure and a narrowing of the mind. Tolstoy concludes that one will never solve the problem of the meaning of life as long as one limits one's thinking to "reason" in this sense. A person must learn to think of his finite life as connected to the infinite and given its meaning by the infinite — by obedience to God and his commandments, and by the prospect of union with God in heaven. And such a thinking that transcends "reason" (or re-conceives it as having a broader scope) seems appropriate to human beings, inasmuch as we cannot *live* satisfactorily if we do not expand our thinking in this way.

The "hidden infinity of human thought" (p. 53) is manifested, at its most authentic, less in terms of discursive, propositional thinking than in terms of deep emotions whose "logic" can be understood retrospectively in propositional form:

> During that whole year, when I was asking myself almost every moment whether I should not end matters with a noose or a bullet — all that time, together with the course of thought and observation about which I have spoken, my heart was oppressed with a painful feeling, which I can only describe as a search for God. I say that that search for God was not reasoning, but a feeling, because that search proceeded not from the course of my thoughts — it was even directly contrary to them — but proceeded from the heart. It was a feeling of fear, orphanage, isolation in a strange land, and a hope of help from someone. (p. 62)

Tolstoy concludes that the only kind of thinking a human being can truly "live with" in full consciousness of himself and his situation is one that connects the finite with the infinite, the world of everyday living with God and eternity. Every psychologically adequate answer to the question "What is the meaning of life?" or "How shall I live?"

> gives to the finite existence of man an infinite meaning, a meaning not destroyed by sufferings, deprivations, or death.... faith is a knowledge of the meaning of human life in consequence of which man does not destroy himself but lives.... If [a person] does not see and recognize the illusory nature of the finite, he believes in the finite; if he understands the illusory nature of the finite, he must believe in the infinite.... It was now clear to me that for man to be able to live he must either not see the infinite, or have such an explanation of the meaning of life as will connect the finite with the infinite. (pp. 50-51)

We are reminded of Kierkegaard's characterization of the human self, penned some thirty years earlier, as "a synthesis of the finite and the infinite, of the temporal and the eternal . . ." (*Sickness unto Death,* p. 13).

Though Tolstoy sees clearly that it is not rational, in a broad sense, to leave the infinite out of one's thinking about human life, he continues to find strongly compelling the strictures imposed on belief by what he takes to be scientific rationality. In particular, while he feels vividly the need to be related to God and eternity, his concept of rationality makes many of the central beliefs of orthodox Christianity repugnant to him. This thralldom to a constrictive ideology of reason exists side-by-side with his hunger for God, creating strong conflicts and extreme emotional shifts:

> "He exists," said I to myself. And I had only for an instant to admit that, and at once life rose within me, and I felt the possibility and joy of being. But again, from the admission of the existence of a God I went on to seek my relation with Him; and again I imagined *that* God — our Creator in Three Persons who sent His Son, the Savior — and again *that* God, detached from the world and from me, melted like a block of ice, melted before my eyes, and again nothing remained, and again the spring of life dried up within me, and I despaired and felt that I had nothing to do but to kill myself.... Not twice or three times, but tens and hundreds of times, I reached those conditions, first of joy and ani-

mation, and then of despair and consciousness of the impossibility of living. (pp. 63-64)

Tolstoy finally resolves the tension between what he takes to be "reason" and faith by trusting *both* his God-libido *and* his positivistically motivated repugnance for traditional Christian theology. Accordingly he rewrites the Gospels, excising from them anything that offends his "reason," but leaving enough of the "infinite" to satisfy the cravings of his spirit. We may specu-late that if he had enjoyed a "postmodern" situation like our own, in which the cultural relativity of the most constricting claims of "reason" has been exposed, he could have left the Gospels un-rewritten and accepted a more traditional Christianity that would have been even more psychologically satisfying than his revision was.

Tolstoy's authorship of short stories and novels of astounding psycho-logical lucidity recommends him as something of an authority on questions about the meaning of life and the requirements of psychological well-being under conditions of very high self-transparency. And the witness of Tol-stoy's need for God is all the more impressive for his intellectual resistance to religious ideas.

FREUD'S INTERPRETATION

Sigmund Freud has offered an interpretation of the human need for God that is in some ways like Tolstoy's but would in the end debunk it and draw a very different picture of the basic human psyche. Freud too sees the moti-vation for religious beliefs in emotional needs that derive from the per-ceived inadequacy of the finite world. Like Tolstoy, Freud idealizes the nat-ural sciences of his day as the standard of reason, and uses this standard to reject religious ideas, though, again like Tolstoy, he finds it necessary to compromise this standard in his own thought: psychoanalysis is a very dif-ferent kind of enterprise than the natural sciences, yet Freud thinks it yields knowledge. On these points our two authors agree; but they are also in fun-damental disagreement. While Tolstoy finds the God-libido to be a basic and ineradicable feature of the human psyche, one that must be satisfied if persons are to live an emotionally healthy and yet fully self-transparent life, Freud takes the need to be transitory, one that is outgrown in the full adult-hood of the individual and the culture. Religious ideas, says Freud, which are given out as teachings, are not precipitates of experience or end-results of thinking: they are illusions, fulfillments of the oldest, strongest and most urgent wishes of mankind. The secret of their strength lies in the strength of those wishes. (*Future of an Illusion,* p. 47; subsequent quotations are from this book)

We human beings find ourselves in an intrinsically threatening and inse-cure world, in which the forces of nature place us at their mercy. But by *our* nature we want security and safety. We grow up with parents who function as means by which we get some control over our environment, and thus a reduction of our anxiety. So it is natural that we should project personality onto nature and see in our calamities and fortunes the anger and the ap-proval of the gods. This is how we see the world in such a projection:

> Over each one of us there watches a benevolent Providence which is only seemingly stern and which will not suffer us to become a plaything of the over-mighty and pitiless forces of nature. Death itself is not extinction, is not a return to inorganic lifelessness, but the beginning of a new kind of existence which lies on the path of development to something higher. And, looking in the other direction, this view announces that the same moral laws which our civilizations have set up govern the whole universe as well, except that they are maintained by a supreme court of justice with incomparably more power and consistency. (p. 26)

Monotheism arises out of polytheism

> as a return to the historical beginnings of the idea of God. Now that God was a single person, man's relations to him could recover the intimacy and intensity of the child's relation to his father. . . . when man personifies the forces of nature he is again following an infantile model. (pp. 27, 31)

The motive of security, filtered through child-parent interactions, produces the concept of God:

> . . . the mother, who satisfies the child's hunger, becomes its first love-object and certainly also its first protection against all the undefined dan-gers which threaten it in the external world — its first protection against anxiety, we may say.

In this function [of protector] the mother is soon replaced by the stronger father, who retains that position for the rest of childhood. But the child's attitude to its father is colored by a peculiar ambivalence. The father himself constitutes a danger for the child, perhaps because of its earlier relation to its mother. Thus it fears him no less than it longs for him and admires him. The indications of this ambivalence in the attitude to the father are deeply imprinted in every religion. . . . When the growing individual finds that he is destined to remain a child for ever, that he can never do without protection against strange superior powers, he lends those powers the features belonging to the figure of his father; he creates for himself the gods whom he dreads, whom he seeks to propitiate, and whom he nevertheless entrusts with his own protection. (pp. 34-35)

So the "need" that Augustine and Kierkegaard and Tolstoy interpret as the indication that man is spirit, that he is in the image of God, Freud interprets as an illusion, the product of rationalized wishful thinking. Our question is, What can be said in favor of the one interpretation over the other? How might a dialogue go, between Tolstoy and Freud?

On Freud's account, the concept of God (and thus God himself) is a *creation* of the human mind in response to the pressures of an *infantile* need. On Tolstoy's account, the concept of God is an idea to which the human psyche is *compelled* by *self-transparency* (an aspect of human maturity) to give credence, on pain of despair.

When Freud speaks of the mind's "creating" God he means to imply that nothing in reality corresponds to the concept of God. But the mere fact that a concept is created by human beings implies nothing one way or the other about whether something real corresponds to the concept. In some sense, perhaps all concepts are created by human beings; in any case, no one will infer the non-existence of quarks from the fact that the concept of a quark is a human creation; nor will contemporary scientists, prior to the verification of quarks, charge believers in them with irrationality because positing their existence satisfies a human need — the need to explain something in physics.

Freud's account of the origin of the concept is largely acceptable to the Christian psychologist. Under the pressure of emotional needs, and on the model of human parents, we come up with the idea of God (I am not saying that each of us invents the concept out of whole cloth; it is a product of tradition, of countless *generations* of human beings' thinking about their place in the universe). But instead of inferring from our "creativity" in this respect that God is only a figment of our minds, the Christian psychologist will say that God intended us to go through this developmental process by which we gain psychological access to Him.

Freud's other main strategy for discounting our sense of need for God is to call it "infantile." This too is acceptable to the Christian psychologist. Some aspects of the attitude of the child are commended in the Christian tradition as features of human maturity (Mark 10:13-16), inasmuch as denying them is dishonest and ungrateful and lacking in a proper perspective on our human situation. We are to become like little children because that is what we are: derived, dependent beings. From the Christian standpoint Freud's proposal that we accept a model of maturity that contains no transcendent comfort is the one that is unrealistic, a distortion of our nature. Freud calls our need for God infantile, and thereby denigrates it; the Christian psychologist calls our need for God infantile, and thereby commends it.

Freud and Tolstoy disagree, perhaps, on a) how momentous, and b) how eradicable, these needs for the transcendent are. Freud thinks the need can be pretty readily outgrown, while Tolstoy is unable to outgrow it. Freud does not think it very important to human life, while for Tolstoy it is all-important. They may also disagree about rationality (though Tolstoy *writes* as though he agrees with Freud). Tolstoy is perhaps more like William James, who adopts a principle of optimism about profound human instincts. He assumes that it is unlikely that human nature has in it a deep need that the universe, which gave rise to the human organism, refuses in principle to satisfy. So if there is a general human urge to connect with God, it is unlikely, according to James, that nothing exists in reality that satisfies this need.

Some individuals, like Tolstoy, find that they cannot (psychologically) live without God (Simone Weil, Kierkegaard, and Augustine are other examples). Others, like Freud, seem to adjust to atheism; they don't go nutty or kill themselves. What may these two classes of persons say about each other? Tolstoy will say that the atheist is not fully conscious of self and situation. Something in his self and situation is being repressed or toned down or shaded or intellectualized or otherwise "defended" against. (For an argument that Freud was less comfortable with his atheism than biographers like Ernest Jones have represented him to be, see Paul Vitz, *Sigmund Freud's Christian Unconscious.* See also Ernest Becker's interpretation of Freud's life in *The Denial of Death.*) In other words, Tolstoy accuses Freud of being immature. Freud, in response, will say that Tolstoy is immature, given to wishful thinking, short on courage and resignation; he lives in his illusions, in a fantasy world. He may think that he cannot live without God, but that is either because he has not summoned enough resignation, or because he has been so damaged by religious training that such resignation is beyond his capacities. In either case, Tolstoy's religion is a consequence of his failure to function fully as a human being. Freud leans heavily on his concept of maturity:

> But surely infantilism is destined to be surmounted. Men cannot remain children for ever; they must in the end go out into "hostile life." We may call this *"education to reality."* (p. 81)

THE CHRISTIAN PSYCHOLOGIST'S JUDGMENT

Who is right? Can we adjudicate between these rival ways of understanding the human need for God, which our two authors otherwise describe in remarkably similar ways? We can adjudicate, no doubt, but I do not think we can find a theoretically neutral standpoint from which to do so to the satisfaction of both sides. The rival standpoints will continue to be occupied by reasonable people.

Rival conceptions of maturity are a fact of life in contemporary psychology (see my *Taking the Word to Heart: Self and Other in an Age of Therapies*), so it should come as no surprise and no alarm that Christians do not fully agree with atheists about what counts as psychological maturity and mental well-being, and in particular how the relationship to God figures in the mature personality. Personality theories and psychotherapies are based on conceptual commitments that are never fully underwritten by the data except insofar as those data are construed in terms of the conceptual commitments. It seems that psychology, as an intellectual enterprise (a science?), depends more on contestable conceptualization than such sciences as chemistry and physics. Throughout this book I take the position that certain kinds of psychology (personality theory, psychotherapy, the kind of psychology being promoted these days under the banner of "Positive Psychology") is really a branch of ethics, and that ethics, insofar as it is about the virtues and vices, is really a branch of psychology. This state of affairs does not stem from psychology's lack of scientific development, but rather from the nature of its subject matter: psychology is necessarily about such issues as development and maturity, which are inextricable from moral and religious commitments. Freud's conscious commitment is to atheism and a corresponding model of maturity; Tolstoy's is to theism and an attenuated Christian model of the mature person as a trusting child of God.

To the Christian it will seem that Tolstoy is right: Freud really does need a God-relationship, and is at some unconscious level kidding himself. The Christian psychologist agrees with Freud and Tolstoy that we have a desire for God, and agrees with Tolstoy against Freud that that need is a basic drive of our nature, and to deny it is to deny something fundamental about ourselves. To try to eradicate it, to class it with dispositions that we must outgrow if we are to become mature, is precisely *not* to move towards maturity, but to arrest our development and pervert our nature, to foster vice and not virtue, immaturity and not maturity. The Christian psychologist disagrees with both Freud and Tolstoy in their judgment that Christian doctrinal belief is irrational and incompatible with science. With positivism behind us, perhaps the major reason since the Modern period for thinking that Christian belief is epistemically substandard has been undermined. The Christian psychologist today is able to give doctrinally orthodox and biblically rich readings of the human desire for God and for its frequent failure to be well developed or conscious. That will be the policy of this book.

CHAPTER FOUR

Something Eternal in the Self

ORIENTATION

In the previous chapter I laid out the general idea of an innate human need for God. In the next three chapters I want to explore the passion for the kingdom of God that may develop from this innate need, and is the basis of the Christian emotions. My account is in a sense evolutionary. I begin, in this chapter, at the bottom of the scale, with the suggestion of a yearning for eternity or for something abstractly resembling the kingdom of God on which the Christian pins his hopes; what I describe in this chapter is not the Christian passion, but a concern out of which the Christian passion can develop. In the following two chapters, I work gradually toward the description of a passion that is adequate and fitted to the Christian teachings. Something like this evolution might occur in the life of individuals, but I am not claiming that all Christians actually go through something like this development or the thought processes that underlie it. Many different patterns of development can lead to a mature Christian passion. My account is therefore not designed to reflect individual development, but is instead a framework by which to organize the psychological and conceptual points I wish to make about the nature and growth of the passion that underlies the Christian spiritual life.

INFINITE TIME

Søren Kierkegaard puts in the mouth of his persona Anti-Climacus the comment that "as a rule, imagination is the medium for the process of infinitizing" (*The Sickness unto Death,* p. 30). 'Infinitizing' refers to a process in the maturation of the individual's self-consciousness. By this process one becomes aware of a dimension of oneself that sets one apart from organisms that live entirely in terms of their finite relationships, such as animals and very young children. An essential and important dimension of the human self — in terms of his needs and obligations — is that he can soar in thought beyond the immediate circumstances of his life. Before one meditates on it, this capacity may seem a small thing, but it has enormous consequences for what a human self is.

Humans are, as far as we know, the only animals that can be transported by a novel or a movie into another world, with its loves and hates, enchantments and terrors, cozy comforts and unnerving suspense. We alone can know, ten years in advance, that the moon will be full on a given day, or sixty years in advance, that we will one day molder in the ground. Only a human life can be shaped by an ideal, such as the life of Christ, or an ideology, such as Marxism, or an obsession, like making money. Only for a human being can a multi-colored piece of fabric flapping in the wind mean the complex of geography and culture that is America. By imagination the actor brings himself to see the world through Hamlet's eyes. By imagination the richest woman in the world may put herself in the shoes of a beggar dying in the streets of Calcutta, and so be moved by compassion. A man dying in a prison cell can be happy, because he sees himself as suffering for a righteous cause, while another in the bloom of health, free and surrounded by opportunities, may blow his brains out because he feels that he is trapped in a hopeless future. Let me describe some exercises of the imagination that Christians will take as manifesting the Godward side of our nature. Then I want to consider some questions about them.

Many years ago I went to the funeral of an old lady who had been a friend of my wife and me. Then I came home and hugged Elizabeth, whose womb was becoming very full with our first child (later to be known as Nate). I said, "In seventy-seven years (that was the age of the lady) this unborn child may be weak and wrinkled and bent over too." The image of that rosy-cheeked, perfectly coiffured, pickled corpse lying so still among the satin and the lilies served to focus an undeniable aspect of that little kicker whose plumpness and gurgling and play would soon delight his parents. It served to contain in a single moment of thought the lifespan of that little person who was already becoming dear to me. To survey a life that is very important to you, to catch it all in a moment, is to get a sense of the futility of it — if that is all there is to it. It is to feel a kind of desperate emptiness about it, a cosmic sadness, and perhaps to reach out in longing for another world in which the beauty of life should be better given its due. My own experience has been that the entire business of bringing a child into the world and rearing him, of contemplating his naïve enthusiasms and the beauty of his little body, is an occasion for many desperate sensations of the futility of life apart from God.

The prophet Isaiah says,

> A voice says, "Cry!"
>   And I said, "What shall I cry?"
> All flesh is grass,
>   and all its beauty is like the flower of the field.
> The grass withers, the flower fades,
>   when the breath of the Lord blows upon it;
>   and surely the people is grass.
> The grass withers, the flower fades;
>   but the word of our God will stand for ever. (Isaiah 40:6-8, RSV)

Isaiah distills in a simple image a truth that can never be far from the mind of a thinking adult. You are grass: your life is a blooming and a fading, a flourishing and a withering, a birthing and a dying. This thought frequents the human mind — though mostly in its recesses. Walking to work, peeling potatoes, chatting at a cozy party over a glass of wine, holding hands with your spouse, playing silly games with your children. And there's the lurking thought: flesh fading and disappearing, withering grass.

But at times this truth comes home with a special shock, and what is only a nagging uneasiness changes into outright terror: the sudden absurd death of a friend, a close brush with accidental death in the midst of play, a pain that I interpret as the first symptom of a dread disease. Sometimes a more purely reflective event can trigger this look at reality. My mind, otherwise accustomed to cunning self-deception in matters relating to death, is sometimes thrust into honesty by reading or hearing astronomy. This probably works only because I do not very often think astronomically; if I did, I suppose I would soon become jaded and objective in my thinking here too, the way doctors and army lieutenants and funeral directors do. But for me, occasionally thinking about the vast expanses of time that it takes for the stars to do their things, or even for the planets to go through certain of their cycles, gives me a visceral new perspective on the time from my birth to my death. For example, Pluto takes about three or four human lifetimes to revolve once around the sun. And it goes round and round and round.

It is easy to survey the life of a blade of grass; *of course* it springs up fresh and firm and green in the springtime and then withers with the winter freeze, and rots in the following season. That's just how it goes with grass, as can be seen by a being who survives the changes of many seasons — maybe seventy or eighty or even ninety such changes. But astronomy stimulates the imagination to take a larger perspective, something like Isaiah's. From here I comprehend, as in a tiny droplet of the universe's time, that moment in the process of flourishing and disappearance that belongs to my very own flesh. All flesh (my flesh) is grass. But here I'm not inclined to say, "*Of course* that's how my life is. That's just the way it is with flesh." No, when I apply it to myself, the thought of withering appalls.

A person who is inclined to view his own life honestly and admit without casting his eyes aside that all flesh is grass will welcome the thought of an enduring rock amidst the flux of things. Isaiah's preaching, if we really hear it, touches our deepest need. He ministers to the worry that pervades all our thoughts. But why does he say that the word of our God endures forever? Wouldn't it be enough to proclaim that *God* is eternal, that *he* stands forever?

Probably not, if Isaiah intends to speak comfort and good tidings to those who are dying. To a very philosophical mind, maybe it would be some comfort to believe that, amidst the flux of things, at least God endures forever. But I doubt it. Wouldn't such a philosophical attitude really be a cover-up for despair? Most of us, anyway, wouldn't find much in the doctrine of God's eternity to feed on, especially if it seemed that God wasn't well disposed toward us and that he didn't include us in his enduring. But in the Christian perspective Isaiah is preaching the really good news that God's loving disposition toward us — his word of mercy and comfort — endures forever and cannot be turned aside.

INFINITE MEANING

Another way this kind of truth gets focused is through reflection on the activities that fill our lives with meaning. We all know what a miserable thing *ennui* is. Having suffered through long, tedious school assignments in which we could see no purpose, or a nearly eternal night stuck in an airport because of storms, we see that meaningful activity is a kind of food for our souls. The emptiness and impatience we feel at such times show that we need to be able to engross ourselves in activities, to give ourselves to them more or less wholeheartedly, if they are to fill our lives with meaning. Consciousness becomes a burden in moments when our activity seems pointless to us, or when we're inactive because we can see no purpose in doing anything. No activity will fill us unless we have an interest in it, and an interest cannot fill us if we don't see ourselves as making some headway toward accomplishing its goal.

Most of us succeed in finding foci for the interests that fill our moments with meaning. We find this in our jobs, our families, our hobbies, in music or competitive sports, in artistic creation or politics, in church work, cooking, sewing, woodworking, firewood gathering, and scholarship. When one such activity begins to bore us, we try to find ourselves in still others, sometimes wandering far and experimenting much in the process. If the activity that becomes empty has been a major focus of my life (for example, a profession from which I have retired or a family that has now grown up), so that it seems hopeless to find a replacement for it, the emptiness can become a generalized despair. The whole of life begins to feel a bit like that night in the airport, only without the comfort of the prospect that daylight will come when the storm will have lifted and a beautiful airplane will carry me into a context of meaningful activities once more.

Even the most trivial activity, if it sufficiently monopolizes my consciousness of purpose, can provide momentary significance. If I am absorbed in splitting a stubborn piece of oak for the fireplace, then for that moment, and insofar as larger thoughts don't enter in, my life is filled with meaning. The hitch here is that it's virtually impossible for a human being always to be entirely absorbed in activities of the moment. Because I am reflective, I am always at least peripherally conscious of a larger view of this moment, and always prone to ask, "Why am I doing this?" "Is this activity to any purpose?" That is, I am always, with one degree of consciousness or another, backing off from the present moment and surveying and evaluating my activities. Often I am not very conscious of going further with this evaluation than the answer, "I'm chopping this wood because I want a fire this evening." If the question, however, is not about firewood but about a career, the evaluation will come closer to being a survey of my life as a whole: "Are the activities that most permanently and pervasively lend meaning to my life really worthy? That is, worthy of me, and worthy in themselves? Am I happy with the kind of happiness I derive from them? Is it enough?" And very often such reflection has time and death in view. Perhaps I look over my past decade with its achievements and pleasures, and say to myself, "Possibly I have two or three such decades left to me. Is that what my life amounts to?"

And if the answer comes back, "Yes, that is what it amounts to, and that is all. That's the whole story," then the sensation is one of despair. In such moments of surveying insight we sense the emptiness of a life that is not rooted in a time frame larger than our seventy or eighty years nor aimed at a goal higher than accomplishments, comforts, money, pleasure, and applause. Thus some very meaningful activities (when considered in their momentary or at least narrower context) are suspended in a web of meaninglessness, unless the individual believes that she does what she does to some eternal glory and in the service (however humbly and indirectly) of some eternal order of things. Because of our imagination — ability and compulsion to survey our lives, to see them for what they're worth — meaninglessness is the destiny of human consciousness, except in the context of eternity.

Are These Reflections Morbid?

You may want to address to me the words a certain Mr. Edwards addressed to Dr. Johnson: "'You are a philosopher, Dr. Johnson. I have tried too in my time to be a philosopher; but, I don't know how, cheerfulness was always breaking in.' True, many people have the experiences you describe, but your tendency to dwell on them just shows what a morbid person you are. Why emphasize negative things like meaninglessness and death and cosmic fretfulness? Let us stress the joys that can be had, the simple pleasures of work and play, hearty conversation, good food, and lovemaking! If we cultivated the kind of thoughts you have described we'd poison the good things life offers. Your morbidity comes from an unwillingness to accept life as it is — a lack of creaturely humility. Besides, much of our life is free from these troublesome experiences. Most of the time we are happily engaged in our work and play, nicely focused down on the present moment where we find meaning and are distracted from the thought of death. We should cultivate this immersion in the present moment, because there we find our happiness, and there we most naturally live our life. But the experiences you have described are farfetched and unnatural and, in the healthy individual, infrequent."

Thank you for your impassioned objections. Let me sort them a bit. First, you say that anyone who dwells on these experiences is morbid. But this is not true. Some persons who show no signs of mental illness are well acquainted with these thoughts. And these experiences lack one of the crucial marks of psychological disease, namely that of distorting reality. They are not at all like the case of the sixty-five-pound victim of anorexia nervosa who believes that if she eats more heartily she will get fat, or that of the paranoiac who believes that everyone he meets is plotting his downfall. The person who reckons by vivid imagination with the fact of his own death and considers what consequences it has for the meaningfulness of a life devoted to getting money and fame may have a balanced view of his condition. It is he who seems realistic and honest, not the person who systematically denies these disturbing thoughts. Surely dysfunction lies in the inability to acknowledge the fact of one's own death, and to feel the meaninglessness of a life that is totally immersed in the passing show. If, however, we hesitate to call most of humanity dysfunctional, we can at least say that they are not very clear, emotionally, about the nature of their life.

But perhaps when you called me morbid, you didn't mean literally that I am suffering from mental disease, but only that I have a rather gloomy outlook. And maybe you are even willing to pay the price of lying to yourself to secure a "happier" attitude. But anyway, I am not counseling you to poison your life with gloomy thoughts. The Christian is not stuck with despair and meaninglessness when she sees that she is left unfulfilled if life in this present time and space is the whole story. For her it's not the whole story. For this reason she can hear in the experiences I have described the voice of God calling her away from a life of immersion in the present passing world, calling her to attach herself in faith and hope and love to himself and his eternal kingdom.

No doubt most of us have a long way to go in getting ourselves attached to God and his kingdom and detached from the world, and so the thought of dying and the survey of our life's meaning does seem gloomy to us, maybe even terrifying. No one who understands will deny that becoming a Christian involves some pain; but neither will he deny that it's worth the price of discipline. And so the Christian who opts to turn away from such experiences as I have described in favor of a "happier attitude" of semi-illusion that he will never die has not only chosen dishonesty. He has also chosen a "happiness" that will let him down, a superficial, passing sense of well-being, fit for animals perhaps, but deadly when adopted by a creature who is spirit.

The "happiness" of one who immerses herself in the passing show doesn't just let her down on her deathbed, so to speak, but creates a life of anxiety and despair all along the way. If she is pretty good at self-deception, she may seem happy to herself and to others. But if she ever looks back clearly on her mental state during those years and sees through to the bottom of her immersion in the passing show, she will have to admit that she was in a more or less dulled state of restlessness and fear. Escape along this route fails because, after all, it is not possible to immerse oneself totally in present moments. Horses and dogs and porcupines, lacking the mental apparatus for having values and ideals, and for scanning themselves from birth to death and beyond, necessarily take the moments of their lives as they come. Their "place" is the present moment, and so they have nothing like the liabilities to error and unhappiness, and the spiritual needs, that we human beings have. Walt Whitman once expressed a wistful longing for this simplicity of animal consciousness:

> I think I could turn and live with animals, they are so placid and
>   self-contain'd,
> I stand and look at them long and long.
> They do not sweat and whine about their condition,
> They do not lie awake in the dark and weep for their sins,
> They do not make me sick discussing their duty to God,
> Not one is dissatisfied, not one is demented with the mania of
>   owning things,
> Not one kneels to another, nor to his kind that lived thousands of
>   years ago,
> Not one is respectable or unhappy over the whole earth.
>   ("Song of Myself," section 32)

The key is in that word "self-contain'd": the animals are not subject to our deepest miseries because they naturally do not live beyond themselves, by virtue of reflection and imagination, as human beings do. We, by contrast, lack the option of *not* scanning our lives and looking for meaning, try as we may to avoid doing so.

We do, of course, have some control over our imagination. We can concentrate on selected thoughts, and disallow or distract ourselves from others. If we did not have this power, Paul's admonition to set our minds on the things of the Spirit and Christ's warning not to lust sexually would be absurd because they couldn't be obeyed. But at the same time we are passively subject to our imagination. Thoughts haunt us; they spring up uninvited; they are triggered sometimes by the most unlikely events. And that surveying function of the imagination, in which we confront our death and the meaninglessness of a life bound-within-finitude, dogs us. It is always present, if not quite in consciousness, then just below the surface.

Being a coward, I may shrink from such thoughts and try to drive them away. "Just don't think that way," I tell myself, "and everything will be all right." And I may succeed in this, over the short haul. I can open the Sears catalog and drift into a reverie about some new tools for my workshop. Or call up a friend and see if we can get a racquetball court. I can, self-deceitfully, compare my professional success with that of a less industrious colleague — as though that were some solution to the problem of cosmic meaninglessness! Or go out for a jog or eat health foods or remind myself that I live in a small town where the air and water are clean, or dwell on the fact that there isn't much heart disease and cancer in my family history — as though ten or twenty years more of life were some solution to the problem of death! Or I may rest my hope on my son's carrying on my ideals and my projects — as if, even if that unlikely event occurred, the same problem doesn't arise in his case, and that of his son, and so on. The difficulty with such expedients of thought is that they are all so patently beside the point.

And even if I am degenerate enough to be comfortable with the lie involved in them, still they will not save me long from despair: my imagination will exercise me in the presence of death, even if I refuse to exercise my imagination in its presence. God has got my scent again and is trailing close behind. I lay me down to sleep, and in the still darkness somewhere just below the surface of consciousness swims that surveying imagination. The ominous truth from which I seek to guard my vision glimmers faintly in the waters of darkness. Then, drowsy, I let my guard down and it comes splashing up to meet me: the specter of my death and the meaninglessness of my life is solid and clear and terrifying. I rouse myself, shake my head, and try to come back to the "real" world by turning on the light. I sit there, propped in a more mastering position with my pillow against the headboard, and think again about how successful my career really is, and how healthy I am, after all, for a man of forty, and what a bright little son I have. It is something of a comfort to be back to reality. But now I am afraid to put my head on the pillow again, afraid that specter will swim back toward me. So I get up and work for an hour on my income tax return, and gradually the impression of terror gets fainter. And finally, before I go back to bed, I take a sleeping pill, to make sure that this time I sink totally into unconsciousness.

IS THE PASSION FOR THE ETERNAL ARROGANT?

In your earlier criticism of my comments you suggested that by immersing ourselves in our finite life, and distracting our attention from the issues that would draw us into the arms of the eternal, we would express a kind of creaturely humility and at the same time keep from poisoning the bit of happiness that we can find in life. I have suggested that your approach has a couple of liabilities: it is dishonest and bound to fail. But now I want to claim that cultivating the sense of our death and the meaninglessness-in-themselves of the activities of this life does not have the liabilities you mention.

Let us start with the matter of creaturely humility. If we are creatures with a religious tendency, then humility would be a matter of accepting ourselves as that. It would be an exaggerated humility, wouldn't it, if we whose hearts are restless till they rest in the eternal denied that fact about ourselves and sought to become more like dogs and horses and porcupines. Creaturely humility is relative to the kind of creature under consideration. If dogs can accept themselves quite happily without any relationship to something beyond this present world, then "humility," for them, is nicely expressed by total immersion in this world. But there is something eternal in the human self, a deep-rooted longing that is difficult, if not impossible, to evade. And if one takes it seriously, as Christians must, then to try to eradicate it must be the most perilous and foolish thing a person can do. Cultivating this restlessness, and letting ourselves become transparent in it, is not a proud seeking to be something we aren't, but just the natural expression of the kind of creatures we are. In seeking the eternal, or welcoming it passionately when it comes to us, we are not being like the emperor who wants to be a god, or the existentialist who wants to be his own moral lawgiver. We are being much more like a collie seriously pursuing the business of being a dog.

Your other objection is that, by dwelling on the kind of thoughts I am discussing in this chapter, we will poison what little happiness we can find. I answer that it is only by finding and assimilating a life view in which these thoughts can be honestly accommodated that we can prevent our natural pleasures from being poisoned. For the truth is that the most exquisite moments in the life of a worldling (and of a worldly Christian) are often deeply compromised. A moment of success in our work, the exhilaration of health in a session of vigorous physical exercise, a moment of intense tenderness with our spouse, a romp with the children, a Christmas feast with family and friends — the very intensity of these pleasures tends to beckon those lurking thoughts to the surface of consciousness. But the anxiety we feel in the face of death is the consequence of our investing this life (from which we must die) with ultimate significance. The despair we feel when forced to reckon with the vanity of all our activities and pleasures is the result of our according ultimate significance to those activities and pleasures — to their being for us the whole story, or the center of the story. If we could manage to see this life as a stage in an eternal life, then it could be accepted honestly and gladly for what it is. If we could see the significance of our present activities and pleasures as deriving from a context beyond this present one of flowering and fading, they could be honestly enjoyed for what they are, no less and no more. If on the other hand we have no larger expectation in terms of which to interpret this life, then since we are creatures who cannot escape our surveying imagination and our deeper longings, embitterment dwells on our doorstep, and we live in constant fear of stepping out into the open.

Christianity is, among other things, the wonderfully good news that this mortal life is not our whole story. We have been redeemed for an eternal kingdom by a Lord who is the first fruits of the resurrection from the dead. The few years that we live in this present body (that blink in the history of Pluto, as it were) are a kind of pilgrimage, a sojourn, a preparatory trip on the way to something much greater. They should be understood as school years. When we are in school we are quite clear (if we are serious students) that our central activities are directed to something beyond school. The quality of our life there is going to be tested by that life for which our school life is a preparation; and the quality of our school life will determine, to some extent, the quality of life after school. We say that school life is a preparation for real life; and so the serious student is conscious of a certain unreality of the present. For the Christian, this present existence is provisional. We are aware that every activity we undertake is schooling directed toward a higher end. The way we comport ourselves at work and play, the way we relate to other people, the use we make of the goods at our disposal;

these are all exercises in preparation for real life. To continue the analogy and balance the account, it needs to be said, too, that school life is in many ways real life; if it weren't, it wouldn't be a good preparation for the future.

Such a consciousness is pure health and pure honesty for a being with a surveying imagination such as we humans have. In such a consciousness time and eternity are related as they ought to be: time is given its full significance (which is great) but not more than that. It is understood entirely in its relationship to eternity. Time is the place where our salvation is to be worked out, and so we take it with the seriousness of fear and trembling (a far greater seriousness, in one sense, than any worldling can take toward it). But since its seriousness is that of a preparation for something else, it can in another sense be passed off somewhat lightly, with a sense of humor and a readiness to depart.

For a person whose roots had begun to dig solidly into the soil of eternity and were so loosely attached to the present soil that he danced lightly on the surface of the earth and so was ready to leave at a moment's notice, dwelling on the thought of death would have little point. Sad to say, however, this mind-set is rarely to be found among those who profess Christ. Most churchgoers are as deeply rooted in this world, and thus as deeply in despair, as those who profess no such hope. For this reason, dwelling, with some pain, on experiences like the ones I described earlier is a necessary, healthy, and humble exercise for us. We must become friends of despair if we are to be drawn above it to genuine and heartfelt hope. Far from being an exercise in morbidity or arrogance, a deepening acquaintance with our death and with the vanity of human wishes is for our worldly hearts a needed path to perfect health.

CHAPTER FIVE

The Salvation of Ivan Ilych

ANOTHER OBJECTION

Consider another source of discomfort with what I outlined in the last chapter. People with a certain deeply moral view of the world, a view that has been with us in various forms since the eighteenth century, may feel that the fear of eternal discontinuation is hardly worthy of us and is, or ought to be, completely submerged in another concern. And ultimately, for this heroic stance, the prospect of absolute annihilation is the gracious beneficence of the universe towards us. Wittgenstein has this to say towards the end of his *Tractatus Logico-Philosophicus:*

> Not only is there no guarantee of the temporal immortality of the human soul, that is to say of its eternal survival after death; but, in any case, this assumption completely fails to accomplish the purpose for which it has always been intended. Or is some riddle solved by my surviving forever? Is not this eternal life itself as much of a riddle as our present life? The solution of the riddle of life in space and time lies outside space and time. (6.4312)

It sounds a little odd to say that the doctrine of immortality was intended to solve a "riddle," but the thinking seems to be this: life really ought to be immortal. Indeed, until we reach a certain age and experience, we probably live on the practical assumption that we are immortal. But then it becomes clear that we aren't. For the individual the passion for life is so great that it seems to him a contradiction that he is going to die: *I, an immortal, am going to die!* Then the doctrine of immortality comes along and resolves this "riddle" by asserting that what seems to be the death of the person is really only the sloughing off of the body.

But, responds Wittgenstein, this is really no solution, not primarily because we have no reason to believe it, but because it trades on a shallow analysis of the problem. Our life is compromised not by death, but by something lying in us, within the power of our will. To a superficial view it may look as though all our troubles would be over if only we could live a healthy life without end. But down deeper, we want not just more life, but a worthwhile life. The immature suppose that the yearning for immortality is a yearning for endless existence, but really it is the yearning for a morally worthy existence. Our current life is unworthy, and its extension beyond the grave will not solve the problem that fact poses. The sting of life is not basically that it comes to a temporal end, but that we are guilty; we have failed to become what we ought, to achieve worthiness. The riddle of life is constituted not by our mortality, but by our unrighteousness.

We cannot but admire the seriousness of this attitude. It is so thoroughly ethical that it can look in the teeth of the most terrifying natural and historical facts and say, as it were, "their terror is nothing in comparison with what I feel when I compare what I am with what I ought to be." How much more penetrating is this attitude than the cringing, whining view that we are essentially victims of fate, whether fate takes the form of our department head, nature, the price of oil, globalization, the thinning of the ozone layer, or the knuckleheads in the White House — and that we, while we may have made a few mistakes, are essentially innocent! Wittgenstein inquires about the apple that's causing all the rotting in the barrel, and answers by pointing his thumb at his own heart. And he invites each of us to do the same. In this understanding of things, the sins of others cease to be inscrutable abysses of alien darkness and look instead like mirrors in which we see our deepest selves. This outlook produces not the self-righteousness that accuses and alienates the other and confirms us in our evil, but instead a sense of solidarity with all persons. Hitler is somebody I could have been, given the appropriate context and temptations.

But this is not an easy, gliding solidarity such as you find among those who need each other for mutual survival or profit — the members of a ball team, a corporation, or a nation at war. It is a solidarity in which each, looking at the other, sees in himself the most stinging riddle of life. And paradoxically, in this pain of self-accusation and self-alienation a person finds, unstably, something of the righteousness of which he has bereaved himself.

For in it he has been humbled and reconciled, in a way, to every brother and sister he meets, in whatever may be their condition. Envy, vanity, pride, enmity, and selfishness have been tortured from his heart, and something not wholly unlike love has been put in their place. But I say "unstably" because this resolution of the riddle by the sting of the riddle itself is at best fleeting and partial, and the individual who has been momentarily saved by his contrition soon falls back again into the attitudes that make him such a riddle to himself. He must look elsewhere than to the strength of his moral passion for a savior from himself.

Some thinkers have thought to find this savior in the prospect of absolute death. Thus the interpretation of death that I attempted to explicate in the last chapter is, according to them, erroneous and morally degrading. The prospect of death should not be taken as an occasion for cutting oneself loose from this present existence and pinning one's hopes on eternal life in God's kingdom. This is only to short-circuit the process of salvation, to give an illusion of cure rather than a real one. Only by facing absolute death can we gain the character that the morally sensitive person sees to be the single thing in life worth achieving. So in the present chapter I want to consider this objection to the direction our thought took in Chapter 4.

The Salvation of Ivan Ilych

Leo Tolstoy's short story "The Death of Ivan Ilych" suggests the kind of spirituality I want to discuss. All my quotations are taken from *The Death of Ivan Ilych and Other Stories.*

Ivan Ilych is an ordinary man of the middle class, a civil servant who has been rather successful in working his way up through the ranks. His life is entirely devoted to pleasure. Ivan Ilych is fastidious about proprieties, and derives the standards by which he lives from his superiors. From those who are placed under him he gets his sense of power: "and he liked to treat them politely, almost as comrades, as if he were letting them feel that he who had the power to crush them was treating them in this simple, friendly way" (p. 107).

He marries a pretty young woman, and for a while married life enhances his pleasures. But then a child comes, and his wife, bored from being cooped up at home, becomes demanding, jealous, and irascible, poisoning Ivan Ilych's life. He meets this problem with a well-considered strategy:

He only required [of married life] those conveniences — dinner at home, housewife, and bed — which it could give him, and above all that propriety of external forms required by public opinion. For the rest he looked for light-hearted pleasure and propriety, and was very thankful when he found them, but if he met with antagonism and querulousness he at once retired into his separate fenced-off world of official duties, where he found satisfaction. (pp. 110-11)

Thus Ivan Ilych and his wife become personally distant, but he succeeds nicely in keeping his life pleasant.

After a minor setback in his career, he is promoted to a well-paying position in Petersburg. He buys a comfortable house, and so intense is his interest in the decoration of it that he even sometimes finds his mind wandering while he presides in the court. One day, standing on a ladder demonstrating to the upholsterer how he wants the hangings draped, he slips and falls, hitting his side against the knob of the window frame.

At first he seems to have sustained only a bruise, but over the next few weeks the pain in his side becomes increasingly bothersome, and he starts to experience a strange taste in his mouth. He becomes irritable and quarrelsome, and visits doctor after doctor, who prescribe various medicines and give conflicting opinions. Ivan Ilych becomes less and less able to convince himself that he is not dying. The activities in which he formerly delighted seem to have lost their point. One evening at cards "his partner said 'No trumps' and supported him with two diamonds. What more could be wished for? It ought to be jolly and lively. They would make a grand slam. But suddenly Ivan Ilych was conscious of that gnawing pain, that taste in his mouth, and it seemed ridiculous that in such circumstances he should be pleased to make a grand slam" (p. 126).

His impending death brings on a sense of loneliness that is the most tormenting part of the ordeal. At work, he perceives that the chief significance of his coming demise is that certain of his colleagues will gain promotions. His family and friends continue their round of social engagements, their outings to the theatre, their dinner parties at home. His daughter becomes engaged to marry. They evade the subject of his death, and largely evade him too. His wife pretends that if he would only follow the doctor's orders, he would be just fine. He begins to see that because he is dying, he is an annoyance to his family. He is taking the edge off their fun: "'Is it our fault?' Lisa said to her mother. 'It's as if we were to blame! I am sorry for papa, but why should we be tortured?'" (p. 151). What to Ivan Ilych is the most cataclysmic event in the history of the universe is to these self-centered pleasure-seekers a minor vexation to be addressed with the deceits of convention: "The awful, terrible act of his dying was, he could see, reduced by those about him to the level of a casual, unpleasant and almost indecorous incident (as if someone entered a drawing-room diffusing an unpleasant odor) and this was done by that very decorum which he had served all his life long" (pp. 137-38).

There are two exceptions in Ivan Ilych's house. His young son seems genuinely to have pity on him. But the more outstanding exception is Gerasim, a young peasant who is the butler's assistant. Gerasim is cheerful, candid with Ivan Ilych about the fact that he is going to die, and displays a loving willingness to help the sick man and comfort him. Gerasim's candor and love seem to be connected with his own acceptance of mortality; it is as though he, alone of all the people in the house, sees that this matter of illness, humiliation, weakness, and death that Ivan Ilych is suffering is our common lot, a tie that binds us into a brotherhood. Gerasim sees that the bell tolls not just for Ivan Ilych, but for himself as well. So instead of fleeing to his own comforts and pleasures, Gerasim is drawn in compassion to the disgusting, helpless, dying Ivan Ilych, who finds comfort in the presence of this strong, healthy young man. Sometimes he sits through the night with Ivan Ilych's legs propped on his shoulders, because the dying man feels that this eases his pain. "Health, strength, and vitality in other people were offensive to him, but Gerasim's strength and vitality did not mortify but soothed him" (p. 137). Gerasim's love is evidently an important factor in Ivan Ilych's "salvation."

The disease progresses, the loneliness deepens. The next stage in his salvation is that he begins to question his former life: "'Maybe I did not live as I ought to have done,' it suddenly occurred to him. 'But how could that be, when I did everything properly?' he replied, and immediately dismissed from his mind this, the sole solution of all the riddles of life and death, as something quite impossible" (p. 148). Then he asks himself what he really wants. To live, and not to suffer, he answers. But how? And his mind is carried back in a survey of his life, and he finds that really he would want to live little of it again, except for some scenes in his childhood. All the rest has been so artificial, so much a matter of doing things and being something to please others, to get ahead, or establish superiority over others. His life had contained little genuine human living. It begins to dawn on him that despite all its proprieties, his life has not been proper, and a suffering even greater than his physical sufferings comes over him: "His mental sufferings were due to the fact that that night, as he looked at Gerasim's sleepy, good-natured face with its prominent cheek-bones, the question suddenly occurred to him, 'What if my whole life has really been wrong?'" (p. 152). The next morning, when he sees one by one his footman, his wife, his daughter, and then the doctor, this conviction that he has missed life by overlaying it with trivialities, by exchanging it for things that are not life, is confirmed. He sees a reflection of himself in their deceitfulness and self-deceit, in their attitude that death belongs to Ivan Ilych and not to themselves; that is how *he* lived, and it is the antithesis of life.

A struggle in Ivan Ilych's consciousness ensues, in which the issue is whether he will acknowledge the truth that he has missed the point of life. He feels that he is being thrust into a black sack, and he struggles against this, but at the same time feels that his greatest agony is that he cannot get right into it. The black sack is of course death, but now not physical death. It is spiritual death, the absolute renunciation of any claim to have lived life properly. The threat of physical death has brought him to this point in dying spiritually, but physical death is only a means to this greater and more important — indeed, all-important — death. Giving up his claim to "righteousness" is an agony all right, but he has got far enough in the process to see that his "righteousness" is the real burden on his soul, the thing that is really killing him. The real enemy is not physical death, but that ego that makes itself the center of the universe, turning other people into instruments and slaves, making claims of righteousness and immortality, and surrounding itself with illusions in the service of this great lie. So great an enemy is that ego that its death is life, and the prospect of physical death has brought Ivan Ilych to the point of seeing this truth.

Then he is carried beyond merely seeing it. Outwardly he is screaming and flailing his arms about. One arm falls on the head of his young son, who clutches it and, weeping, kisses it:

> At that very moment Ivan Ilych fell through [into the black sack] and caught sight of the light, and it was revealed to him that though his life had not been what it should have been, this could still be rectified. He asked himself, "What is the right thing?" and grew still, listening. Then he felt that someone was kissing his hand. He opened his eyes, looked at his son, and felt sorry for him. His wife came up to him and he glanced at

her. She was gazing at him open-mouthed, with undried tears on her nose and cheek and a despairing look on her face. He felt sorry for her too. (p. 155)

In this moment Ivan Ilych, almost for the first time since his childhood, loves another human being. He has died to the self that clung to its claims — of righteousness and of the right to live and to live on its own terms — and so is now able to be humanely conscious of his son and wife. The inexorable prospect of utter annihilation has left him naked and stripped of every defense, causing every artificiality with which he has hidden life from himself to fall away. And when all is stripped away, he finds not nothing, as he had feared, but himself, the self he had betrayed all these years, and denied and safely jammed into oblivion by decorum: "'And death . . . where is it?' He sought his former accustomed fear of death and did not find it. 'Where is it? What death?' There was no fear because there was no death. In place of death there was light. 'So that's what it is!' he exclaimed aloud. 'What joy!'" (pp. 155-56). Ivan Ilych remains in this state of joy for another two hours, and then dies.

Two Objections to the Christian Hope

Ivan Ilych dies contented, indeed joyful, despite having no notion at all of being delivered from the permanent annihilation of his consciousness. The joy he experiences in the last two hours of life does not stem from the hope of resurrection, but from a sense of being released from his insatiable, grasping, and haughty ego, which the prospect of annihilation has gradually caused him to feel as an intolerable burden. He has no more fear of extinction, not because it has been forestalled or short-circuited by belief in a life after death, but because the concern for continuation of life has been utterly submerged in a greater concern, which we might call the concern for authenticity. In a paradoxical turn of events, triviality, disingenuousness, and lovelessness, which seemed at first to be the acceptable order of the day, have become the hellish horror of horrors; while death, which at first seemed the ultimate enemy, has put on a mild face and a beckoning voice and become the savior.

In the remainder of this chapter I will reflect on two objections to the proposals I made in Chapter 3, objections of a sort that might very well lie behind Tolstoy's story as its ideological starting point. The high-minded people I mentioned at the beginning of this chapter will object to the Christian scheme not just because they believe there is no such thing as eternal life, but for what to their minds are much more important reasons. They will hold that the belief in eternal life — and thus also the Christian's salutary use of the prospect of death — is morally degrading, for two reasons. First, the belief in heaven cannot be divorced from a reward mentality, and a reward mentality is the very antithesis of an authentic and moral life. Second, the egocentrism that lies at the foundation of all moral failure is so deep and tenacious that nothing can save us from its misery short of looking straight in the teeth of unconditional obliteration, as Ivan Ilych was forced to do. In the next two sections, I examine these claims.

Is the Love of the Kingdom an Unworthy Motive?

The first objection goes something like this: the reason it is so difficult to assess the ethical value of an action is that the value lies not just in the observable action, much less in its consequences, but in its motive. In some cases, of course, a motive is obviously bad: someone writes a check for $100,000 to a charitable organization and then demands her money back when the society informs her that it is not their policy to publicize the names of donors. This donor seems to desire primarily not the humanitarian purposes of the organization but her own public glorification. Her desire is not a moral one, but a desire for a certain kind of reward. This is an obvious case, but many cases are more subtle than this. We sometimes wonder about even our own motives in doing some good deed: Was I just afraid I'd feel guilty if I didn't do it? Would I have done it had I known that nobody would ever know about it? Did I do it primarily because I looked forward to the expressions of gratitude from my beneficiary? Or worse yet, did I do it to make myself feel superior to my beneficiary? And so on and on. The great difficulty of acting in a *wholly* moral way comes out when we begin to distinguish moral from non-moral motives. Most of us don't even come close to passing the test most of the time. We are a lot like Ivan Ilych in his "prime."

But many philosophers in the last couple of hundred years have taken this ordinary but very important distinction between moral and non-moral motives and twisted it into something quite different. They say that considerations of advantage (what I have called more crudely "reward") and moral considerations belong to entirely different categories. They mean that the desire for some advantage or reward can never be a moral desire. Immanuel Kant, the apparent father of this view, avers convincingly that a shopkeeper who for lucre's sake refrains from overcharging children is not by that token an honest man. He is moved by the prospect of gain, not honesty. But a couple of paragraphs later, exemplifying what to his mind is the same point, Kant tells us that humane actions are also without any genuine moral worth, insofar as they arise from the doer's concern for the happiness of others. We can tell for sure that a person's acts of benevolence have moral worth only if he lacks the desire for another's happiness and acts merely from duty. Kant makes the same point with a distinction between practical love and pathological love. Pathological love is the kind we have for friends, family, and perhaps even strangers if we happen to wish for their welfare and want to do them good. Pathological love has no moral worth because, he suggests, in exercising it we are only fulfilling our own desires. We exemplify practical (i.e., moral) love when we do something good for someone not because we have an inclination to do it, but simply because it is our duty (see *Foundations of the Metaphysics of Morals*).

It is easy to see how this artificial and austere theory of moral psychology would lead to criticism of the Christian virtue ethics we are considering. In such a scheme of things the eternal kingdom for which the Christian hopes is seen as an "advantage," even a "reward." Thus if a person chooses his behavior and lifestyle in this life because he desires to be a fit member of the promised kingdom, then according to these thinkers such a person cannot be acting morally. He cannot be acting as an authentic human being. Not only (so goes the objection) is the person acting out of a desire (like the individual who takes pleasure in relieving the suffering of others); he is even acting out of an *extrinsic* desire. For the person who simply enjoys seeing people relieved of their suffering, at least the object of pleasure is something closely connected with the benevolent action. But in the case of the Christian who acts in hope of the kingdom, the object of desire is something different, and distant, from the action itself. In doing acts of charity for the sake of the future life he is just like the shopkeeper who performs acts of fairness for the sake of money. (Kant himself did not use his theory of ethical motivation as an argument against believing in immortality; that inference has been added by others.)

This first objection has two stages, and each is mistaken. First, the dis-

tinction between moral considerations and considerations of advantage is
false when it is made absolute. Often, when we act for our advantage, our
actions are without moral worth. But this is not always so. Sometimes
moral considerations and considerations of advantage overlap. For persons
in whom justice has become a character trait rather than just a duty, seeing
injustice will be a painful thing. We will love justice, desire it, and in its absence long for it. In the compassionate person the sight of a hungry or mis-
treated child will be cause for emotional pain. The moral life is a life of passions, as I used the word in Chapter 2. The successful alleviation of the
hungry will be to the compassionate person as much a reward or advantage
as making lots of money is for the avaricious. To the just person the rectifi-
cation of injustice will be a satisfaction of his personal longing, and an emotional delight. The more deeply a person develops, the less important does
the concept of duty become. We act from duty only because we are not yet
spiritually moral. The perfected saint feels few duties, but many joys and
sorrows. So these philosophers are wrong in thinking that desires and considerations of advantage are ruled out in the person who has truly become
himself. And if this is so, why couldn't one of the moral person's desires, indeed the summation of all his deepest desires, be the kingdom of God?

The second stage of the objection is the claim that the desire for the
promised kingdom is even worse, morally, than other desires, because it is
extrinsic to the moral life. In a book entitled *Death and Immortality,* which
should really have been called *Death and Authenticity,* the philosopher
D. Z. Phillips says,

> It has been seen that construing belief in the immortality of the soul as
> the final state which gives men good reasons for acting in certain ways
> now falsified the character of moral regard. It certainly allows no room
> for anything that might be meant by the spirituality of the soul. It seems
> to me that if people lead a certain kind of life simply because of the final
> set of consequences to which it leads, they are indifferent to that way of
> life. (p. 30)

But this objection rests both on the Kantian mistake that I examined above,
and a misconception of "the final state which gives men good reasons for
acting." If you picture eternal life as a context of endless surfing, card playing, gin drinking, and coeducational hot-tubbing, and then figure that the
way to get your hands on this jackpot vacation is to deny yourself, take up

your cross, and embark on a short but painful ministry to the headhunters of New Guinea, then Phillips's objection has fouled your eschatology. But in Christian thinking, surely, eternal life is the consummation and perfection of love to one's fellow personal creatures and of loving obedience to God. It is a state of perfect justice and peace, the perfection of the moral life itself. It may include hot tubs and surfing, for all I know, but it is above all a context of obedience and love. So selfish people, people who have no compunction about acts of cruelty and injustice, people who want to live independently of God and to be left to their own pleasures, cannot desire the kingdom of heaven as it is conceived by Christian faith. They may think they desire it, but they would find it a very unpleasant place to be if they somehow landed there. (See C. S. Lewis's *The Great Divorce* for an imaginative depiction of this situation.)

Phillips is wrong to think that leading a life of love is incompatible with believing that such a life leads to the immortal kingdom of God. The eternal kingdom is the reward of a spirit who has developed in such a way that such a kingdom can look like a reward to it. So it is every Christian's duty to combat worldliness in himself, to open himself to influences of holiness, and to practice the practices that will nurture him toward being the sort of person to whom the kingdom of heaven really looks like an advantage and a reward. But a life of growing moral sensitivity and toughness is more than just *compatible* with the hope of this reward. It is positively *nourished* by this hope. It is very easy to get discouraged in the moral life. As soon as the going begins to get rough, one is tempted not just to violate the standards, but to lower them. The temptation is to say, "It can't be done; it is hopelessly idealistic. Justice and love are a dream dreamt of by youths and fanatics, but a grown man knows better; a little tinge of justice here and there, a hint of love, this is the most that one can or ought to expect. For the rest, let us enjoy ourselves. We must be realists." Against such dulling compromise, the resolute preaching of the kingdom of heaven can be a powerful antidote. It says, "Don't give up. Indeed, you'd better not give up. For God, who is in control of things, is going to make complete justice and perfect love the very structure of the world. In trimming down your moral vision, you're setting yourself at odds with the Creator of heaven and earth."

CAN ONLY ABSOLUTE DEATH KILL SIN?

The other moral argument against the Christian hope goes like this: because of the vanity of everything that humans accomplish under the sun, the only thing of real worth is something that does not show by the light of the sun: the moral virtue of the individual human heart. But the systematic obstacle to every virtue is human selfishness, what Iris Murdoch calls "the fat relentless ego." Ambition, scorn, envy, greed, injustice, cruelty: the disease in every case is traceable to the same source — the self's nonnegotiable claim to be Number One in the universe. The ego is a very hard nut to crack, so hard, in fact, that nothing short of confronting its absolute annihilation will bring it to the humility that is the foundation of all the virtues. In *The Sovereignty of Good,* Murdoch says,

> Goodness is connected with the acceptance of real death and real chance and real transience and only against the background of this acceptance, which is psychologically so difficult, can we understand the full extent of what virtue is like. The acceptance of death is an acceptance of our own nothingness which is an automatic spur to our concern with what is not ourselves. The good man is humble . . . (p. 103).

Belief in immortality, according to Murdoch, harms human beings, because it gives them an out from the only remedy that is radical enough to make them good.

I agree both that humility is central to human goodness, and that confronting death can foster it. Death levels. The most successful businessman, the most powerful politician, the most popular Hollywood star are, with respect to death, in the same boat as the poorest, most inept, and despised human being on earth. It is our duty, in honesty, to dwell on the shortness of our life. When we do, we find that the edge is taken off our worldly ambitions, our greed, our ruthlessness, our cruelty, our willingness to scorn and despise those who are less virtuous, wealthy, intelligent, or popular than we. A heartfelt reflection on our own death can help us in our pilgrimage toward seeing every person we meet as our brother and sister.

But must the death we confront be conceived as utter annihilation for it to have this effect? If the only way to conceive the afterlife were as a continuation of the present order of things, where the rule is dog-eat-dog for the survival of the ego, then perhaps so. But I have suggested in the last section that this is not the only way to conceive it, and indeed is very far from the Christian view. The kingdom is a context (with some distant analogies in the present order) in which people whose fat relentless egos have not been killed will be very uncomfortable. For most of us, looking forward to this kind of afterlife is itself a kind of death, and can have the same humbling effect as the prospect of physical death.

But I would note too that death, whether understood as utter annihilation or as the passageway to judgment, is not the only and maybe not even the chief way that people are freed from themselves and empowered to live in selfless obedience to God or love of their fellow creatures. Perhaps the most powerful solvent of the self-encased self is another's relentless love for it. "We love because he first loved us," says the apostle. In the face of the irresistible affirmation of oneself by a lover, it becomes almost impossible not to open up and forget oneself in responsive love (see the conversion of Raskolnikov at the end of Dostoevsky's *Crime and Punishment*). Nothing drives us more deeply into egoism than the feeling that if we don't look out for ourselves, no one else will. Even the most humble can sometimes be tempted into self-assertion by the relentless assaults of a social setting governed by the rule that each person is to establish his or her worth at the expense of others. And when, into such a context, a person comes who resolutely accepts another not by these standards, but in love, she enters as a liberating ray of grace into a world of darkness, casting down the other's defenses and lighting up the other's neighbors in his eyes. The story of Ivan Ilych's transformation would be implausible without the roles played by Gerasim and Ivan Ilych's young son. Even Tolstoy could not convince us that facing death could, by itself, make a loving, self-abandoning person of Ivan Ilych.

In the present world, liberating experiences of love are rare. Egoism is the formula for survival. This is a world where most commodities and social positions and personal qualities are prized because not everybody can have them, and so they engender envy in those who lack them and pride in their possessors. And the envious and prideful fuel one another's sin and harden the encasement around each that prevents them from communion. But in the new world to which Christians look forward, all these pressures that foster the entrenchment of the fat, relentless ego, all these encouragements to selfishness and lovelessness, will be gone and in their place will be an overpowering presence of love. What Ivan Ilych experienced in a small but powerful way in the person of Gerasim, the less-than-perfect individual entering the new world will experience as irresistible grace. Love is just as irresistible as death, with one proviso — that the individual to whom love is offered not be completely without love himself. If one is entirely self-enclosed, without any sensitivity to the claims of other persons on him, but treats them only and always as means to his private ends, then even the love of God and of all the saints will not affect him. Ivan Ilych's susceptibility to be changed by the love of Gerasim shows that he was not beyond redemption. A faulty psychology or a lack of imagination, or both, lie at the basis of the claim that only the confrontation with absolute death can make a person good.

But beyond this, Murdoch's position harbors a certain absurdity. Heroically, she says "a genuine sense of mortality enables us to see virtue as the only thing of worth" (p. 99). But if virtue is the only thing of worth, and we must face "real death and real chance and real transience" (p. 103) if we are to come to this realization, then there is not even a grain of truth in the intuitions we explored in Chapter 3. The perception of death as an enemy is entirely mistaken, and is completely due to the fat, relentless ego. Only insofar as we are selfish, immoral, and unfulfilled do we perceive death as an enemy. The truth is not, as Christianity holds, that death is both an enemy and a friend. Utter annihilation is simply the best and only real friend a person ever had.

But isn't it outrageous to make virtue "the only thing of worth" and at the same time to hold that the universe is so constituted that those beings in whom virtue is possible (and occasionally actual) flourish for a while and then sink into nothingness? Murdoch rightly conceives virtue as loving other people. But if absolute death is not only my destiny but also the destiny of those people who are the object of my virtue, is there not something deeply sad about virtue itself? I am not pointing to anything like a logical contradiction here, but rather to a contradiction of how, in our heart of hearts, we must feel that things ought to be. Something is offensive, fundamentally shocking, about a universe that allows a being capable of love to be annihilated.

Let me put the matter another way. The love of virtue seems to imply the love of life, since a dead person is not capable of virtue. So even for Murdoch, who believes that virtue cannot be achieved apart from believing that one is confronted with absolute death, it would be preferable if we were not in fact destined to it. That is, the ideal situation would be one of deceit — the situation in which we all believe that we are going to be obliterated, but in fact we are going to live on to exercise our virtue. Or, to put the point another way, Murdoch cannot really believe that virtue is the only thing of worth. She must believe that life too is of worth, even if it is worthless without virtue. But if life is worthless without virtue, surely virtue is also worthless without life. Tolstoy had to give Ivan Ilych at least a bit of time (those two hours of joy before he died) in which to be virtuous.

The Christian does not believe that virtue is the only thing of worth; of worth also is the life that is the only context in which virtue can be exercised: a conscious life of fellowship with God and his creatures. And so for the Christian (as, I think, for many non-Christians), it would be an inexpressible pity if death were the eternal annihilation of the self. For if it is, it is also the annihilation of virtue, the annihilation of a child of God. It is natural for us to grieve on the occasion of death, and more so if we are without hope. But if Murdoch is right, we have here a transformed and deepened sadness, the gloomiest and most incongruous of pictures. It is not now the screaming protest of the fat, relentless ego against the ultimate threat to its godhead, but instead the quiet grief of love at the prospect that something as precious as a child of God should be obliterated. And now I want to admit to a certain thinness in the feelings I described in Chapter 3. Much in those feelings is the screaming protest of the fat, relentless ego. But the protest contains something else too, which prefigures the Christian apprehension. And that is the sense that in absolute death something of priceless value is slated to be snuffed out.

So Wittgenstein's suggestion that the "riddle" of death is completely submerged in the "riddle" of our unworthiness is not right. Death remains a riddle, an incongruity and an embarrassment on the face of the universe, unless it is conquered, as Christians believe it has been. But Wittgenstein's emphasis is right, even if his declaration is not. For Christians, the fact of death and the hope of life are inextricably tied up with the passion for moral worthiness, the hungering and thirsting for righteousness.

LOOKING BACK AND AHEAD

In this chapter and the last two I have attempted to say a little about the basis of the Christian emotions, a passion we might call the heart's seeking for the kingdom of God. My account has been progressive, in that the present chapter has approximated more nearly the description of Christian maturity than the previous one. In the previous chapter I described an embryonic passion for the kingdom of God, the yearning for a life beyond this finite existence, and defended it against some obvious objections. Then in the present chapter, in the course of answering a profound moral objection to the desire for eternal life, our understanding of this passion deepened and took on the second major aspect of correspondence to the Christian gospel: just as Christianity is a message about God's triumph for us over the twin evils of sin and death, so the Christian's passion must be not only a desire for life-despite-death but also a desire for righteousness, a desire for a world of justice, peace, and love. For the life that is offered us in the Christian gospel is essentially a moral life, one of love for God and neighbor; in the Christian conception of the kingdom, the living and the being worthy are not separable. In the next chapter I try to increase our understanding of the Christian passion still further by beginning to look inside the moral life. If I succeed, the account will give a yet deeper insight into the passion basic to the Christian emotions: an overriding enthusiasm for the life of perfect fellowship with God and neighbor in the promised kingdom.

I shall focus my discussion on humility both because of its great intrinsic interest as a virtue of the Christian life and also as a way of making clear the connection between moral striving and Christian spirituality. My concentrating on humility does not suggest that this is the only virtue worth striving for (though I do think it very basic to the Christian outlook); it is, for our present purpose, an example. I hope to show that moral striving is both an essential part of spiritual growth (that is, spiritual growth is moral growth) and a ground of self-despair that sensitizes the individual to the grace of Jesus Christ. The more serious you become about attaining moral goodness, the more serious you have become about God's kingdom. And the more actively you get involved in the endeavor to straighten yourself out morally, the more deeply do you perceive the grace of Jesus as food for your spirit.

Chapter Six

Humility as a Moral Project

Humility as Pride

The classical Christian virtue of humility has fallen on hard times. Even people who believe, because Christ says so, that the meek are blessed, sometimes get uneasy about humility. This may be due to the self-esteem movement in pop psychology, the feminist emphasis on assertiveness, the influence of the Nietzschean philosophy in our culture, and the many ways competitiveness is built into our institutions. Maybe we are uneasy because we have so taken our culture's ways of thinking into our self-understanding. Humility seems so often unrealistic, impractical, or downright demeaning — not a virtue at all. We may find it repugnant because it conflicts with deep-seated personal values — even if it accords nicely with our spoken ones. It is so natural to conceive ourselves in terms of power over others; our confused hearts are convinced that the pursuit of self-respect is the same as the pursuit of advantageous comparison with our fellows. We are committed to building our egos on a foundation of inferiority — the inferiority of others. So the distaste for humility may be traced to both cultural distortions and natural, sinful inclinations.

It can also be traced to one or more confusions about what humility is. So I want to clarify the concept of humility as a virtue, and to begin by distinguishing it from some things that are clearly not virtues, with which it is often confused. Behold Uriah Heep, a particularly disgusting character in Charles Dickens's *David Copperfield:*

> Father and me was both brought up at a foundation school for boys. . . .
> They taught us all a deal of umbleness — not much else that I know of,

from morning to night. We was to be umble to this person, and umble to that; and to pull off our caps here, and to make bows there; and always to know our place, and abase ourselves before our betters. And we had such a lot of betters! Father got the monitor-medal by being umble. So did I. Father got made sexton by being umble. He had the character, among the gentlefolks, of being such a well-behaved man, that they were determined to bring him in. 'Be umble, Uriah,' says father to me, 'and you'll get on ...' 'Be umble,' says father, 'and you'll do!' And really it ain't done bad! ... I got to know what umbleness did, and I took to it. I ate umble pie with an appetite. . . . 'People like to be above you,' says father; 'keep yourself down.' I am very umble to the present moment, Master Copperfield, but I've got a little power! (pp. 604-5)

Umbleness, as Uriah Heep practices it, is a strategy for getting ahead in the world. It is a pattern of deferential and self-demeaning behavior calculated to play on other people's invidious desire for self-importance, thereby procuring for its practitioner advancement in rank, medals and honors, and suchlike. The desire to beat out all the other servants in the contest for the monitor-medal is clearly not humility. In Uriah, at least, umbleness does not involve a humble attitude of heart: he is quite aware of seeking power over others and the advantages that self-demeaning affords on that score. The hostage of a terrorist may practice umbleness with his captor as a means of "getting on," all the while consciously despising him as the very scum of the earth.

Uriah Heep's umbleness does not utilize self-deception, at any rate not much. The philosopher Friedrich Nietzsche is famous for having noted a subtler form of Uriah's trait that does involve self-deception. He pointed out that what seems like humility is often (he thought always) motivated down deep by the desire to topple people who are stronger, or more intelligent, or higher in rank from their positions of strength. "Humility" is a strategic device used by the weak in the competition for ascendancy over other human beings. If a person (or group) finds he cannot compete successfully in terms of worldly success, he does what he can to change the terms of competition to something in which he can succeed. And, of course, what he really excels at is mediocrity. The perverse genius of the "slave morality," as Nietzsche calls it, is to make a virtue of failure (namely weakness, lowliness, degradation) and to make what is naturally virtuous (namely success, power, intelligence, nobility, haughtiness, flagrant self-approval) appear to be failure. Thus the losers and misfits of the world try to become winners by convincing everybody that losing is really winning. God especially favors the poor in spirit. If those with weak and slavish natures can make this illusion stick, then those who have worldly success will see that their power and excellence is not so great after all — indeed, it is pride, selfishness, arrogance, callousness, and other vices — while people who think themselves meek and lowly sinners undeserving of what little they have are the good people, the noble characters, the real winners in the game of life. Blessed are the meek, for by their strategic weakness they will wrest the reins of power from the great and inherit the earth.

So, according to Nietzsche, at the root of all humility is a very unhumble motive: the desire to rank oneself superior by putting down the mighty from their thrones and exalting those of low degree. But Nietzsche thinks that people who use this strategy are seldom fully conscious of what they are doing. In trying to deceive the powerful into thinking that power is bad and weakness good, the Christians who practice this vice are also deceiving themselves: they are hardly aware, or at best half-aware, that they are humbling themselves *in order to be exalted.* They half-believe their own lies about the disvalue of pride and dominance and lording it over others.

For Nietzsche, humility is despicable, but not because it is an effort to establish one's superiority over others. He regards that as a natural, inevitable disposition of the human heart, not at all to be despised in itself. In the noble and powerful ones who recognize glory in themselves and have no compunction about asserting it, this predilection for ascendancy and domination is a natural and innocent attitude; what we call arrogance is really a virtue. Humility is despicable not because it is unhumble, but because it is a reversal of true values, a lie in which what is really bad (lowly, degraded, weak, sickly) is made out to be good. Humility is disgusting because it propagates mediocrity.

Nietzsche thinks that human nature dictates that humility always is and must be merely "humility" — self-abasement deceitfully aimed at self-exaltation. He seems to dismiss the possibility that people might abdicate the power-play model of life altogether, getting their self-value some other way than by deriving it from their power over others. If we believe that we can be freed, even in part, from the competition for power, and if we believe that the power-seeking view of life is intrinsically evil, then we will want to resist Nietzsche on this point and hold out for both a better conception of humility and for the possibility of realizing it. But we must also admit the justice of his analysis as a criticism of much that passes for humility. Much of it is the despicable device he says it is. We, like Uriah Heep but with greater self-deceit and greater psychological sophistication, do in many subtle ways debase ourselves to establish our ascendancy over others or to protect ourselves in a competition for power that we are very reluctant to lose and almost as reluctant to admit. Our "humility" is not really humility, and has the double defect of deceitfulness and invidious pride. Nietzsche's is a deep criticism of many people whose moral life is outwardly Christian (and of many who have no interest in Christianity).

HUMILITY AS SICKNESS

Humility is also confused with low self-esteem, submissiveness to other persons, or seeing oneself as inferior to others. Unlike the confusion of humility with umbleness, this confusion does not necessarily involve deceit, or make humility into a device for getting something. It can be a perfectly honest (though pitiable) self-assessment, and nothing more. William MacDougall's view is typical. Humility, he says,

> may be due to the original strength of the submissive tendency, or may be the result of much chastening, of rebuffs and failures which gradually induce in a man a lowly estimate of his qualities and weaken, by repeated discouragement, the self-assertive impulse. (*Character and the Conduct of Life,* p. 129)

The picture here is that of a person limited by genetics or beaten down by failure. He does not have much confidence in his own abilities and judgments. He does not initiate projects and human relationships. He would rather follow orders than give them, would rather have others make the decisions in his life. His failures (or his genes) have rendered him a psychologically passive personality, a Mr. Milquetoast who does not object to being told where to sit and wait, or even to being utilized as a convenient wiping-place for muddy feet. Anyone who undertook to cultivate this disposition in his children would be doing them a momentous disservice. This is not humility, but rather a deeply engrained and ramified humiliation. Humility, by contrast, is not incompatible with assertiveness, self-confidence, and a high view of one's own abilities; indeed, as I shall soon argue, it is a transcendent form of self-confidence.

Sad to say, Christians have indulged — even reveled — in this confusion about humility. In mystical and ascetic Christian literature, we sometimes meet the view that the truly humble person sees himself unfavorably in comparison with his fellows and as incapable of anything good. Note the following remarks from Walter Hilton's *The Stairway of Perfection* (a mystical treatise of the fourteenth century):

> First of all, this is how you must practice meekness. You must judge yourself in your will (and in your feelings, if you can manage it) to be unable to dwell among men and unworthy to serve God in conversation with His servants. Further, you must consider yourself unprofitable to your fellow-Christians, lacking both the intelligence and the strength to perform the good works of the active life and help your fellow-Christians as other men and women do. . . . You shall judge yourself more foul and more wretched than any creature alive, so that you'll hardly be able to put up with yourself for the greatness and number of your sins and the filth that you'll experience in yourself. (pp. 80, 81)

We must reject this picture for several reasons. First, it confuses humility with contrition. Humility has nothing essentially to do with being sinful. Jesus Christ is the most perfect exemplar of humility (see Philippians 2), but he could not exhibit contrition, which involves sorrowing over one's sin (see Chapter 7). Second, if one who is humble has to believe that he is lacking both the intelligence and strength to do good works as other men and women do, then not everybody's humility can be based on a true belief. But it doesn't seem fair for a virtue to require some people to believe a falsehood about themselves. The unfortunate ones who excel in the intelligence and strength to do good works would then be condemned to choose between humility and truth; true humility would be reserved for people lucky enough to be genuinely mediocre. And third, Hilton's conception of humility requires that the individual indulge in precisely the activity that so easily slides into pride — building one's view of oneself on comparisons with others. Unlike the straightforwardly proud person, he does not seek a flattering comparison with others. And yet the humility he achieves by this means he still achieves, in a sense, at somebody else's expense; for if it is true that he is more wretched than any creature alive, then no other creature will be in quite such an good position for cultivating the virtue. Humility, strangely, turns out to be an elitist virtue.

HUMILITY AS HUMILITY

It would be better to try to conceive of humility as a matter of viewing everybody as ultimately or basically equal. The belief in people's ultimate equality will probably have to be one that transcends appearances, since from all that is obvious, people are so unequal. But if such a belief can be integrated into a person's emotional life, it will allow humility to be compatible with people's believing the truth about themselves, and also allow them to eschew the whole dangerous business of building self-assessments on watching to see how they're doing in comparison with others. Such a view would not have to deny obvious individual differences of beauty, ability, and virtue, since its conception of human equality would turn on a feature of the self that transcends such differences.

'Humility' comes from *humus,* Latin for earth. This origin of the word might suggest that being humble is being down to earth, not trying to be up in the clouds where one doesn't belong. It need not mean groveling in the dirt while others are standing erect and dignified; it might mean being solidly a member of the earthy human family by not trying to opt out of it upwardly (and in fact, by God's standard, opting out of it downwardly, thus ending one's endeavor to be more than a member of the family by becoming less).

I propose that the opposite of humility as a virtue is not self-confidence, initiative, assertiveness, and self-esteem, but instead pushiness, scorn of "inferiors," rejoicing in the downfall of others, envy, resentment and grudge-bearing, ruthless ambition, haughtiness, shame at failure or disadvantageous comparison, and the need to excel others so as to think well of oneself. Humility is the ability, without prejudice to one's self-comfort, to admit one's inferiority, in this or that respect, to another. And it is the ability, without increment to one's self-comfort or prejudice to the quality of one's relationship with another, to remark one's superiority, in this or that respect, to another. As such, humility is a psychological principle of independence from others and a necessary ground of genuine fellowship with them, an emotional independence of one's judgments concerning how one ranks vis-à-vis other human beings. Next I want to reflect on the idea of a spiritual relationship and show that humility is necessary for such relationships.

Humility and Spiritual Relationships

Most of our associations with people are largely instrumental and external. By 'instrumental' I mean that one relates to the other person for some other purpose than fellowship with him or her. Many of our relationships with others in our daily lives aim at making money, acquiring information, getting some job done, etc. To say that a relationship is largely instrumental is not to say that it is wholly so. My engagement as a teacher with students is largely aimed at getting a job done — namely, teaching them something. Yet part of what motivates me to stick with the teaching profession may be the friendships I enjoy with my students. By 'external' I mean that I relate to others by conventions, by behavior that is judged proper or improper without regard to my motives or attitudes. Thus in hiring someone to mow my lawn, I am thought to have been impeccably decent if I treat her respectfully and pay her fairly. The question of the propriety of my thoughts about her doesn't arise (or so it seems) even if, for example, I take a mild, fleeting joy in the fact that she is having financial troubles or silently rejoice in how advantageously my own daughter compares to her in beauty and intelligence.

My relationship to her may seem to me entirely instrumental and external, that is, entirely without a spiritual dimension. After all, I just want to get the lawn mowed. But if I am a Christian, then I do not believe that any of my relationships can be merely instrumental and external. I am called on to love my neighbor. And yet even Christians fall into thinking in purely instrumental and external terms; this is, in a way, natural, for most of our interaction with others is to get some job done or for some other external purpose.

But even the non-Christian, who may think it entirely proper for some of his relationships to be merely instrumental, will have to admit that the most significant ones in his life are not merely instrumental. These are relationships of friendship and love, ones whose point is fellowship, and whose substance is attitudes fundamental to fellowship. The young woman who mows my lawn may say, "I don't care what Roberts thinks about me, as long as he pays me," but my daughter Beffie cannot say, "I don't care what Papa thinks of me, as long as he's a good father to me." And my best friend can't say, "I don't care what attitudes Roberts takes towards me, as long as he remains a good friend." I demand not just loving behavior from my lover, but a certain enthusiasm for my person, a heartfelt devotion, a tendency to rejoice and grieve with me at appropriate moments, a deep respect. Here, the attitudes of the parties to the relationship are its very substance, and this is why a lack of humility destroys a person's spiritual life; it subverts his spiritual relationships, the deepest and most important relationships of his life. Pride cuts a person off from fellowship with others. It isolates him and, however little he may recognize the fact, degrades him. He who exalts himself will be humbled.

Invidious, competitive pride is most likely to manifest itself in relationships in which the two individuals are close enough to equality in worldly terms to feel themselves competitors, and yet not very close friends or lovers. The most famous and brilliant philosopher in America is not likely to get much satisfaction when his analytic ability is considered superior to that of a graduate student from Northeastern West Virginia State Teachers College, but he may get intense satisfaction from contemplating his superiority to another member of the Harvard philosophy faculty. (He may, in fact, feel himself less alienated from, and be less alienating to, the graduate student than the colleague.) Similarly the graduate student from NWVSTC is less likely to feel malicious envy of the brilliant philosopher than the philosopher's colleagues are, since she is not even in the running, so to speak. If the NWVSTC student feels envious of anybody's philosophic abilities, it is more likely to be those of some fellow graduate student.

But the symptoms of competitive pride (envy, superciliousness, putdowns, condescension, scorn) may be absent between two persons who are in the running with one another if the two are very close friends or lovers. This is possible if they identify with each other. The superior one does not nourish his ego from his superiority to the other, because the other is almost an extension of himself (just as he would not take malicious pride in the fact that he is a better mathematician today than he was ten years ago, because he identifies with the self that he was ten years ago). Similarly, the inferior one does not take offense against the superior, envying and hating him for the degradation he feels at being rendered inferior by the comparison, because he identifies with the superior one. He can take a sort of pride in the other's superiority, because he feels that the other is part of himself. A wife, traditionally, has seen the achievements of her husband in this way; even if she herself is in the running, she doesn't succumb to envy of her husband, but instead takes pride over others in his superiority; his ascendancy over others is hers through identification. (In our time, most wives in this situation probably have mixed feelings; they are proud to be associated with their hotshot husband, but at the same time a little envious of his ascendancy.)

It is not difficult to see why people who lack humility are spiritually bankrupt. Their capacity for human relationships — the spiritual ones that are the most important of their lives — is poisoned by the tendency to climb to eminence at someone else's expense. The proud person is one who feels good about himself only if he has somebody who compares disadvantageously with himself. He says to himself, "I may be stupid and ugly, but all is not lost; compared to a guy I see at the YMCA, I'm a combination of Albert Einstein and Brad Pitt." Since the comparison builds the self, there is always another person, somewhere in the background at least, who is supporting the weight of my ego with the suffering of his failure to make the grade relative to me.

Is It Really That Bad?

Now you may object: "First you said relationships of fellowship and love are the important, the spiritual ones. Then you observed that the proud individual gets his self-confidence by comparing himself with others who are less advantaged than he. But your conclusion, to the effect that pride ruins the most important relationships, doesn't follow from these two observations. That would follow only if the same people upon whose shoulders of weakness you construct your glory were the people with whom you are purporting to have these important relationships. But that needn't be so. In fact, we tend to build our friendships with people who are our equals, and are therefore not very good candidates to become, by their wretchedness, the cornerstone of our self-esteem. So I don't see how these important relationships are spoiled by invidious pride."

I will admit that the parasite strategy of the proud person's bid for self-esteem is not as obviously directed to his close friends as it is to the others about whom he and his close friends invidiously gossip. People who are clearly beyond the pale make good candidates, in one way, for pride fodder, because they don't offer serious competition with us. But in another way they make poor pride fodder, because being superior to them doesn't count as much in ego-building as superiority to someone roughly equal to us in whatever matter is the basis for comparison. So our closest friends are likely to be just the kind of people whose inferiority holds out the greatest promise of serving to build our pride. Their being our friends, and not merely our rivals, means that we have come to some kind of understanding with them in the matter of superiority/inferiority.

Perhaps you play the role of acknowledged inferior and your friend that of superior. You find this understanding acceptable, because your very association with him enhances your superiority to some other person or group. But now ask yourself: what if suddenly you were promoted to a position of prominence and power in the company, and in the eyes of the world you had clearly established your superiority over him? If you are a proud person, it is likely that the superciliousness you once directed to other inferiors will now be turned directly on your friend. You will begin to rejoice in your superiority to him; he will become now the fodder for your pride. Maybe you won't admit this to yourself; perhaps you exercise, in the name of the spiritual relationship, a certain chaste self-deception. But still, in your heart, you know it feels very good to have one-upped the old boy and reversed the roles. This sort of imagined case seems to say that pride makes a person *ready* to eat his "friends"; it gives one's friendships a very unstable character, for given a slight shift in the circumstances, suddenly the "friend," who was not fodder for one's competitive pride, becomes such.

Or let's suppose that the understanding the two of you "friends" had was that you were the one in ascendancy, and he the acknowledged inferior. And now let it happen that the roles are reversed by some circumstance. Maybe you don't admit to yourself that your self-comfort was invested in being the big brother in that relation, the one to whom your "friend" would come for advice, looking up in admiration. After all, you do have a dim sense that this is a spiritual relationship, and that your parasitically feeding on his inferiority is not good for it. But now he has been catapulted to fame, and you are left in relative obscurity. Will your relationship go on undisturbed? Not, I think, if you are an invidiously proud person. Instead, your reaction will be envy — a certain hatred of your friend now that he has usurped your place and "put you down." Of course you may try to hide this, from him and from yourself. But still, that love has been poisoned. And my point is that what seemed to be love was already spoiled by your pride. It was not your friend's sudden rise to fame that spoiled everything; the relationship was spoiled already because pride was in its foundation.

It is hard to be close friends with an unrepentant cannibal. Even if he is not at the moment eyeing my musculature with a fond view to the tenderloins, still the fact that my tenderloins are the kind of thing on which he feeds threatens to spoil everything. I may not notice that the relationship is spoiled. For one thing, I may be so crass that I accept this mutual cannibalism with equanimity; perhaps I don't have an inkling what spiritual friendship is. Dog-eat-dog is just the name of the game; what does it matter if after we've had some nice meals together, one of us ends up in the other's pot? Only I'd better watch out that if that happens, it's me who makes a meal of him, and not the other way around. On the other hand, if I am not so crass, I may achieve equanimity by deceiving myself a little about the mutual cannibalism. I say to myself, "I would never eat him, for he is my friend; and I'm sure he wouldn't eat me, either. It would never come to that. No, I'm sure it wouldn't." But the way to avoid all these doubts and troubles is to give up cannibalism.

EXPEDIENTS OF HUMILITY

Humility is not itself an emotion, like joy or gratitude or contrition. A person could be a wonderful exemplar of humility without ever feeling humble; in fact, one who frequently feels humble is probably not very humble. But humility is an emotion-disposition — primarily a negative one, a disposition *not* to feel the emotions associated with caring a lot about one's status. As an inclination to construe as my equal every person who is presented to me, humility is a disposition not to be downcast by the fact that someone is clearly ahead of me in the games of the world nor to find any satisfaction in noting that I am ahead of someone in those games. It is the ability to have my self-comfort quite apart from any question about my place in the social pecking order (whether the criterion is accomplishments, education, beauty, money, power, fame, or position); it is the absence of a spiritually cannibalistic appetite. Humility is cannibal-anorexia, as we might say. It is thus a self-confidence, one that runs far deeper than the tenuous self-confidence of the person who believes in himself because others look up to him.

If this is humility, two things follow. First, if adults are to cultivate it, we need some way of conceiving of ourselves and our neighbors jointly, by which they will appear to us as equals. If we have no other way of seeing our neighbors than in terms of the competitive games the world plays, we have little hope of becoming humble. Our inclination to succumb to invidious comparisons is so great, and the means of making these comparisons are so ready-to-hand, that a necessary part of our defense against spiritual cannibalism will be an equally clear conceptualization of our neighbor as our equal. And second, we need some basis of self-acceptance other than our success in competition with others. We cannot escape the need to believe ourselves valuable, nor would we want to lose that capacity if we could. To believe ourselves worthless is a terrible and unchristian thing; and not to care that we are worthless is perhaps more woeful still.

Christianity offers to satisfy both these conditions, and this is a psychological recommendation for it. I do not deny that other philosophies or worldviews may satisfy these conditions. For example, Kant's philosophy tells us that rational beings must always be regarded not merely as means to ends, but as ends in themselves. The Stoic philosophy tends to see all persons as equal in that their circumstances (in terms of which the inequalities are so obvious) are not the source of peace; instead, the source of peace is an inner renunciation of which all perhaps are (initially) equally capable. Likewise, existentialism sees death as the great equalizer, and thus the basis of a kind of humility (see Chapter 5).

But we are concerned with Christian spirituality, and Christianity is eminently well qualified to engender the evenhanded, deep self-confidence that I am calling "humility." For it challenges us to see every person as a brother or sister whom God so loved that he humbled himself to equality with the lowest human being, and to death on a cross, to reconcile with himself. The equality in terms of which a Christian is equipped to see every other person is not that of inalienable rights (see the Declaration of Independence), of rationality (see Kant), of the potential for resignation (see Stoicism), or of mortality (see existentialism). It is that we are all equally the objects of God's great love, all equally children (or potential children) of his household, members of his kingdom. The Christian understands that she is precious before God — however much a sinner, however much a failure (or success) she may be by the standards of worldly comparisons — and that every other person she meets has the same status.

This vision not only levels every distinction by which egos seek a glory that really demeans them. When it becomes entrenched in one's outlook, the vision is also the ultimate ground of self-confidence. The message is that God loves me for myself — not for anything I have achieved, not for my beauty or intelligence or righteousness or for any other qualification, but simply in the way that a good mother loves the fruit of her womb. If I can get that into my head, or better, into my heart, then I won't be grasping desperately for self-esteem at the expense of others, and cutting myself off from my proper destiny, which is spiritual fellowship with them.

Anyone who has had a normal upbringing has some psychological basis for humility, however much he may have neglected it for a worldly under-standing of himself. That basis is the love he has received in his childhood (and any genuine love received since then). Unless a parent is perverse, her child will sense that he is treasured simply for himself. In countless ways, and usually without words, this love is communicated. But an explicit model is this: she looks into his eyes and says "I love you, Nathan," not be-cause she always wanted a boy and he is a boy, nor because he has just picked up his toys, nor still less because he aced out the other kids in the coloring contest, but quite out of the blue. Thus he grows, feeding his soul daily on an unconditional affirmation of his value. This implicit and inarticulate sense of his own worth, if carried into adulthood by becoming articulated in a definite life view, would be the radical self-confidence that Christians call humility: a self-confidence so deep, a personal integration so strong, that all comparison with other people, both advantageous and disadvanta-geous, slides right off him. And this is the psychological structure of the kingdom of God. That kingdom is a society in which each member is so sur-rounded by and conscious of focused love — both the love of his God and of his fellow creatures — that measures and inequalities of the kinds that preoccupy us in the current order of things fade into a background of inat-tention. Competitiveness, other than of the most unserious and playful sort, ceases; superiority and inferiority in every respect cease to touch any-one's self-evaluation.

People experience in their childhood varying amounts and qualities of this analogy to the kingdom of God. Some have been more or less systemati-cally taught, by their upbringing, that their worth is conditional on acing out the competition. They have experienced love being withheld from them when they performed badly, or were naughty, or came in second in the race. No upbringing could be better calculated to produce a spiritual canni-bal, for two reasons: first, it has been engrained in her mind that the way to self-value is the achievement of comparative excellence; and second, the deeper sense of self-worth that a person must have if she is to give up invidi-ous ego-building has not been established. In the extreme case of a pervert-ing and depriving upbringing, the person has been so damaged that she can-not be held responsible for her perversity. She is like a person who has been trained to think that stealing is normal and then so deprived of the oppor-tunity to get food by respectable means that her only choice is to live by theft or starve. Even if an inkling descends on her mind that stealing is wrong, she can hardly be much condemned if she chooses not to starve. In building our self-value at others' expense, we are all a little like the starving woman who, to survive, violates another's property. We are all socially damaged. But to the extent that we have known love, precisely to that extent can we be held responsible for our gluttonous, destructive, and ill-considered policy of building our self-esteem at the cost of fellowship.

HUMILITY AS A MORAL PROJECT

No one is inducted into the kingdom of God on the strength of his parents' love. Those of us who have known love well enough to see that dog-eat-dog is a degradation of the spirit have, in participating in it, responsibly violated a trust. God has created us for fellowship with one another, and we have chosen instead to forsake it for something unsatisfying and despicable. Despite our parents' love, not one of us is humble, not one is innocent of the crime of spiritual cannibalism.

The church is a society of people who have undertaken the struggle to love one another with a spiritual love. We teach one another, week in and week out, the beauty and duty of humility. We cultivate ourselves and one another in the consciousness of a calling to perfect fellowship, and in responsibility before God we struggle against the evil in our hearts. The gospel has taught us we are children of God, and the fittingness of that conception for our deepest social needs has not been lost on us. So we struggle to view one another not as competitors, but instead as brothers and sisters all equally beloved of the Father, all equally and graciously bestowed with membership in his family.

The picture sketched in the preceding paragraph may have a ring of unfamiliarity. Perhaps it doesn't sound much like any church you have ever attended. But then the church I sketched isn't anything a person would *attend;* instead, it is a provisional, struggling foretaste of the kingdom of God, a little group of persons who have been touched by the vision of the kingdom included in the gospel of Jesus Christ. And many Christians may be familiar with this church, though probably only with fleeting instances or hints of it. At any rate, it is within such a church that we are most likely to undertake the struggle for humility in all seriousness.

What happens when humility is seriously accepted as a moral project? What happens, over the years, to the heart and understanding of one who reflects on the brother- and sisterhood of believers, and tries in the light of this to become humble? We are not speaking here of the Average Presbyterian, for whom the church may be nothing so momentous as a foretaste of the kingdom of God — who may not even be acquainted with the church, though he knows by regular participation about the baptisms and organ music and potlucks that go on "at the church."

This is what happens: to the extent that I agree with the worldly cannibalistic attitude toward others, I will just accept it as normal. But as I become more ethically sensitive, this complacency changes into a growing discontent with my attitudes. When I feel envious toward another, or experience a passing scorn for one who is "below" me, or take delight in a certain person's failure, I no longer give myself wholeheartedly to the attitude, but learn a kind of disgust for it and for myself. And now, if I believe that God's intention is that I should be a member of his kingdom and rejoice in every brother and sister who likewise and equally are members of it; and if I believe that my spiritual cannibalism is a degrading and hateful thing, a ruining of the perfect fellowship that God intends for me; then I will become all the more concerned to eradicate it from my heart. And the more I participate in the life of the church (in the above defined sense), the more precious and desirable does this state of fellowship appear to me and the more horrible my own complicity in spoiling it. Thus the ethical struggle begets a deepening of my passion for the kingdom of God. But it is a universal testimony of the saints that the more enthusiastic they become for the things of the Spirit, the more deeply aware they become of the evil in their hearts, until at last they experience what Christian thinkers have called bondage to sin. They come to realize that the struggle is hopeless, and that hope, if there is hope, must reside in some rescue operation. At this point of spiritual awareness, the individual is at a maximum of desire for the kingdom of God, and simultaneously at a minimum of his confidence to gain it by struggle.

But in the possession of the very same church that struggles for a spiritual love that is rightness before God, is the good news about the rescue operation that God has performed in Jesus Christ. It is the message that our yearning for eternal life, which started growing perhaps independently of the church and then was nurtured and deepened and directed by the church, is to be satisfied. And in a sense, it is already satisfied, in that for the sake of Jesus, the perfectly humble one who humbled himself to equality with the lowest of human beings and loved with a pure spiritual love, God has counted us (the spiritual cannibals) fit for this kingdom. We can hope for it because Jesus pleads our case before the Father and the Father listens to his Son, and is of one heart with his Son. To the person who has gone through the spiritual development I have described in the last three chapters, the gospel of Jesus will be as food to the hungry and water to the thirsty.

I argued in Chapters 1 and 2 that emotions are "construals" of things in terms that impinge on our concerns. The gospel offers us a way of reading ourselves, our neighbors, the creation, and God himself; it is a conceptual lens, a principle of understanding, by which we see the world in a new focus and frame. Through the gospel, God intends to bear fruit in people's hearts; the fruit of joy, peace, hope, thanksgiving, love, and more. But to the extent that this fruit of the message is emotions, it cannot be expected to arise if the hearer is not actively concerned about the things to which the message speaks. The gospel "speaks" to the issues of sin and death, and says that the kingdom of God has been and will be established; and thus it speaks only to people whose hearts are more or less deeply exercised about these matters. In recent chapters I have attempted to sketch the passion that would make emotional sense of the gospel of Jesus Christ: a yearning for an eternal life of moral purity. To people (even regular churchgoers) who are concerned only about their health, pleasures, reputation, real estate, and bank account, the gospel will not be greeted with joy and gratitude. But to those who have opened themselves to the fact of their death and who have become deeply enough developed ethically to know what sin is and hate it, the message of the kingdom can be the source of a new emotional life. In the third part of this book I will examine six aspects of that new life, six kinds of "fruit of the Holy Spirit": contrition, joy, gratitude, hope, peace, and compassion.

PART THREE

Christian Emotion-Virtues

CHAPTER SEVEN

Contrition

THE LOGIC AND LYRIC OF CONTRITION

The main character of Isaac Singer's *The Penitent* is a man suspended in agony between two worlds, the fast modern world of money and pleasure and sexual promiscuity, and the timeless world of ancient Jewish holiness. Joseph Shapiro is thereby suspended between two selves, two sets of passions that bid to define him as a person: the lusts of the flesh and ambition on the one side, and the love of God and his eternal law on the other. His agony consists in the difficulty of identifying decisively with one of these incompatible selves. There is no real doubt, at any point in the novel, that the real Joseph Shapiro is the ancient Jew, the one who looks with revulsion on that other, New World self; but there *is* doubt whether the ancient Jew in him will ever be actualized, will ever win out over the tawdriness and stupidity and sickness of American "civilization," and its corresponding character.

When Joseph goes to buy a prayer shawl and phylacteries, the shopkeeper asks, "Have you become a penitent?" and his answer is "I want to be one" (p. 131). The mere fact of being torn between these worlds, of feeling the pain and confusion, the regret, the fear, the sorrow, is not enough to make him a penitent. Even the feeling of guilt is not enough. Needed is a solid identification with the new self that will be nurtured by earlocks and phylacteries that proclaim to the world that he is not of it, but allied to a different order of things. Penitence is a solidity of character nurtured by action after action, insight after insight, that consolidate the self in the terms of contrition. Shapiro's experience makes painfully clear that the feeling of emotion, however finely tuned it is in itself, and however dramatic may be the actions that issue from it, is no guarantee of genuine penitence. And yet

97

an emotion (our traditions have called it contrition) is the centerpiece and moving force of the process of repentance and the formation of a new self. Contrition is not named in any of the apostle Paul's various lists of canonical spiritual traits, though he certainly endorses the practice of repentance; and the theological and psychological basis for such a trait seems to be laid in Romans 7. In this chapter I aim to clarify the concept of this emotion-trait and to make some corresponding suggestions for the Christian practice of confession.

Contrition has both a "lyric" and a "logic" that must be respected if the church is to prosecute responsibly its calling to form selves fit for the kingdom, souls genuinely transformed by the gospel of grace. As to its logic, contrition is not just any old feeling that one may have on the occasion of thinking about the improprieties of one's own life. It is, in quite definite ways, related to and distinguishable from such neighbor-emotions as fear, regret, embarrassment, and guilt. Some of these neighboring emotions are enough like contrition, in one respect or another, that we may think of them as aspects of contrition; but none of them *is* contrition, and I think it is not, finally, quite right to regard contrition as made up of other emotions like regret, guilt, and hope. The understanding of emotions proposed in this book seems to me to make it unnecessary for us to think of some emotions as made up of more basic ones. By specifying the logical features of the concept, we "define" contrition and thus a central phenomenon of the Christian spiritual life. Contrition must be kept definite, and definitely Christian, by preserving the logic of the language in which we express and teach contrition in the church. Our prayers of confession are an important instance of such language. But it is not enough just to get contrition's logic right; if people are to be positively moved with it, our language of contrition must be properly affecting, which is to say that it must display an appropriate poetic, rhetorical, or lyrical quality, one fitting the fact that contrition is an emotion. In addition to a logic, contrition has a mood; and this mood needs to be reflected in the standard ways this emotion is nurtured and expressed in the church.

My central illustration will be a fanciful reading of the encounter between King David and the prophet Nathan in the 12th chapter of 2 Samuel.

CONTRITION, FEAR OF PUNISHMENT, AND REGRET

King David impregnates Bathsheba, the wife of Uriah, and then, finding himself unable to conceal his sin, arranges for Uriah's death on the battle-field. As the writer tells the story, David seems remarkably ruthless in his ac-tions and insensitive to his immorality. Perhaps he half-believes such behav-ior to be a kingly prerogative. To awaken David to his sin, the prophet Nathan does two things. First, he tells the story of an atrocity that elicits the king's indignation, and surprises him by pointing out that David himself is the offender in the story. And second, he prophesies the punishments that David's sin will bring him.

A rich man with many flocks, says Nathan, gets a visitor, but doesn't want to use up one of his own lambs for hospitality. Instead, he takes a lamb from a poor neighbor, indeed the only lamb the neighbor has, which "grew up with him and his children. It shared his food, drank from his cup and even slept in his arms. It was like a daughter to him." And he slaughters the neighbor's lamb and roasts it for his visitor. David responds to the story with strong, righteous anger: "As surely as the Lord lives, the man who did this deserves to die!" Nathan invites David to turn that anger on himself: "You are the man!" Furthermore, says the prophet, you will have continual military troubles with neighboring nations, and someone will disgrace you by having intercourse with your wives in public, and the child you have en-gendered in this affair will die.

David responds to Nathan's prophecy of the child's death by begging God, fasting, and lying all night on the ground, but as soon as the child dies he gets up, washes and anoints himself, dresses, worships, and then goes home and has a meal. Surprised at David's sudden recovery when the child is dead, the servants ask,

> "Why are you acting this way? While the child was alive, you fasted and wept, but now that the child is dead, you get up and eat!" He answered, "While the child was still alive, I fasted and wept. I thought, 'Who knows? The Lord may be gracious to me and let the child live.' But now that he is dead, why should I fast? Can I bring him back again?" (vv. 21b-23)

David's behavior bespeaks fear of punishment more than contrition. The concern characteristic of contrition is not aversion to punishment (in fact, the contrite person may welcome punishment), but aversion to turpitude.

Since the death of the child does not decrease David's turpitude, we would not expect it to affect his behavior, insofar as it expresses contrition. So the quick change in behavior suggests that it expressed some other emotion.

One can imagine that on learning of Bathsheba's pregnancy, David regretted that he had yielded to his urge. To regret an action is to see it as a mistake, an action that would have been better left undone, most likely because of its untoward consequences, as in the present imagined case. To be contrite, by contrast, requires seeing one's action as a culpable offense. If David were contrite about lying with Bathsheba, he would not only wish that he hadn't; he would wish this for a particular kind of reason, namely that in doing so he offended against God, her, and Uriah. Nathan's parable is calculated to arouse David's *anger* against the rich man — to bring this man into judgmental, condemnable focus, not as one who has made a regrettable mistake, but as one who has culpably wronged the poor man; and contrition is like anger in this respect, except that the penitent takes himself to be the offender.

We regret particular misdeeds, such as an illicit sexual union, but it is not quite right to say we are contrite about particular deeds. Whatever the writer of Psalm 51 has done, his emotion goes beyond his action. It is about his very being as a person:

> Surely I was sinful at birth,
>   sinful from the time my mother conceived me. (v. 5)

He begs God to create in him a new heart, a new center, a new spirit (v. 10). Feeling sullied by what he has done, he asks God to wash him clean of his iniquity (v. 2). It's a mark of contrition that its object is not directly the illicit deed or thought, but the self. It generalizes from the sinful action to the sinful person, feeling the sin as a condition or state of the self; the sinful deed or thought is *that in terms of which* the self is construed, as an indicator of the character of the broken-boned self.

EMBARRASSMENT

We have discussed two emotions, fear of punishment and regret, and have distinguished them from contrition. Our latest comment, that contrition takes the whole self as object, suggests another emotion in the neighborhood of contrition, namely embarrassment. Embarrassment is also an uncomfortable awareness of oneself, often occasioned by something one has done. Imagine, for a moment, that King David is chiefly embarrassed in his encounter with Nathan. He doesn't take seriously the prophecies of punishment, nor care about having wronged God, Bathsheba, and Uriah. But he doesn't want to be thought of as a spoiled adolescent who can't keep his pants up, or as so panicky as not to stop even at murder to cover up his mistakes. So he is alarmed to discover that his adultery and homicide are known. His chief concern is to make sure that the news does not get beyond the present walls. He will swear Nathan to secrecy. He will avoid Nathan's company in the future, for whenever he is with Nathan, or thinks about him, he sees himself through Nathan's eyes: I am a king known to have done unseemly things; I look small and foolish to my people.

The concern characteristic of embarrassment is to avoid being seen in an uncomplimentary light. Thus embarrassment differs from contrition, whose characteristic concern is to be righteous, to have a "clean heart." Yet contrition and embarrassment resemble one another in a certain respect. In general, the paradigm cases of *feeling* guilt are those in which we stand face to face with the one we have wronged, stared at, as it were, by our victim, in his status of victim-accuser. Guilt is enhanced by a sense of the accuser's presence, and thus tends to beget dreams and imaginings of it; but these are not *necessary* for guilt, as the sense of the other's observing presence is for embarrassment. If David feels guilty about murdering Uriah, he may still feel so even if no one knows that he has done it. But if David is really *only* embarrassed about the incident, then when he satisfies himself that no one knows, his embarrassment will disappear.

Jewish and Christian contrition, however, is more than guilt. It is a perception that one has offended against *God:*

> Against you, you only, have I sinned,
> and done what is evil in your sight. (Psalm 51:4)

We Christians and Jews feel our contrition most sensibly in the moment of prayer, when we are actually in fellowship with the God we have offended. And we remind ourselves that there is, in reality, no escape from the seeing eye of God. Remember the plea of the *Book of Common Prayer,* "Almighty God, to whom all hearts are open, all desires known, and from whom no secrets are hid: Cleanse the thoughts of our hearts by the inspiration of thy Holy Spirit. . . ."

Where can I go from your Spirit?
   Where can I flee from your presence?
If I say, "Surely the darkness will hide me,
   and the light become night around me,"
even the darkness will not be dark to you;
   the night will shine like the day;
    for darkness is as light to you. (Psalm 139:7, 11-12)

Shall we say, then, that Jewish and Christian contrition, unlike ordinary humanistic guilt, is really just a form of embarrassment? Perhaps it is a more primitive emotion than guilt, more infantile, indicative of a lower stage of moral development, a greater degree of dependency and less of autonomy? Are religious people unable to be serious unless they think God is watching?

Christianity does not have the same ideal of autonomy as modern moral outlooks. Christian ethics and psychology affirm that we are fundamentally dependent on God and that maturity is a certain *kind* of dependence on God, rather than some radical autonomy. So it should not embarrass us that Christian ethics involves, in a very basic way, a sense of being watched by God. But this admission does not imply that contrition is a form of embarrassment in the sense that I have been contrasting with guilt. First, God is not *accidentally* privy to the actions and thoughts of the contrite person, in the way that other human beings are to the actions and thoughts of the embarrassed person. It is in God's nature to see in secret and with unavoidable gaze. Second, to have a mature sense of standing in the presence of the Holy One is a spiritual achievement, requiring self-denial, courage, purity, honesty, and love. Being embarrassed, by contrast, requires only the most minimal and ordinary sense of being under the watchful eyes of some other human beings, plus concern for what others think. In itself, embarrassment does not discriminate along lines of holiness, righteousness, and goodness. By contrast, the One before whom the penitent is contrite is holy; he is the very standard of righteousness and goodness. So contrition is a distinctly moral perception, while embarrassment is not.

HATRED OF SIN, DISMAY AT SIN, PLAIN GUILT

Another couple of emotions in the neighborhood of contrition, which by their contrast will help us to locate contrition on the logical map, are hatred of sin and dismay at sin. When the psalmist addresses the "mighty man," saying

> Your tongue plots destruction;
>   it is like a sharpened razor,
>   you who practice deceit (52:2)

he expresses hatred of sin, but not contrition. He hates somebody else's sin, but contrition is hatred of one's own. This last remark is not precise enough to distinguish hatred of sin from contrition. The apostle Paul says

> I see another law at work in the members of my body, waging war against the law of my mind and making me a prisoner of the law of sin at work within my members. What a wretched man I am! (Romans 7:23-24a)

He expresses hatred of his own sin (or perhaps more precisely, dismay at his sin), but not contrition. To distinguish these emotions we must sharpen the concept of "one's own" sin that operates in the two self-construals. Paul sees the sin that he laments as "his" in the sense that it is in *his* "members." That is, it is not somebody else's sin; it is attached to *him,* hindering him from doing the good that he wants to do. But in this passage he insists that it is not his in what we might call a moral sense: "it is no longer I myself who do it, but it is sin living in me" (vv. 17, 20). We might say that his sin belongs to one of Paul's selves, but not to the one with which Paul himself morally identifies — the self that loves Jesus and identifies with him. The sin belongs to "the flesh," "the old man," to a besetting "body of death" from which Paul dissociates himself. This is understandable in light of the intensity with which Paul identifies with the crucified and risen Christ: "I have been crucified with Christ and I no longer live, but Christ lives in me" (Gal. 2:20). But this seeing of his sin as something alien, to the point of seeing it as something that *he* does not even do, prevents his emotion from being contrition, however dismayed he may be.

The matter is even more complicated than this. It is not as though just any dissociation from one's sinful self precludes contrition. After all, something of a dissociation from sin is *required* for contrition. Joseph Shapiro hates his fast, loose American self, and as he becomes more solidly contrite, he sees it as more and more alien. And yet contrition requires that he take responsibility for that self, that he own up to being its author, that he construe

that modern self (which is more and more a self of his past) as morally contin-
uous with the present Joseph Shapiro, who is more and more an ancient Jew.
Even as he becomes a new man, he must be and experience himself as the old
man — not a person with the *traits* of the old man, but as the agent of those
traits and the actions that sprang from them. Thus contrition requires an ap-
plication of humility that we do not see in Romans 7, and do not often see in
the apostle Paul — a willingness to acknowledge that, however different I may
now be, and however hateful I may find my former sinful self, *I* am responsible for the actions, the thoughts, and the personality of that former self. In
most of Paul's writings, the perception of being a new creation in Christ Jesus
is so strong that it mitigates Paul's impression of himself as the agent of that
former life. His indomitable sense of being a new creation is a rare and beautiful thing in the history of Christian spirituality, and was strategically essential
for the development of the church. But if contrition is a Christian virtue, the
sense of discontinuity with the old self's character must be integrated with an
equally strong sense of the continuity of agency between old and new.

In contrasting the logic of contrition with that of fear of punishment,
regret, embarrassment, and hatred of sin, I have sometimes used the word
'guilt' to indicate contrition. This is possible because contrition is like guilt
in a number of significant ways. I want to bring my discussion of contrition's logic to a close by contrasting it with what we may call plain guilt. It is
highly characteristic of Christian and Jewish prayers of confession to begin
with an acknowledgment of God's mercy, love, and forgiveness: "Have
mercy on me, O God, according to your unfailing love" (Psalm 51:1). "Almighty and most merciful Father; We have erred, and strayed from thy ways
like lost sheep" (*Book of Common Prayer,* 1945, p. 6).

Contrition, as contrasted with plain guilt, is characterized by confident
hope in God's mercy — in other words, the construal of oneself as not lost
because of one's guilt, the construal of God as benevolent and a source of
help, as well as angry and offended. Contrition can even shade into joy, the
full perception of God's goodness to oneself, acceptance, and forgiveness.
Indeed, the difference in emotion during the prayer of confession and during the absolution is a matter of shading, for prior to the absolution the
penitent perceives God as well disposed to himself (though the dominant
content of the emotion is the perception of oneself as offender), while during and after the absolution the penitent does not lose sight of himself as offender, though the dominant content of the perception is that of his forgiveness by God and God's approval and acceptance.

Nothing like this sense of mercy is in the emotion that I am calling plain guilt. It is simply a perception of oneself as sullied and offensive through one's own responsible agency; if God is involved, guilt is a perception of him as simply angry. Being without joy and hope, plain guilt is an emotion that eminently invites recoil and urgently tempts to repression and self-deception. Contrition, by contrast, while it may be agonizing, is not without its lighter side. It is a gracious affection, a gospel emotion. Jews and Christians see themselves not only as sullied by their own responsible agency, and not only as standing before an angry and judging God, but equally as having the prospect of being cleansed and forgiven, and as standing before a God who listens with love to those who call on him for mercy. The difference between Jewish and Christian contrition lies in the way of conceiving God's mercy. The Christian penitent construes God as one who, as the man Jesus of Nazareth, has mercifully stood before God in the place of all sinners and borne the suffering and alienation that attend sin. The mercy that the Christian currently prays for is that one act of mercy that God has already performed. The Jew, by contrast, thinks of God's mercy as primarily exemplified in God's countless acts of mercy to Israel, the crowning one of which lies still in the future — the coming of Messiah. The mercy that is currently prayed for is a further example of this general disposition of God toward his people.

Many types of emotion motivate action by having a consequent desire, a desire that arises, by the terms of the construal, out of the concern on which the emotion is based. For example, anger is based on a concern that justice be done, either to oneself or to others. From this concern, transformed in the construal of someone as having culpably offended against oneself or another, a consequent desire emerges logically: the desire to see the offender punished, this action being a way to restore justice. Similarly, from the concern to be righteous, as it is transformed in the construal of oneself as having offended against the holy God, spoiled oneself, and having nevertheless been made the object of God's mercy, etc., emerges a desire to amend one's life, to express one's allegiance to God in holy living. Note that whereas plain guilt, if very intense, may paralyze its subject by casting him into despair, the good news that is incorporated into Jewish and Christian contrition liberates the penitent by giving him a way out, thus encouraging in him the formation of an intention to amend his life.

THE LOGIC OF CONTRITION

It may seem odd that one and the same emotion can be both painful and pleasant, that it can represent its object (oneself) as both ugly and attractive. The horror of one's offense against God and the beauty of one's reconciliation to him seem to be so opposite as to require different emotions — perhaps plain guilt on the one hand, and plain joy or relief or hope on the other. Perhaps these alternate in the Christian's consciousness: feeling guilt (ideally) as he confesses his sins, and then joy (ideally) as he receives absolution. A similar question is raised by my method of articulating the logic of contrition. Some of the emotions whose logic I have contrasted with contrition may seem to be aspects of it. Would it not be better to think of contrition as a compound of several more basic emotions, such as regret, embarrassment, hatred of sin, and joy at forgiveness?

As to the idea that contrition might be just the alternation of horrific guilt and pure joy, this description does not seem true to Christian experience. I have noted that prayers of confession often contain *within* them, prior to the words of absolution, an acknowledgment of God's love and forgiving disposition; forgiveness comes as no surprise with the words of absolution, and has its effect on the experience of coming before God in confession. Similarly, the experience of joy that is especially tied to the words of absolution does not dispel the penitent's aversion to his sin; rather, the aversion to his sin is presupposed by the distinctive character of this joy, which is joy *about the forgiveness of one's sins*. As to my method of articulating the logic of contrition, I would point out that the analysis has shown, not that contrition is a compound of other emotion-types in some pure and basic form, but that it bears some logical similarities to these other emotion-types. That a raccoon bears some similarities to a fox, and some to a bear, and some to a monkey, does not imply that raccoons are a compound of fox, bear, and monkey. Also, if emotions are construals — a sort of "seeing-as" shaped by a complex of thoughts — then it is not surprising that an emotion can contain, within itself, a complex of attitudes. A summary of the thought content of Christian contrition can now serve two purposes: to recapitulate the logic of contrition that I have outlined, and to illustrate what it is for an emotion to be a construal, and thus to capture rather diverse thought content in one perceptual experience.

The concern characteristic of contrition is for righteousness (not, for contrasts, the concern to avoid getting punished or looking foolish to others); contrition is based on a hunger and thirst for righteousness, a seeking for the kingdom, the passion that I outlined in Chapters 3–6. This concern can be expressed in a proposition: Righteousness is excellent, good, right for me. To be contrite is to see the action or thought or feeling that occasions my contrition not as a mere mistake (as in mere regret), but as a culpable offense, a sin. But the real object of my contrition is not, as in regret or remorse, a particular action, but myself: the psalmist of Psalm 51 construes himself as besmirched, sullied, compromised, spoiled. Contrite Jews and Christians experience ourselves as in the unavoidable presence of the Holy One. We see the actions, thoughts, or feelings that occasion our contrition, or the self about which we feel contrite, as alien to our true self, and yet as falling within our responsibility. However different in character we may now be than when we did, thought, or felt those things, still it was we who authored them. If I am contrite, rather than just feeling guilty, I experience myself as forgiven or having the prospect of forgiveness; I construe the God in whose presence I stand as merciful, loving, forgiving. And last, desiring righteousness and seeing myself as sullied by sin but nevertheless loved and forgiven by God, I form the intention to amend my life.

If an emotion is a construal, an experience of something *in some terms,* then it is possible for it to bring together in experience a rich complexity of thought. And if, in the Christian view, it is both painfully true that we have sinned against God and spoiled ourselves, and pleasantly true that God has forgiven us and restored us to himself in Jesus Christ, the emotion of contrition brings these truths together into one experience. Thus the thoughts in terms of which one construes oneself when contrite could be listed:

1. Righteousness is good, excellent, and right for me.
2. I have culpably done wrong.
3. Thus I have spoiled myself.
4. That spoiled self is not the real me.
5. In doing wrong I have offended you.
6. I cannot escape from your gaze.
7. You are merciful and will forgive (have forgiven) me.
8. I must amend my life.

The logic of contrition is made up of these thoughts, based on the concern for righteousness. If so, then none of the emotions that neighbor on contrition has quite the same logic, though they may share some of these thoughts, or have closely analogous ones in their logic. Quite a lot of Christian theology is enfolded in the emotion of contrition, and if you get the theology wrong, you get the emotion's logic wrong, and if you get that wrong, you don't get the distinctively Christian emotion of contrition. And if the emotion is not right, then the Christian virtue of penitence disintegrates, along with many other Christian virtues that are interdependent on it — virtues like joy, hope, and gratitude.

I am not saying that whenever a person feels properly Christian or Jewish contrition, these thoughts are discursively rehearsed in the auditorium of his consciousness. Nor am I saying that all eight propositions will be equally prominent in the mind of each contrite person on each occasion of feeling contrition. Rather, these are the thoughts that will come out when an articulate Christian is called on to explain what he is feeling in feeling contrition. They are the propositions in terms of which he sees himself when he experiences himself in that peculiarly immediate, perceptual, quasi-sensory way that we call the *emotion* of contrition. In some instances the most prominent thought will be that I have spoiled myself; in another that I cannot escape from God's gaze, etc. But whatever thought may be most prominent, the others will need to be lurking in the background of the mind for the emotion to be, in the fullest sense, Christian contrition.

If the emotion does not imply the explicit rehearsal of these thoughts, neither does their rehearsal, even a sincere one, guarantee the occurrence of the emotion. The emotion is a "seeing-as" in terms of these propositions, and I have pointed out (Chapter 2) that seeing-as, while partially and sometimes within the command of our will, is not always so. It sometimes comes unbidden, and sometimes, when bidden, does not come. But something can be done to promote contrition among those who are disposed to think about themselves in the terms of Christian theology. In the practical wisdom of the church, one of the expedients for promoting contrition has been well-crafted prayers of confession.

The Lyric of Contrition

A good prayer of confession will reflect, within itself as well by its resonance with its fairly immediate liturgical surroundings, the logic of contrition. Such prayers become in this way not only an aid in the expression of contrition, but also a device for the emotional/spiritual education of the congregation. If the prayer is fixed, as in a book of worship, it becomes also a norm of character for the congregation.

It is not enough that a prayer reflect the logic of contrition. No one would think we could make a good prayer of confession just by stringing together the eight statements I numbered above. In that bare logical form, a prayer would not be very affecting, and thus would not bear the appropriate relationship to emotion, even if it displayed quite accurately the logic of contrition. The language of emotion is not just logical, but also rhetorical, lyrical, expressive, mood-producing. As Jonathan Edwards points out in his *Religious Affections,*

> No other reason can be assigned, why we should express ourselves to God in verse, rather than in prose, and do it with music, but only, that such is our nature and frame, that these things have a tendency to move our affections ... God hath appointed a particular and lively application of his Word, to men, in the preaching of it, as a fit means to affect sinners, with the importance of the things of religion, and their own misery, and necessity of a remedy, and the glory and sufficiency of a remedy provided; and to stir up the pure minds of the saints, and quicken their affections, by often bringing the great things of religion to their remembrance, and setting them before them in their proper colors, though they know them, and have been fully instructed in them already. (pp. 115-16)

The language of prayer is a language of imagery as well as concepts, and must encourage the concrete reference to the speaker(s) that is characteristic of lyric poetry. The vocabulary must be dramatic enough — and this will include direct and indirect reference to emotions — to evoke more than the judgments specific to contrition; it must promote the construal, the perception with the eyes of the heart, that I have responsibly spoiled myself, that my spoiled self is not the real me, that God is merciful. . . .

When the American *Book of Common Prayer* of 1928 was revised in the 1970's, two orders for Holy Eucharist were provided in place of the one earlier service. Rite One is reminiscent of the older prayer book, while Rite Two uses modern language and presumably appeals more to contemporary sensibilities. The more modern service replaces the prayer of confession by a shorter and simpler prayer. The original Eucharistic confession was rich in the lyric of contrition:

We acknowledge and bewail our manifold sins and wickedness,
which we from time to time most grievously have committed,
by thought, word, and deed, against thy divine Majesty,
provoking most justly thy wrath and indignation against us.
We do earnestly repent,
and are heartily sorry for these our misdoings;
the remembrance of them is grievous unto us,
the burden of them is intolerable (p. 75).

Dramatic words like 'bewail' and 'grievously' and 'intolerable burden' strongly express the pain and moral seriousness (frustrated love of righteousness) characteristic of contrition. The references to God's majesty, wrath, and indignation express the sense of having offended a holy God. By comparison with the colorful language of the older prayer, the 1977 replacement is simple and prosaic — except for the last line, a minimalist statement of fact:

We confess that we have sinned against you
in thought, word, and deed,
by what we have done,
and by what we have left undone.
We have not loved you with our whole heart;
we have not loved our neighbors as ourselves.
We are truly sorry and we humbly repent (p. 352).

If we look at the 1928 confession for Morning and Evening Prayer, from which the new Eucharistic confession derives, we see that what was left out is chiefly the emotionally expressive elements of the prayer:

We have erred, and strayed from thy ways like lost sheep.
We have followed too much the devices and desires of our own
    hearts.
We have offended against thy holy laws.
We have left undone those things which we ought to have done;
and we have done those things which we ought not to have done;
and there is no health in us.
But thou, O Lord, have mercy upon us, miserable offenders (p. 6).

The metaphor of wandering, lost sheep; the reference to the violated laws as "holy"; the acknowledgment of the damage we have done ourselves in forfeiture of health and accrual of misery; these are all expressive of the regret, the guilt, and the grief characteristic of contrition. Without these elements, the prayer is less likely to convey and express the texture of contrition.

At their best, the high liturgical worship forms characteristic of the Roman Catholic and Anglican churches have their own way of expressing and shaping the enthusiasm for the kingdom of God that I found in the Baptist church on which I reported in Chapter 1. Anglican enthusiasm is less flamboyant and less obvious, and perhaps in one sense less intense (it would be interesting to hook up equally pious worshiping Baptists and Episcopalians to blood-pressure and skin-conductance monitors to see whether they differ on physiological markers of emotion). But what it lacks in exuberance and perspiration, the Anglican approach gives back in theological and lyrical fine-tuning. Prayers like the older Anglican prayers of confession and thanksgiving wonderfully balance theological richness and precision with lyric and mood. The pity is that these resources of emotional formation seem, often, so little supported and exploited by those who have them closest to hand. Why, do you suppose?

Why Do the Prayers Make Us Uneasy?

It does seem to us an exaggeration to confess that there is no health in us and to call ourselves "miserable offenders." Surely we have *some* health in us; and even if we have offended, we may not really feel very miserable about it, and may prefer not to contribute further to whatever misery we may be experiencing, by making a point of it. If we must confess our sins, we prefer to do so calmly, factually, without melodrama and without heat. Why do we feel uneasy with a sumptuous rhetoric of contrition? In attempting to answer this question, I speak only for myself, not for the revisers of the prayer book. (I am entirely unacquainted with their biographies.) But some others may recognize my sentiments in themselves.

First, I think I am squeamish about full-blooded expressions of contrition because I have "forgotten" the holiness of God and the glory to which he has destined us. My preferred god is a friendly little fellow, more indulgent than the God of the older prayer book. Not only the terms descriptive of *us* have changed from the 1928 prayers to the 1977; so also has the description of God. For the two conceptions — of what we have done, and of whom we have done it to; of who we are and of who God is — are insepara- ble. In the earlier prayers our offense is characterized as "against thy divine Majesty, provoking most justly thy wrath and indignation against us." And we admit having offended "against thy holy laws." But in the more recent prayer God's majesty and wrath and holiness have all disappeared, and the only description of him is "merciful." The misery of my wickedness has be- come emotionally less clear to me because God's majesty and holiness are re- duced, along with the glory of the life to which this majestic and holy God has called me. Or shall we say that God's holiness is less visible to me because I've lost the full awareness of being a sinner — or because I have lost the pas- sion for the kingdom of God?

Our society is very conscious of the demand to feel good and be func- tioning properly, and the sense of being sinners is anathema in a therapeutic culture. It has become a matter of pride, even a pseudo-morality, to avoid what is unhealthy. These days, people who want to smoke feel often ashamed and do so on the sly. Health freaks disfavor guilt, but the Christian aggrava- tion of guilt into manifold sins and wickedness before the face of a holy, righ- teous, and wrathful God is beyond contemplation to many people. Taken quite literally, the phrase "there is no health in us" does exaggerate. There must be some spiritual health in us for us even to notice that we are sinners, and still more for us to care about that fact (contrition is a Christian virtue). But the lyric of contrition, like any other lyric, affords a certain license; hav- ing a poetic quality, good prayers don't have to be precise psychology at every turn. However uncomfortable we may feel with it, the phrase expresses well that we have fallen very far short of the glorious life to which God has called us — that we are badly spoiled, even if not quite completely.

If people like me feel a certain morbidity in the phrase, or become mor- bid through thinking about themselves in its terms, surely the solution is not to excise the phrase, but to help us understand it. A bit of careful preaching on the prayer of confession may be in order. The God in whose presence the Christian feels contrition is not *merely* holy, righteous, and wrathful. He is also "the Father of our Lord Jesus Christ, who desireth not the death of a sinner," as the words of absolution declare. When the Chris- tian confesses to the "almighty and most merciful Father," she does so in the hope of the atonement. This is the distinctively Christian and Jewish way of keeping contrition from going morbid, and a good preacher, employing the lyric of Christian faith within the full scope of its logic, should be able to make God's loving mercy perceptible enough to the congregation that we can also perceive our misery in full color.

A Final Word about Joseph Shapiro

Most of us don't make as dramatic a change in personality as Joseph Shapiro, and so our "old self" is a less well-defined thing to rue; many of us are cradle Christians who in outward ways do not stray very far from the path. Yet even for us, contrition is not a minor virtue or incidental corner of the Christian life, something to be passed over perfunctorily on the way to joy; for we, too, like lost sheep, have erred and strayed from God's ways. Contrition is that state of mind in which we perceive with the eyes of the heart, and thus in a truly spiritual way, the issues of our selfhood. We see that the self of our sin is not our real self and that we belong, through God's forgiveness, to God and his kingdom. Contrition is that state of mind in which we appreciate with our spiritual viscera what God has done for us in Jesus Christ, and in which we are moved to depart from our sin and consolidate ourselves in him. It is that state of proper pain, that experience of fitting misery, without which our joy is not a joy in our Redeemer.

CHAPTER EIGHT

Joy

AN EPISODE IN THE LIFE OF ISRAEL

Their temple and holy city destroyed, the Jews spent seventy years exiled in Babylon, grieving for their own country. Then Persia came to dominate Babylon, and King Cyrus sent the exiled Jews back to Jerusalem with instructions to rebuild the temple. After almost three years in Judah, the builders began work on the new temple,

> And when the builders laid the foundation of the temple of the Lord, the priests in their vestments came forward with trumpets, and the Levites, the sons of Asaph, with cymbals, to praise the Lord, according to the directions of David king of Israel; and they sang responsively, praising and giving thanks to the Lord,
>
> > "For he is good,
> > for his steadfast love endures for ever toward Israel."
>
> And all the people shouted with a great shout, when they praised the Lord, because the foundation of the house of the Lord was laid. But many of the priests and Levites and heads of Fathers' houses, old men who had seen the first house, wept with a loud voice when they saw the foundation of this house being laid, though many shouted aloud for joy; so that the people could not distinguish the sound of the joyful shout from the sound of the people's weeping, for the people shouted with a great shout, and the sound was heard afar. (Ezra 3:10-13, RSV)

The one group shouted for joy, the other wept with grief, and both were responding to one situation: the new temple of God emerging in outline as its foundation took shape. Both groups believed the words of praise with which they sang to God: 'For he is good, for his steadfast love endures for ever toward Israel.' How, then, can their emotions be so different, the one group feeling joy, the other grief? The answer is that they *saw* different things in this situation, or to put the matter another way, they didn't quite see the same situation, or they didn't see the same meaning in the situation, or they were not seeing the situation from the same angle. By their pleasure, the joyful group saw the coming fulfillment of their fondest hopes, the wonderful goodness of the prospect: to worship God in his holiest place. The grieving group did not deny that prospect, but they saw something different in the emerging figure of the new temple. With vivid pain they saw what they had lost. They remembered the glory of the old temple, its cruel destruction, and the seventy years of exile. For them — at least for this moment — the rebuilding of the beloved temple signaled the dark evil that had befallen them.

Shall we say that the one group was wrong, the other right? Is the difference in emotion a difference of blessedness? These two responses to the situation reveal a unity of mind among the celebrants. However opposite the pain of the one group is to the pleasure of the other, the two groups agree in the fundamental orientation of their hearts. They both love God and the worship of God; they both love the temple as a place where that worship was (and will be) enacted. Scripture tells us that the older people had a greater tendency to the grief-response, and we can easily see why; but there is no reason why a particularly imaginative younger lover of the temple worship could not also feel the grief. In fact, we may plausibly think that every one of the celebrants had often grieved for the old temple and all that it stood for, in the years of their captivity. The possibility of sadness is tightly bound to the capacity for joy. A godly sadness is as precious in the eyes of the Lord as the joy that corresponds to it. Furthermore, though they saw opposite things, both groups grasped, in their emotion, a truth about the situation: joy saw the real goodness in the new temple's coming into being and the goodness of the Lord, and grief saw the real tragedy of the old temple's destruction and the people's exile.

PLEASURES

Throughout history and in all cultures, pleasure has been very popular. Some philosophers and psychologists have even thought it the only motive, or the only proper one, the final reason we do whatever we do, or anyway the best reason for doing what we do. But even if we disagree about that, we must admit that pleasure is a big attraction in life. What is it? To answer this question, we need to see that there are several kinds.

Let's first distinguish physical pleasures from spiritual pleasures. Physical pleasures are *sensations.* They have a location in one or other part of the body, and the pleasures are feelings of states of those body parts. Thus the pleasure of having your back rubbed is a feeling *in* the back, the pleasure of stroking a cat's fur is *in* the hand that is stroking the cat, the pleasure of eating and drinking is in the tongue and throat and nose, the pleasure of sexual intercourse is largely in the sex organs, and so forth. Many human pleasures are not physical in this sense. I call these non-physical pleasures spiritual, but I could also call them psychological. They are spiritual in a very broad sense, not in the more narrow sense that Christians have in mind when we talk about spiritual matters — not in the sense, for example, in which the pleasure the Hebrews took in the thought of worshiping the Lord in the new temple was a spiritual pleasure.

Spiritual pleasures in this broad sense are pleasures in *meaning.* When your doctor tells you that your newborn baby is perfectly healthy, you take pleasure in the *news,* in the fact that your baby is healthy. You don't feel this pleasure in any part of your body. It is true that you may feel a leaping in your midsection, an impulse to dance, and a big smile may come over your face. These are all sensations — located in your gut, your legs, your face. But such sensations are not where the pleasure of the joy comes in. The sensations are neither especially pleasant nor especially unpleasant. They are more or less neutral, while the emotion is intensely pleasant. This is what I mean by saying that the emotion is a spiritual pleasure. It is not a sensation, but a delight in the way the world is: my darling baby is in good shape and I am so pleased. We call this emotion joy. As this example and that of the Hebrews in the Book of Ezra suggest, joy is a kind of *satisfaction.* You care about something — your baby, the temple — and you *see the situation as satisfying your care,* as being very good from the standpoint of your care. You don't rejoice in the health of other babies in the way you rejoice in the health of your own beloved baby; and the non-Hebrews in Jerusalem did not rejoice in the prospect of the new temple (quite the contrary!) because it didn't satisfy any concern of theirs.

So joy is one kind of spiritual pleasure. Aristotle emphasizes another kind in his *Nicomachean Ethics.* He points out that when people become very good at some activity, like playing tennis or piano, or building brick walls, or doing scientific research, they enjoy the *activity*. He points out that this will be so only if the conditions under which they perform the activity allow it to be performed really well — without "impediment," as he says. So the tennis player must have a good live ball and an excellent racquet, the bricklayer has to have good materials and not be trying to lay the wall in sub-zero temperatures, the pianist has to have an instrument whose keys all work and is decently in tune, and so forth. When an excellent agent expresses her excellence in performing an activity and does so without serious impediment, she takes pleasure in the activity. Like emotional pleasure, this pleasure is not located in any particular part of the body, though it is true that the pleasure is, in part, the pleasure of moving one's hands across the keyboard, of handling the trowel, and so forth. But even so, the pleasure is a pleasure of meaning (of the task, of oneself as agent, of the excellence of the performance), and is not a sensation like that of an orgasm or a fine port sloshing over the tongue. Aristotle applies this insight to virtues like justice: when an agent has the virtue of justice, then he is good *at* doing justice. When he acts justly in circumstances that don't impede his activity — for example, in a political system that gives scope for the just person's efforts — then the agent takes pleasure in acting justly. If the circumstances present impediments to doing justice — if one is being persecuted for doing it, if all sorts of obstacles are thrown in one's way — then one may take little pleasure in the activities of justice, yet if justice emerges from the situation, one may still take joy in that. Joy is compatible with quite a bit of frustration and pain. We will see illustrations of that in a moment.

Two more kinds of spiritual pleasures are the pleasure we take in music and our enjoyment of humor. These are somewhat like joy and activity-pleasure, but are also different in ways that we will not go into here.

So physical pleasures differ from spiritual ones. But in the life of a human being, the spiritual and the physical interact and influence one another in many important ways. The pleasure of a fine port is enhanced by the thought of the port's fineness. More importantly, for us, sexual intercourse is never just a matter of sensations. It is always a matter of the meaning that the partner and the act have for oneself. So the pleasure one takes in intercourse is enhanced by one's joy in the beloved, and one's joy in the beloved is enhanced by the pleasure of intercourse. Or, as it may be, the physical pleasure is spoiled (without ceasing to be physical pleasure) by the shame of betrayal. The pleasant sensation of one's newborn child's soft skin is taken up in the joy of the child's being alive and healthy. The pleasures of the palate become an aspect of the joy of fellowship over a meal with friends. Activity-pleasure also interacts with joy in ways that mix the spiritual pleasure with the body. When the apostle Paul encourages the members of the church in Rome to offer their bodies as a living sacrifice, which is their spiritual service (Romans 12:1-2), he is suggesting that Christian work (which is best done with joy) consists of bodily activities: waiting tables, standing up in front of crowds, shoveling manure, tending the sick, writing letters, visiting prisons. When these activities are done with "grace," the joy and the activity-pleasure intermingle so that body and spirit become one in the enjoyment of God.

BAD PLEASURES

I said that pleasure has been quite popular, and that some philosophers — they are the hedonists and utilitarians — have even thought it the chief good. But the best philosophers have disagreed, and have suggested that pleasure, and particularly the kind the Bible calls joy — is by no means always good. It is as wrong to think that joy is always good as it is to think that sorrow is always bad. We have seen that to feel joy is to see a situation as good, but sometimes people see bad situations as good. So when someone delights in the public humiliation of a brain-damaged person, his pleasure is evil. Scripture tells us that Judas Iscariot went to the chief priests to betray the Lord to them, and that when they saw what he was offering to do, "they were delighted *(echarēsan)* to hear this, and promised to give him money" (Mark 14:11). The terrible evil of facilitating the crucifixion of an innocent man was for them an intense spiritual pleasure. I use the mild expression "the crucifixion of an innocent man" because the chief priests may not have known "what they were doing" (Luke 23:34) — that is, probably they did not know that they were facilitating the crucifixion of the Son of God, the savior of the world, the only thoroughly good man in the history of the planet. But what they thought they were doing was bad enough to make their joy deeply vicious, an evil joy that shows the corruption of their hearts.

The joy of the chief priests is vicious on a grand scale. But less dramatic nasty joys are a common occurrence in the lives of most decent people. We not only take joy in the healthy birth of our child, but sometimes our hearts leap with a quick twinge of pleasure at the sight of a gory highway accident.

We may enjoy hearing the latest dirt about our next-door neighbors. We relish the troubles of people we don't like. We are vulnerable to a kind of joy that the Germans call *Schadenfreude,* which is taking pleasure in somebody else's misfortune. We experience this kind of joy when someone we envy suffers a setback, and this is one of the main reasons that envy has such a bad reputation among the wise.

But most of us are not so corrupt as to endorse these foul joys when we think about them. We may enjoy them in an unreflective moment, but we know, intuitively, that they are shameful and show shameful things about our character, and we don't want to live shamefully. We know that a person's joys reveal his heart by showing what he cares about. And so our souls are divided. We enjoy our wicked joys, but the more we reflect about them in a moral and spiritual mood, the more pain they cause us. We are pained by our pleasures. If the pleasure is bad, then the pain we feel about it is good — *if* our reason for feeling pain is that the pleasure is wicked. (If our reason is just that somebody thinks ill of us for feeling a wicked pleasure, then our pain about our joy is not worth much.) And if the pain is good, we must pursue it.

Among us human beings, pain is unpopular to the same extent that pleasure is popular. We naturally avoid it. So we do not automatically welcome the kind of reflection I have just described. It takes seriousness of spiritual purpose and courage to engage in the kind of reflection about our joys that could lead, ever so gradually, to their transformation. But that is a goal of the Christian life: to become the kind of person who takes joy in what is genuinely good, and is pained by what is genuinely bad. And for this process to move forward, pain is required.

In addition to the nasty joys, both grand- and small-scale, are the trivial and the unhealthy joys. The antique car buff rejoices when his antique car magazine comes each month, and the wino rejoices when the street affords an opportunity to get a bottle. The trivial and the unhealthy need to be kept distinct, though they can overlap, as we will see. It is not in itself unhealthy to have trivial joys; in fact, in a life that is not trivial, trivial joys have an important and healthy place, the kind of place that hobbies and other diversions have in a life that is otherwise intense and strongly goal-directed. But when the trivial joys are the only kind a life has, then the life is neither healthy nor admirable. When Leo Tolstoy wants to sketch for us the character of a thoroughly trivial man, he describes someone whose greatest activity-pleasure is playing bridge and whose greatest joy in life is a grand slam at the card table.

The pleasures connected with his work were pleasures of ambition; his social pleasures were those of vanity; but Ivan Ilych's greatest pleasure was playing bridge. He acknowledged that whatever disagreeable incident happened in his life, the pleasure that beamed like a ray of light above everything else was to sit down to bridge with good players, not noisy partners, and of course to four-handed bridge (with five players it was annoying to have to stand out, though one pretended not to mind), to play a clever and serious game (when the cards allowed it) and then to have supper and drink a glass of wine. (*The Death of Ivan Ilych and Other Stories*, p. 119)

Ivan Ilych did not find joy in his marriage, or his children, or in God, nor did he take any intrinsic joy in his work. As we have seen, Tolstoy's novella is the story of Ivan Ilych's deepening (rather suddenly near the very end of his life) through pain and love — and that deep emotion in which his life culminates and in which he discovers life's meaning is also joy. Ivan Ilych's joy at a grand slam is not by itself an indication of spiritual poverty, in the way that someone's enjoyment of malicious gossip is. But it is an indication of spiritual poverty by virtue of its status within his narrative. We come to appreciate the triviality of Ivan Ilych's life by grasping the sweep of the narrative in which this joy is a sort of emotional high point. Seen from that point of view, it is evident that Ivan Ilych's joy is a symptom of pathology, though he probably does not fit any of the categories in the *Diagnostic and Statistical Manual*. In a different life narrative — one, say, characterized by deep enthusiasm for real goods such as family, friends, the well-being of humanity, and the kingdom of God — an intense pleasure at the bridge table would not be in any sense pathological.

Joys that Reveal Virtues

We have been looking at joys that are evil, sick, or trivial. For the rest of this chapter, I will strike a happier note and talk about joys that are good, healthy, and significant. Excellent joys often reveal more than one virtue, and joy is a characteristic of several of the other emotions discussed in this book. Gratitude, hope, and peace are joyful emotions; we have seen that spiritual pleasure is an aspect even of that rather somber Christian virtue of contrition; and Christian compassion, though it involves discomfort, has a joyful aspect.

I mentioned Aristotle's comment that anyone who has the virtue of justice will take pleasure in doing just actions. Someone who acts justly without pleasure, or even with grudging discomfort, falls short of fully exemplifying the virtue of justice. (If he takes no joy in doing justice, perhaps he is doing it out of a sense of duty — a different virtue, but still a virtue.) Aristotle understands this point chiefly in terms of activity-pleasure, but the point could also be made with respect to the emotion of joy. The just person rejoices to have brought about justice because he loves justice and justice is therefore a satisfaction to him. But he rejoices not only in the justice he brings about, but also in justice accomplished by others. As the book of Proverbs (21:15) comments, "When justice is done, it is a joy to the righteous, but dismay to evildoers" (RSV). The just person takes pleasure in contemplating just institutions and laws, and in the character of people who have the virtue. The just person is most likely to rejoice in justice where a contrast is clear — say, where injustice has been corrected, or injustice threatens, or he merely thinks about the alternative to justice.

Consider next the generous person. She "sacrifices" for another by giving the other something that is valuable to herself, the giver. If the giver didn't care about the well-being or satisfaction of the recipient, then giving away what is valuable to herself might be a pure sacrifice — just plain discomfort, the pain of wrenching her goods from herself. But since the generous person does care about the well-being and satisfaction of the other person, and sees the transfer of good things — money, time, attention, the benefit of a doubt — as bringing about such well-being or satisfaction, she takes pleasure (joy) in giving to the other, and so in this sense her generous actions are less sacrificial, or perhaps not sacrificial at all in the sense of causing pain. If it is hard for her to part with what she gives, the joy she takes in the other's satisfaction is at any rate a major compensation for the sacrifice.

Consider how the words of John the Baptist express the virtues of faith and humility:

> You yourselves bear me witness, that I said, I am not the Christ, but I have been sent before him. He who has the bride is the bridegroom; the friend of the bridegroom, who stands and hears him, rejoices greatly at the bridegroom's voice; therefore this joy of mine is now full. He must increase, but I must decrease. (John 3:28-30, RSV)

An important part of the virtue of faith is the love of the Savior. This goes as much for any of us Christians as it does for the first ones who were devoted to Jesus. John the Baptist, one of Jesus' very first disciples, here expresses his love for Jesus in the joy that he feels when he sees Jesus coming out into the world to preach, to teach, and to do the works of his mercy that indicate the new reign of God. He foresees a fulfillment of his expectations and hopes, and his heart fills with gladness. But this increase in the activity and prominence of Jesus, his stepping forth as the center of attention, signals a diminishment of John's role as herald. He has made his announcements, cleared the way for the coming of the king, and now it is time for him to "decrease." We would attribute a virtuous humility to someone who, without rancor, gave up his place of prominence to another, greater than he. But John accepts his own decrease, not with resignation and equanimity, but with positive joy out of his love for Jesus and the coming kingdom. This joy shows that whatever bit of vanity or desire for dominance and being the center of attention may have been in the heart of John (John was, after all, a sinful human being more or less like the rest of us), was utterly swamped in his enthusiasm for God's program.

As our last example, let us look at the place of joy in adversity-facing virtues such as courage and perseverance. Scripture several times refers to joy that disciples feel in circumstances quite opposite the ones that usually occasion joy. The two passages that I will present identify the reasons for the joy, and in each case the reasons are ones that non-believers would not have, reasons that connect the adversity to features of the world that are highlighted in the Christian take on reality. The capacity to feel joy — real, delicious emotional pleasure — in these circumstances and for these reasons is an extraordinary achievement of character formation, one that we see in the first disciples and occasionally in later Christian history.

You will remember my discussion in Chapters 1 and 2 of the extraordinary spiritual joy the apostles experienced at being threatened and beaten up by the authorities in Jerusalem (see Acts 5). Prior to describing that episode, Luke points out that acting like a disciple in Jerusalem was such a dangerous business that "no one else dared join [the disciples], even though they were highly regarded by the people" (v. 13). The apostles' joy shows their attitude toward the threats that call for courage and the adversities that call for perseverance. Without exactly ceasing to see whipping as a threat and adversity, they see it in the light of their Lord's suffering and thus as honorable in the circumstances, something good, a satisfaction of their desire to be like their Lord, who had taught this very doctrine and drawn the emotional inference:

Blessed are you when men revile you and persecute you and utter all kinds of evil against you falsely on my account. Rejoice and be glad, for your reward is great in heaven, for so men persecuted the prophets who were before you. (Matthew 5:11-12, RSV)

Courage is a disposition to act well in the face of threats, and perseverance an ability not to be derailed from one's purpose by adversity. But if one thinks of the threatened adversity as itself a blessing of sorts, as a badge of membership in the community of the most excellent, then the adversity is not, for oneself, quite as threatening as it would be without this reading of the situation. One has a handle on the adversity. The apostolic disposition to joy is a very special kind of courage that involves a deep internalization and emotional integration of the central story of the New Testament. It makes people who possess this courage strange and difficult to deal with, vis-à-vis people with an ordinary worldly emotional formation.

Joy and activity-pleasure mingle in the joy of stewardship. I will end this chapter with a discussion of this kind of Christian joy.

THE JOY OF STEWARDSHIP

When I was a child, a book sat on the shelf just above the sink where we washed the dishes in our kitchen. As my childhood waned and adulthood emerged within me, that book became more and more tattered and soiled from usage. The title was *The Joy of Cooking,* and I think that title expresses well my mother's attitude. Not that she took delight in every meal she made us; she was sometimes under stress and frustrated, and occasionally the cooking didn't work out so well, but on the whole meal-making was a joy to her. Mom liked to eat, but the main thing for her was the persons for whom she was cooking, her husband and kids. Her joy of cooking was the joy of family life, and she took special delight when we were especially delighted by the food she prepared for us. Mom's joy revealed her heart — her love for us, her enthusiasm for the things of the family. And this is generally true about people's joys: we delight in the success of what we care about, and in the activities by which we achieve that success.

Jesus tells the story (Matthew 25:14-30) of a master who gets ready for a long absence by doling out some of his property to his three servants, with the idea that they use it fruitfully. He gives five talents of money to one servant, two to another, and one to a third. When at last he returns, the first presents him with a return of five talents, and the master says, "Well done, good and faithful servant! You have been faithful in a few things, and I will put you in charge of many things. Enter into the joy of your master!" When the second servant comes and presents him with a return of two talents, the master says, "Well done, good and faithful servant! You have been faithful in a few things, and I will put you in charge of many things. Enter into the joy of your master!" Then the servant with one talent comes and reports that he just buried the talent in the ground because he knew that the master was harsh; and he brings the talent he has dug up and hands it back to his master. The master is not pleased, and orders this servant's talent to be turned over to the servant who has earned five talents, and sends the cautious servant into the outer darkness.

Jesus' parable is about stewardship — responsible servanthood — and the story connects stewardship with joy. The master says to each of the good stewards, "Enter into the joy of your master." This joy is surely one of those virtuous joys of which I have been writing. Let us think a bit about the virtue of stewardship.

The first chapter of the first book of the Bible answers the question of Psalm 8, "What is man that you are mindful of him?" (v. 4) by saying that we are special in God's sight because we are created in his image (Genesis 1:26). People have explained the idea that we are made in God's image in many ways: they have talked about our ability to reason and to plan and to think big thoughts about our lives and the nature of the universe. They've talked about our capacity for moral responsibility and free action. They have talked about our creativity — our ability to concoct art works and inventions and schemes of social life that did not exist before we came up with them.

But the book of Genesis itself explains the idea that we are in the image of God by saying that to be in the image of God is stewardship. It is basic human nature, says the Bible, to stand in this special relationship *between* God, on the one side, and the rest of what he has created, on the other side.

> Let us make [humankind] in our image, in our likeness, and let them rule over the fish of the sea and the birds of the air, over the livestock, over all the earth, and over all the creatures that move along the ground. (1:26)

A steward, then, is a caretaker, who has quite a lot of responsibility, but who is not herself the final boss or owner of that for which she has responsibility.

A steward is a person who takes the belongings of another, just as the three servants of our parable took the talents of their master, and "rules" over these, but all the while acting as the master's agent. The steward acts on his own, but not on his own behalf.

To say that stewardship is basic to human nature is to say that we find fulfillment in behaving and thinking as stewards, and that if we fail to think and behave as stewards, we will live a crippled and incomplete life. Imagine someone who says, "I don't want to be responsible for the well-being of anything in creation. I just want to amuse myself, to the disregard of all consequences to the environment and to the well-being of my fellow human beings. I can't be bothered with stewardship. I am not a caretaker. I think the world owes me a living." Or imagine somebody who says, "I am going to rule over the things of my life. I am going to develop my land and cultivate my animals. But I am not a steward. I am an *owner,* and am going to do these things for myself, not for God."

Both of these people reject their nature as stewards. If the Bible is right about human nature, these people are like someone who comes home to his wife one evening, and rather casually after dinner says, "Honey, I've decided to have one of my legs removed." She says, "Oh? What gave you that bright idea?" "Well, I just thought it would be interesting to see what it's like. The kids do have their noses pierced, after all. And also, you know I've been trying to lose a little weight." This is a man who fails to understand something about human nature — its basic two-leggedness. He doesn't seem to understand what it will mean for his functioning to have one of his legs off.

The two-leggedness of human nature is pretty obvious to everybody, a lot more obvious than our stewardliness. We find quite a few who deny their stewardliness, but very few like the husband in our parable, who deny their two-leggedness. But apart from that difference, the person who refuses to function as a steward and the person who refuses to function two-leggedly are similar. If you refuse to take any responsibility for anything but your own amusement, or if you work only for yourself and your family, but not for God, you are headed for a crippled life, a life of incompleteness or disaster. If you seek irresponsible amusement, you are headed for a kind of basic disorientation in life, a sense of being lost in the cosmos without an identity; if you take responsibility, but only for yourself and your family, you are headed for despair in face of the end of life. If you have lived your life as a steward of God, working not ultimately for yourself, but for God and his kingdom, you have laid the groundwork for a sense of identity and a sense of having a solid place in a universe that is much larger than your own life.

In Jesus' story the man who makes his servants his stewards takes their abilities into account. The servant with greater ability is put in possession of five talents of money, and the other two receive two talents and one talent, respectively. The master is very pleased with the first two servants and says to each of them, "Enter into the joy of your master." Notice that he commends these servants equally, even though one produced five talents, and the other only two. The point is that they were both working for him. His approval is not measured to the *amount* that is done for him, but to the spirit in which it is done, in particular the spirit of stewardship.

He tells them to enter into the joy of their master. And what is this joy? Just before telling them to enter into the joy of their master, he tells them he's going to give them even more responsibility. Now some servants might respond to this by saying, "What? Even more responsibility? Do you call that a reward? Am I supposed to be joyful about that? What I need is a vacation!" It is true that people need a vacation now and then, but it's the spirit of the true steward that he takes joy in acting on behalf of his master. That is why entering into the joy of his master means, for him, being able to act even more as the master's steward. These two good stewards were experiencing joy all along the way. Each day, while the master was gone, they were working in the awareness that it was for him they were working, and because it was for him, their work was a joy to them. Maybe the work was intrinsically enjoyable, like running a bakery or teaching school or practicing law or medicine or rehabbing old houses or administering a bank or doing social work or trimming trees or being a secretary or running a print shop or programming computers or working in a lab or a good factory. But the work had a joy that went beyond the immediate pleasure of the work itself, and that delightful meaning was that the work was for the master.

Just as the joy of cooking is less in the cooking than in the beloved people who will eat the cooking, so the joy of all work is, for the person who does it for the Lord, not just in the work but also in the Lord.

A Servant without Joy

In the case of the third servant the special relation to the master comes out very clearly. When he explains why he did nothing with the talent that the master entrusted to him, he begins by accusing the master of injustice and harshness.

> Master, I knew that you are a hard man, harvesting where you have not sown and gathering where you have not scattered seed. So I was afraid and went out and hid your talent in the ground. (Matthew 25:24b-25a)

He seems to have quite a different "take" on the master than his two fellow servants. Maybe he is rationalizing, trying to justify his irresponsible behavior; but more likely he really does see the master as harsh.

If we take the master in the parable to symbolize the Lord, then the wicked servant has certainly misinterpreted the master. In the last analysis, the Lord doesn't need any of us to make money or computer programs or trim trees for him. What he really wants is *us* as his stewards. Imagine the third servant in a different scenario. He takes the one talent and works his fingers to the bone with it, so as to please the master, and everything is going swimmingly until the sweet potato crop fails and he loses all he's gained, and the original talent to boot. Now the master calls for a reckoning, and the servant comes to him empty-handed. If the master is the Lord he won't say, "You wicked and useless servant. You lost my money. If you'd been more conservative and invested with the bankers, I'd still have my money. Go to Hell." No, he won't say that. He'll say, "Well done, good and faithful servant. Your heart was with me, both in the joy of your early success and in your sorrow about the failure of the sweet potato crop. You have been faithful in a little, and I want you to continue to be my servant. Take one of the talents earned by the servant with five talents, and give it to this boy so he can get started again. Enter into the joy of your master."

But in the real parable, I'm sorry to say, the third servant didn't even try to make anything of the talent his master had provided him. He let himself be paralyzed into inaction by his harsh interpretation of the master — inaction on behalf of his master, that is. Jesus doesn't say that the wicked servant did nothing at all while his master was away. He probably looked out for himself. He invested his own money and worked hard to get ahead, built a retirement fund, and supplied himself with a number of the luxuries of life. He was not generally lazy; he was only lazy when it came to his *master's* affairs. In other words, he didn't lack the virtue of industriousness; he lacked the virtue of stewardship. Maybe he didn't even believe his line about the master being harsh and unjust. Maybe he just wanted to excuse his own selfishness in working only for himself and not for his master.

ON STEWARDSHIP IN THE
CONTEMPORARY SENSE OF THE WORD

In contemporary church life, 'stewardship' has come to have a rather narrow, churchy sense. It is not really considered, by most churchgoers, as a trait of character, a virtue. Annually, we have a stewardship drive, and that means a time for encouraging one another to contribute money to the church. But giving money to the church of Jesus Christ is part of the larger life of Christian stewardship. Everything we do is to be done in the spirit of service to God. Nothing we have is quite our own, but we pursue all our activities as servants who have been made responsible for some of God's belongings, to nurture and protect and cultivate and make something of them. What is true of all our "talents" is true of our money, and so we devote a part of our income to the particular work of the church — the support of a place of worship, of the clergy, and the church's various mission and outreach activities.

And if we really have the proper spirit of stewardship, we do this with a lavishness that corresponds to the joy we experience in the pursuit of our master's work. We don't look grudgingly on this stewardly giving as though it's some kind of annoying duty to fulfill. Rather, we do it with joy. I said that, for my mother, the joy of cooking was largely the delight in seeing her family eat well and happily. The joy of cooking was for her the joy of love. And the joy that the good steward experiences in doing the work of his or her master is like that: like the Israelites when they celebrated the foundation of the new temple, he remembers the goodness of the Lord, and loves the things of the Lord's kingdom. He counts it a privilege and a delight to contribute to this glorious enterprise of the kingdom of God. He thinks of the children of the parish, whose lives will be touched and shaped by the Sunday school teachings of the Word of God, who will carry into their adult life this beautiful influence and affect others in countless ways. He thinks of the young married couples who find in the parish a healthy spiritual context for nurturing their early life together. He thinks of the people who come each week to hear the gospel of forgiveness and eternal life and to receive the body and blood of the Lord. He thinks of the single mothers and their children who are served by New Neighbors Transitional Housing, and the people who come to the Morgan Park Food Pantry to supplement their larders. He thinks with joy of the college students who are served by InterVarsity Christian Fellowship and the seminarians at Trinity School for Ministry. He thinks of his own pastor, his or her needs, and the countless hours she devotes to fruitful ministry.

As a spiritual exercise, perhaps you could imagine yourself coming before the Lord Jesus on a day of reckoning. He asks you, "What have you made of the 'talents' (including the money) with which I supplied you, my steward?" Your answer, I hope, will indicate a life of stewardship, a life of love for his kingdom. And if it does, it will elicit a response from him for which you have been prepared by many happy experiences of service along your life's way: "Well done, good and faithful servant. You have been faithful over a little. I will bless you with further opportunities of stewardship. Enter into the joy of your master."

CHAPTER NINE

Gratitude

WHAT IS GRATITUDE?

Esther Summerson, the heroine of Charles Dickens's *Bleak House,* is a model of gratitude. She is the illegitimate daughter of a wealthy and noble lady who thinks Esther died at birth. Early in the story, her puritanical god-mother (actually the sister of her mother) tells her, "Your mother, Esther, is your disgrace, and you were hers," and that it would be better had she not been born.

> I went up to my room, and crept to bed, and laid my doll's cheek against mine wet with tears; and holding that solitary friend upon my bosom, cried myself to sleep. Imperfect as my understanding of my sorrow was, I knew that I had brought no joy, at any time, to anybody's heart, and that I was to no one upon earth what Dolly was to me. (p. 65)

Soon she is taken to a boarding school where, after a time, she earns part of her keep by teaching the other girls what she has learned. By her gentleness and solicitude for the girls, she earns their affection, which makes her very happy. "I felt almost ashamed to have done so little and have won so much" (p. 73). After "six happy, quiet years" at the school she receives a letter, insti-gated by her secret benefactor, summoning her to become the companion of an heiress. The letter, and her consequent departure, occasion great ex-pressions of affectionate regret in the school:

> "Oh, never, never, never shall I forget the emotion this letter caused in the house! It was so tender in them to care so much for me; it was so gra-

cious in that Father who had not forgotten me, to have made my orphan way so smooth and easy, and to have inclined so many youthful natures towards me; that I could hardly bear it. Not that I would have had them less sorry — I am afraid not; but the pleasure of it, and the pain of it, and the pride and joy of it, and the humble regret of it, were so blended, that my heart seemed almost breaking while it was full of rapture. . . . could I help it if I was quite bowed down in the coach by myself, and said 'O, I am so thankful, I am so thankful' many times over!" (pp. 74, 75).

This episode presents an instance of Esther's emotion. This *felt* gratitude is an expression of her *virtue* of gratitude. But throughout Esther's narratives, even where the emotion proper is absent, are found the marks of the virtue, and they involve her way of thinking and feeling about herself, about the adversities and blessings of her life, and about the persons, including God, whose actions and attitudes impinge on her life. This habitual pattern of thought and concern, as it affects her perceptions of the situations of her life and thus her actions and demeanor, constitutes the virtue of gratitude.

The central emotion that Esther feels on her departure from the school is a concern-based construal of the situation in three broad terms: of something as a gift freely given, of herself as the recipient of the gift, and of some person or persons as givers of the gift. We could speak of the interlocking three B's that make the framework of gratitude: the benefit, the beneficiary, and the benefactor. The gift in Esther's case is the love and regard she receives from so many at the school; she is the recipient, and the givers are the members of the school and God.

As all the "benes" in the framework suggest, gratitude is a perception of *good*: to the grateful person, the situation that evokes the emotion appears excellent. This is especially so of the benefit and the benefactor. If either of these does not appear good to the subject, the emotion will not be gratitude. If Esther had taken all the expressions of affection and regret at her leaving not as a blessing, but as a pure and colossal annoyance, an embarrassing irritation from which she would escape as quickly as she could, her emotion would not have been gratitude. Similarly, if she had regarded the members of the school as a bunch of dolts and miscreants from whom she would not feel right receiving even a minor fortune, then she wouldn't be grateful to them even if she were delighted to receive the fortune they gave her. She would be glad for the fortune, but not grateful to them.

Is Christian Gratitude a Mistake?

Christian worship services attempt to promote gratitude because gratitude to God for all his gifts is an attitude of worship. In the departing coach, Esther feels "quite bowed down," in an exalted sort of way, by the burden of a good gift and of the good free givers of the gift. An analogously humble upraising is the experience of Christian worshipers as we celebrate God's goodness to us. The disposition, or readiness, to feel grateful to God and to one's human benefactors is a Christian virtue. The apostle Paul exhorts the members of the church at Thessalonica, "Be joyful always; pray continually; give thanks in all circumstances, for this is God's will for you in Christ Jesus" (I Thessalonians 5:18).

The idea that gratitude applies in *all* circumstances and that it requires that the subject construe himself as recipient of a *benefit* from a *benefactor* creates a problem for Christian gratitude, according to Brother David Steindl-Rast, a monk at Mount Savior Monastery in Elmira, New York (personal communication). The problem takes the form of a contradiction: in some circumstances, we receive not a benefit, but a harm: we lose a job; we fall sick; a loved one dies; our students reject our teaching and dislike us. So we can't be grateful in all circumstances if we think of gratitude as a response to *something good* given to us by *someone*. Brother David proposes, therefore, that we not emphasize gratitude as I have begun to expound it. Instead we should demote it to the status of what he calls "thankfulness," a good but limited attitude we take when people do good things for us. The really important and deeply religious attitude, which he proposes to call "gratefulness," is the sort of experience that many of us have had on the shore of a quiet mountain lake at sunset, or in an open field on a starry night in summer. In this experience we have a positive sense of "belonging," says Brother David, not a belonging to this or that, but a sort of "cosmic belonging," along with a sense of not deserving this belonging ("Gratitude as Thankfulness and as Gratefulness"). A second reason to give up Christian gratitude in favor of "gratefulness" is that "gratefulness," according to Brother David, is an experience common to all religions, and so the new emphasis would promote interreligious goodwill.

But the price of giving up Christian gratitude would be the loss of distinctively Christian character formation. Many of us have experienced something like the transcendent "gratefulness" that Brother David describes, and we value the experience, but it is no substitute for the kind of transcendence that characterizes gospel gratitude: a heart overflowing with thanksgiving to

God for our membership in his people through the sacrifice of Christ on the cross. And the "problem" that is supposed to follow from the fact that Christian gratitude is a three-term construal in which the grateful person construes himself as the beneficiary, God as the benefactor, and God's gift as the benefit, is not a real problem. It depends on making a mistake about the essential nature of the benefit. If we think that the primary benefits for which the Christian is grateful are such things as health, wealth, security, and the good opinion of our fellow human beings, then it is true that we can't be grateful in all circumstances, since not all circumstances contain such benefits. In fact, many of our circumstances contain the mirror-opposite evils. Health and security are certainly good things, and the Christian is grateful for them if he has them; but they are not the primary thing.

The prayer of General Thanksgiving in the Episcopal *Book of Common Prayer* (1979) has the logic of Christian gratitude right:

> Almighty God, Father of all mercies,
> we thine unworthy servants
> do give thee most humble and hearty thanks
> for all thy goodness and loving-kindness
> to us and to all men.
> We bless thee for our creation, preservation,
> and all the blessings of this life;
> but above all for thine inestimable love
> in the redemption of the world by our Lord Jesus Christ,
> for the means of grace, and for the hope of glory. (Daily Morning
> Prayer, Rite One)

The "above all" in the eighth line identifies the order: *above all* the redemption of the world in Christ, *but also* our creation, preservation, and all the blessings of this life. We are naturally glad to be alive, to stay alive, and to have some of the blessings of this life: friends, health for ourselves and those we love, material prosperity, freedom of movement and self-expression, development of our talents, opportunities to explore the world of nature and cultures, good food, a beautiful environment, and so forth. But the absence of these benefits, or their corresponding evils, do not prevent our being grateful for God's central gift. The gift of forgiveness, redemption, and eternal life in Christ is a *transcendent* circumstance, a circumstance that always holds, regardless of the coming and going of the "blessings of this life." And it is a mark of Christian gratitude as a character trait that it has this transcendent feature: it shares the logic of the prayer precisely by *not* ceasing to be felt when the going gets rough and the blessings of this life are reversed or few and far between. Because of the gospel, the well-developed Christian stands, to some extent, emotionally and spiritually above the vicissitudes of human circumstance.

This kind of emotional transcendence is nicely illustrated in the life of the apostle Paul, who comments,

> . . . as servants of God we commend ourselves in every way: in great endurance; in troubles, hardships and distresses; in beatings, imprisonments and riots; in hard work, sleepless nights and hunger; in purity, understanding, patience and kindness; in the Holy Spirit and in sincere love; in truthful speech and in the power of God; with weapons of righteousness in the right hand and in the left; through glory and dishonor, bad report and good report; genuine, yet regarded as impostors; known, yet regarded as unknown; dying, and yet we live on; beaten, and yet not killed; sorrowful, yet always rejoicing; poor, yet making many rich; having nothing, and yet possessing everything. (II Corinthians 6:4-10)

Paul appreciates the difference between good times and bad, between enjoyment and suffering. But his steadfast gratitude for the good that God has done us in Jesus Christ transforms his understanding of both the blessings and the sufferings: both are transient aspects of a temporal world that is encompassed by the eternal world of God's love, a world from which God has visited in Jesus Christ. Paul's gratitude is an emotional connection to that eternal world, one that puts the sufferings *and* blessings of this life in perspective.

Next, I want to explore ingratitude in the hope of deepening our understanding of Christian gratitude. We can often learn something about a virtue by looking carefully at the ways of deviating from it. The examples we will consider illustrate various ways in which a person can fall short of the virtue that Esther Summerson exemplifies, though they all focus in different ways on the aspect of her emotion that she expresses by saying she was "bowed down." After that, we will return to Christian gratitude, applying what we have learned. Let us begin with Richard Savage, an eighteenth-century English poet of whom Samuel Johnson wrote a short biography (in *The Lives of the Poets*).

RICHARD SAVAGE

Johnson tells us that Savage was nearly always in financial straits, and regularly solicited his acquaintances for small sums of money, which mounted up fast due to the frequency of the asking. He was not in the habit of repaying these loans, so people soon became disgusted with the requests and shunned him. But since he moved constantly from place to place and frequented many taverns, he made new acquaintances about as fast as he repelled the old, and so was seldom without resources. Nor was he very grateful for the kindnesses he received:

> he always asked favours of this kind without the least submission or apparent consciousness of dependence, and . . . did not seem to look upon a compliance with his request as an obligation that deserved any extraordinary acknowledgements; but a refusal was resented by him as an affront, or complained of as an injury: nor did he readily reconcile himself to those who either denied to lend, or gave him afterwards any intimation that they expected to be repaid (§227).

People who went so far as to take him into their homes

> soon discovered him to be a very incommodious inmate; for, being always accustomed to an irregular manner of life, he could not confine himself to any stated hours, or pay any regard to the rules of a family, but would prolong his conversation till midnight, without considering that business might require his friend's application in the morning; and when he had persuaded himself to retire to bed, was not, without equal difficulty, called up to dinner. . . . It must therefore be acknowledged, in justification of mankind, that it was not always by the negligence or coldness of his friends that Savage was distressed, but because it was in reality very difficult to preserve him long in a state of ease (§§228-29).

Savage's ingratitude is made, in large part, of a sense of being *owed* the benefit. He treats the benevolence of his friends as though, in helping him, they are doing nothing but minimal justice. When someone sells us a car, we pay her the money, and she "gives" us the car. Unless the transaction has some character of a gift — say, she gave us a *very* good price, or went out of her way to make the transaction convenient for us — then gratitude is inappropriate, because once we have paid for it, she *owes* us the car. People very naturally distinguish gifts and favors, on the one hand, from strict debts on the other. So when we meet someone like Savage, who treats our favors as requirements of justice, we are likely to be offended. And yet there is a kind of debt here: Savage owes *us* a "debt of gratitude" for the favor.

A debt of gratitude differs from a debt of justice. If, as a matter of hospitality, we shelter Savage in our house for a week, we do not expect him to pay *rent,* but we do expect him, at a minimum, to accommodate himself to the rules of the house, and we will feel still better about the whole interaction if he gives us tokens of his appreciation — a word of thanks, and perhaps a bit of help with the dishes. Debts of gratitude are debts of acknowledgement, and that is why they can be paid with mere "tokens" — tokens that express the sense of debt that is characteristic of the recipient's gratitude. They are "spiritual" in this generic sense: we feel that the debt has been paid when the right attitude is taken.

The grateful person feels this debt to his benefactor. He perceives the benefit as gratuitous, as a good the benefactor did not owe him. I use the words 'feels' and 'perceives' to suggest that the grateful person does not merely judge himself to be indebted to his benefactor, but has a strong immediate, heartfelt impression of this indebtedness. It is a kind of weight, a sense of connection in which the recipient feels dependent on the giver. It is Esther Summerson's self-perception of being "bowed down." But not just any sense of this dependence is a part of gratitude; if, for example, one resents being in this "one-down" position of dependency, then one is not grateful. The grateful person is willing, even glad, despite the weight of dependency, to "live with" the indebtedness, not paying it in any strict sense — not paying it *off* — so that he remains indebted to his benefactor and thus bound to him. The grateful person is glad to continue to perceive himself as "irremediably" indebted. Savage seems to have lacked this capacity.

> Once, when he was without lodging, meat, or clothes, one of his friends . . . left a message, that he desired to see him about nine in the morning. Savage knew that his intention was to assist him; but was very much disgusted that he should presume to prescribe the hour of his attendance, and, I believe, refused to visit him, and rejected his kindness. (§230)

Presumably, Savage was disgusted at being prescribed the hour of meeting because it seemed to him a token of his dependence. He was willing to accept the assistance, but only if it was given in the spirit of justice, of perfect equality in the transaction, as something rightly his, something that placed no weight of obligation on him.

Savage's origins bear a certain resemblance to those of Esther Summerson. Like her, he was the illegitimate child of a wealthy and noble mother, a fact that he discovers in adulthood. A difference, which may partially excuse the enormous difference in character between the two, is that Esther's mother did not knowingly abandon her, while Savage's sought actively, over a long period, to make his life miserable and even to destroy him. The exaggerated sense of entitlement that is so prominent in Savage's ingratitude may be explained as an irrational response to the knowledge of his noble and privileged birth, to the awareness of injury in being so unfairly prevented from enjoying it, and to a due sense of his own talent. Esther draws no such resentful conclusion from a similar self-knowledge (though she differs from Savage in underestimating both her beauty and her talents) but steadily presupposes that she does not deserve the many benefits and acknowledgments she enjoys. She tends to see all good things that come to her as gifts, with the result that a life begun almost as badly as Savage's and attended by some analogous difficulties, ends up an unusually happy one, almost incomparably better than his.

ARISTOTLE'S GREAT-SOULED MAN

Samuel Johnson comments at some length on the moral and spiritual wisdom and knowledge of human life found in Richard Savage's writings, while reporting in great abundance his follies in living. Savage regarded himself as a Christian, so we must take his ingratitude not as a general ideological commitment, the consequence of a doctrine about the best way to live, but as a pathology that he ought to have recognized as such. In *Nicomachean Ethics,* Book 4, Chapter 3, Aristotle describes what he takes to be a *virtue* — indeed the crowning one in which all the other virtues culminate — that implies ingratitude. I do not think that if we look at all of Aristotle's ethical writings together we will find him a consistent enemy of gratitude, but in this passage we do find a picture of human excellence that excludes it. It will be interesting, therefore, to consider it as a possibility in the starkest contrast with Christian ethics, which actively and uncompromisingly promotes gratitude.

Aristotle tells us that the great-souled man thinks himself worthy of great things and is right to think so. He has the best possible reason to think highly of himself: he has all the virtues. So the one thing he wants, *as* great-souled, is honor, because it is the only good that could be added to his self-sufficient greatness. But he does not want it from just anyone: he despises honor paid him by common people and on trivial grounds, and even the honor of peers, who judge rightly, is not a big thing to him.

> And he is the sort of man to confer benefits, but he is ashamed of receiving them; for the one is the mark of a superior, the other of an inferior. And he is apt to confer greater benefits in return [for benefits received]; for thus the original benefactor besides being paid will incur a debt to him, and will be the gainer by the transaction. The great-souled seem also to remember any service they have done, but not those they have received (for he who receives a service is inferior to him who has done it, but the great-souled man wishes to be superior), and to hear of the former with pleasure, of the latter with displeasure.

The great-souled man experiences indebtedness of the kind engendered by gratuitous favors as reducing his dignity, and thus as shameful. Behind this kind of ingratitude, then, is a comparative, competitive, and elitist personality ideal: to be excellent is to rank higher than others. It is not just to be excellent of one's kind, but to be better than others of one's kind, and better in a particular way: self-sufficiency. To be really excellent, I need both to be self-sufficient, and to be associated with people who are less self-sufficient than I, people who depend on me without my being dependent on them.

If we are self-aware, we can recognize in ourselves the values of the great-souled man. Our generosity is often directed less at the benefit of the one on whom we bestow it than on the expression of our own importance. We enjoy the role of giver because of the way it ranks us vis-à-vis our recipient. And we sometimes feel a certain discomfort with being put in the role of recipient because of the way *that* ranks us vis-à-vis our benefactor. We feel an impulse to pay back our benefactor, not just with the token of gratitude that would express our indebtedness, but in a superfluity that would turn the tables on her. Unintentionally (perhaps) Aristotle's description of great-souled people shows them to be ridiculous. They are trying to live an ideal that is fundamentally at odds with our nature as human beings. When he says they remember any service they have done, but not those they have received, his supposition is that they have in fact received services from others. They are less self-sufficient than they would like to be, and so to maintain the impression of themselves as self-sufficient, they have to engage in some selective and self-deceptive remembering.

This anxiety to be on top of our benefactors is absent from the spirit of Esther Summerson. She is simply "bowed down" with her indebtedness to her benefactors for the great good she has received from them, and content to dwell happily in that indebtedness. As Dickens presents her, she is not at all a second-class character, by comparison with whom more self-sufficient characters are nobler or more successful specimens of the human race. Juxtaposing Esther with the great-souled man highlights the fact that gratitude has a "metaphysical" background: as a virtue, it belongs to a view of the world in which human beings are by nature and design dependent creatures. Dickens is a Christian writer, who therefore trades on a Christian version of this "metaphysic": human beings depend on God for our creation, preservation, and all the blessings of this life, and we are also made to be dependent on one another: on our parents and other caretakers in childhood, on our friends and colleagues in adulthood, and (if all goes well) on our children in our old age. As Paul comments (I Corinthians 12), the Christian church is a tissue of mutual dependencies. Self-sufficiency, therefore, is at best a very qualified ideal, and the great-souled man's striving for it is a sinful distortion. The heartfelt acknowledgment of dependency embodied in the emotion and virtue of gratitude is therefore an excellent expression of our real nature. Our dignity does not derive from self-sufficiency or (worse) from a greater self-sufficiency than our fellow human beings; our gratitude expresses our dignity as creatures of God whom he made to depend on one another.

ANNIE LITTLEFIELD AND JESSE JOAD

Who's been stealing the toilet paper in Unit Four of the government camp? Nobody, as it turns out. The Joyce children used it up on their skitters. With no money for food, the kids have been stuffing themselves with green grapes. So Unit Four has been suffering shame because Mrs. Joyce wouldn't admit that the family had nothing to eat. But now she's confessed. Ma Joad speaks.

Now you hol' up your head," Jessie said. "That ain't no crime. You jes' waltz right over t' the Weedpatch store an' git you some grocteries. The camp got twenty dollars' credit there. You git yourself fi' dollar's' worth. An' you kin pay it back to the Central Committee when you git work. Mis' Joyce, you knowed that," she said sternly. "How come you let your girls git hungry?"

"We ain't never took no charity," Mrs. Joyce said.

"This ain't charity, an' you know it," Jessie raged. "We had all that out. They ain't no charity in this here camp. We won't have no charity. Now you waltz right over an' git you some grocteries, an' you bring the slip to me."

With some reluctance, Mrs. Joyce agrees to get some groceries on the camp's credit. She departs.

Annie Littlefield said, "She ain't been here long. Maybe she don't know. Maybe she's took charity one time-another. Nor," Annie said, "don't you try to shut me up, Jessie. I got a right to pass speech." She turned half to Ma. "If a body's ever took charity, it makes a burn that don't come out. This ain't charity, but if you ever took it, you don't forget it. I bet Jessie ain't ever done it."

"No, I ain't," said Jessie.

"Well, I did," Annie said. "Las' winter; an' we was a-starvin' — me and Pa and the little fellas. An' it was a-rainin'. Fella tol' us to go to the Salvation Army." Her eyes grew fierce. "We was hungry — they made us crawl for our dinner. They took our dignity. They — I hate 'em! An' — maybe Mis' Joyce took charity. Maybe she didn' know this ain't charity. Mis' Joad, we don't allow nobody in this camp to build theirself up that-a-way. We don't allow nobody to give nothing to another person. They can give it to the camp, an' the camp can pass it out. We won't have no charity!" Her voice was fierce and hoarse. "I hate 'em," she said. "I ain't never seen my man beat before, but them — them Salvation Army done it to 'im." (John Steinbeck, *The Grapes of Wrath,* Chapter 22)

If to Esther Summerson the burden of grace at the hands of others is an almost unbearable joy, and Richard Savage feels no burden at all most of the time, Jesse, Annie, and Mrs. Joyce agree with the great-souled man that grace bestowed by another human being feels like an attack on their dignity.

The great-souled man handles the problem rather easily, it seems, with his little routine of selective memory, but for these ladies if you ever took charity it makes a burn that don't come out. Esther has a sense of dignity. She is not a fawning character, but a self-confident, active, and generous agent who makes positive contributions wherever she goes. But it's an implicit dignity, a sense of self that doesn't require constant maintenance and defense. Unlike the dignity of the great-souled man, hers is not maintained by constant reflections on her accomplishments and excellences, and by repeated actions of putting others in her debt. Her dignity is not exactly self-esteem; she is always a bit surprised at her happiness, her successes, and others' good opinion of her. Despite her sense of dignity, she is inclined to think herself unworthy of these blessings.

Annie and Jesse seem pretty much to have erased gratitude from their emotional repertoire. They defend against it by disguising generosity as something due them as members of the community: "They can give it to the camp, an' the camp can pass it out. We won't have no charity!" With nobody to thank, there will be nobody before whose face we lose our fragile dignity. The Salvation Army was too much for Annie and her husband, because it was all too clear whom to thank.

Let's say that the particular corps of the Salvation Army with which the Littlefields had their run-in was really nasty. Let's say their generosity was like that of the great-souled man, who likes giving to others because he enjoys the sense of self that he gets from the down-looking view. Receiving from a giver with this predatory look in his eye is a real challenge for gratitude, because the grateful person wants to think of her giver as giving from a benevolent attitude towards her. And if she finds it impossible to attribute such goodwill to the giver, her emotion will not be gratitude. (Though she may still be glad to receive the benefit, and she may be able to defend against the attack on her dignity by thinking cynically, "Let him have his little fun, if he's stupid enough to give me a meal in exchange for this petty pleasure.") Gratitude, by its nature, attributes goodwill to the giver. So if the soldiers in this part of the Salvation Army made it unambiguously clear that *their* purpose in giving food to the hungry was to boost their self-importance by looking down on the recipients of their "mercy," then the Littlefields' failure of gratitude (the emotion) is not due to any lack of gratitude (the virtue) on their part.

But seldom are the motives of the giver so pure. Most sinners, especially if we are Christians, have at least some desire to benefit the beneficiary for his own sake, even if we are *also* seeking to promote our own importance.

But if so, then there is something for gratitude to get hold of. "They made us crawl for our dinner." What does that mean? In a person with as fragile a sense of dignity as Annie Littlefield's, that may mean they had to sit through a sermon. We have too little information to judge about Annie, but let's do a thought-experiment. Assume that the Salvation Army in this case represented a middling average Christian charity, as regards motivation. So they were getting some ego-satisfaction in the sinful style of the great-souled man, but they were also really trying to help. They were aiming, in part, at the well-being of those who received their services. Let's say this was the situation the Littlefields fell into. If they felt put down by the soldiers' attitude, it's because they were picking up on the less virtuous part of their motivation, and missing or disregarding the real love that was in it. But in that case, they *might* have focused on the other aspect, and felt some real gratitude for what they were receiving.

Now let's try to imagine Esther Summerson in the same place as the Littlefields: she's desperately hungry, and the same Salvation Army corps takes her in and feeds her, and puts some requirement on her, of the kind that made Annie say, "They made us crawl for our dinner." Now I don't think Esther will react the same way. The reason is that she is disposed to see the loving motive in her benefactors, and to discount or ignore the less noble one. Gratitude, as a virtue, has a kind of generosity built into it, a generosity in attributing motives. Comparing notes with Annie, she might say, "I too noticed that predatory gleam in the eyes of some, but did you see how pleased they looked at the eagerness of the children?" or "Yes, the sermon was pretty poor, and a bit manipulative; but it was well meant."

A difference between Annie and Esther that makes a big difference in their ability to feel gratitude is their sense of dignity. Esther's is serene and secure; Annie's is fragile and defensive. Esther's generous disposition to see the best in givers' motives and to overlook their foibles is possible because she does not feel that she needs constantly to be defending or re-establishing her dignity.

A COUPLE OF OTHER WAYS TO BE UNGRATEFUL

We have looked at permutations of the general resistance to dependency. Let us consider briefly a couple of other ways to be ungrateful, before we apply our insights to the central kind of Christian gratitude.

Let's say I have a friend I love dearly. I am generally happy to receive graces from her. But on one occasion she showers me with a matching set of hungry, energetic, abundantly salivating Labrador retriever puppies. I think with affection about what she has done, that is, the attitude of love she expresses in this awkward gift. But I'm afraid I am not grateful for the gift.

Another possibility is this. I don't suffer from any of the pathologies represented by Savage, the great-souled man, or Annie Littlefield. A benefactor gives me a gift that I value. But I cannot be grateful because I do not want to receive this gift from this particular benefactor. Imagine that a wealthy relative who all her life has sought to remake me in her own patrician image leaves me a large sum of money. I perceive the gift as one last posthumous effort in a thirty-year series of efforts to deliver me against my will from the company of beloved philistines. She has goodwill towards me, in her own way, but her attitude creates an obstacle to my gratitude, because of what I know the gift means to her. A similar situation may arise if someone who is in love with you gives you a gift, but you are not in love with her.

So the conditions for gratitude are the following: The situation is that of two parties and a good. One of the parties is the beneficiary, one is the benefactor; and the good is a gift from the one to the other. Gratitude is the beneficiary's concern-based construal of the situation in these terms. The concerns involved are the desire for the gift and a willingness to receive it from the benefactor. Gratitude is correct, as a construal, only if what is given really is a good, and the attitude of the giver really is benevolent toward the recipient. The transaction creates a debt to the giver on the part of the recipient, and thus a situation of the recipient's dependency, which the recipient acknowledges in his construal of the situation (his sense of being "bowed down"). It is not a debt of justice, since the gift is free, and the debt must therefore not be paid *off;* but it is a debt — a debt of gratitude — that binds the recipient spiritually to the giver, and the recipient "pays" the debt by acknowledging it, by feeling and expressing gratitude.

In this chapter I have emphasized the character-conditions that must be met for a recipient to have the virtuous attitude — the one characteristic of gratitude — about the indebtedness to his benefactor. We have seen that quite a lot can go wrong with this aspect of the construal, and that much of it has to do with the recipient's construal of himself. In particular, human beings are rather strongly prone to take offense at gifts and givers because these seem to them to threaten their "dignity" — their autonomy and their self-importance. If we were to put, in a word, the attitude or character trait whose lack prevents gratitude in Richard Savage, the great-souled man, and Annie Littlefield, that word would be 'humility.'

Let's now apply what we have learned to Christian gratitude.

THANKS BE TO GOD

The Christian understanding of the universe and our place in it is a set of ideas and beliefs that are especially hospitable to gratitude. We owe our life and sustenance to God, who out of his love gives us these gifts. The central event of biblical history is another pure gift: God's redemption of humanity from sin and death, apart from any assistance on our part. God created us to depend on one another, to have a long, dependent infancy and, in many cases, an old age in which we could not live without the support of our younger family members and community. Furthermore, the church is a community in which each depends, for his or her ability to function, on the contributions of the other members. Compare this view of things with one in which our life is not a gift, but a chemical and biological accident; or a view in which strict justice governs all affairs and righteousness: you get what you pay for and you earn what you get; or a view in which the essence of life is a competitive struggle for survival and gain at the expense of others.

Christian gratitude is thankfulness to God for our creation, preservation, and all the blessings of this life; but above all for God's inestimable love in the redemption of the world by our Lord Jesus Christ. The obstacles to Christian gratitude are human resistances to acknowledge our dependence on God, and a failure to appreciate the gifts he gives us and the beauty of a relationship with him.

Certain strains of Romanticism, the philosophy of Friedrich Nietzsche in the nineteenth century, and the Existentialism of Jean-Paul Sartre in the mid-twentieth century, are movements that reflect human resistance to depending on God, movements that still influence the consciousness of many. So important is human self-creation, according to such philosophies, that God must be banished from human life or transformed into something compatible with our radical independence. Nietzsche might call Esther Summerson's experience of being "bowed down" before the goodness of God "slavish," and Sartre might call it "inauthentic" — in any case, unworthy of the best human beings. But these philosophies are just particularly sophisticated expressions of a basic human desire to be the most important thing in the universe, a resistance to acknowledging that we are subordinate creatures beholden to God for everything we have and are.

A moral permutation of this infection is self-righteousness, the insistence that we are basically okay, morally, able to stand on our own merits, not fundamentally in need of forgiveness or the substitutionary atonement of a really righteous one. To maintain this fiction we are willing to pose, to play-act, to deceive ourselves and others — to defend against the humiliation of being forgiven for the life in which we take so much pride.

A more suburbanite version of this resistance to Christian thanksgiving is the pattern of appreciating our prosperity, health, talents, and successes without being grateful to *God* for them. Perhaps we call them our "blessings," but God remains to us a vague principle of their origin, rather than a Giver clear and present to our awareness. Or if God does seem to the individual a vivid personal presence, he is a sort of Super-Size Sugar-Daddy whose function in life is to provide the goodies in sufficient abundance. This kind of person may be a churchgoer, but the telltale mark of ingratitude is that when the "blessings" are reversed, when the hard times come, she tends to get angry at God and feel he has let her down. We might call this the Savage syndrome, since the individual treats God as a convenient source of blessings, rather than as God. It is as though God owes her the blessings. If God fails to serve his essential purpose, he is guilty of the injustice of not doing his job.

In Chapters 3–5 I outlined a process of personal development that would counteract the exaggerated sense of self-sufficiency native to the human breast, the tendency that is also enhanced by Romanticism and Existentialism. The process I outlined is essentially one of becoming honest with ourselves about our vulnerability to loss, harm, and death, and to being forgotten in the world-process, so as to develop a vivid and immediate awareness of this vulnerability. The development is itself a process of being bowed down. The believer in whom this sense prospers grows at the same time a willing awareness of dependency on God, and thus becomes, potentially, a more grateful person.

Then in Chapter 6 I tried to show how someone who combines this honesty with a serious effort to acquire a virtue like humility runs smack into his own unrighteousness and its recalcitrance to being reformed from within his own endeavors. If such a person is a Christian, he knows about the atonement: God's offer of righteousness in Jesus Christ quite apart from what any sinner has accomplished or earned. Again, this is an experience of being bowed down, but now also at the same time of being lifted up by God. And so it is a basis for gratitude to God for what he has done for us in Jesus Christ, that gift for which, "above all," we give thanks in the prayer of General Thanksgiving.

A person who has developed in the foregoing ways will be much less likely to idolize her possessions and successes. She will have come to value God for a goodness that is far from exhausted in his ability to provide the blessings of this life. That is, she will have come closer to loving God for his goodness, for his own intrinsic nature as righteous and as conferring righteousness on sinners in Jesus Christ. She will not have lost her ability to appreciate such goods as health and prosperity, talent and successes in her endeavors. But she will also be able to see God's goodness in the midst of sickness and failure, in loss of ability and in the absurdities of misfortune and waste. And this will be because she thanks God, above all, for his inestimable love in the redemption of the world by our Lord Jesus Christ.

Let me close this chapter with two further observations. The first is that Christian gratitude, like other emotions, is a construal, a way of "seeing the world," a way in which things "strike" the subject. In Christian gratitude, things tend to strike you as gifts of God, as wonderful, undeserved blessings from his benevolent hand. Given this perceptual character of gratitude, one obvious way to develop it is to *practice* seeing things this way. How does one practice seeing? By *looking.* Looking is active seeing, and as we succeed in seeing what we are looking for, we train our seeing into conformity with our looking. The developing Christian, for example, looks for blessings in adversity. When troubles come into his life, he may at first see nothing but troubles, and these overwhelm his gratitude. But then he practices looking with grateful eyes. He looks for ways that adversities may actually draw him closer to God; he tries to see in them occasions for a growing sensitivity to the things of the gospel. He learns to see the adversities of life in the larger perspective of God's good ways. What look like disasters to the immature, he learns to see as among the "normal" difficulties of life on earth, just the usual run of human troubles, not at all incompatible with God's goodness and the fact that life abounds in good gifts. Thus the "seeing" Christian weans himself from the perfectionism of insisting that life be a flawless weave of worldly blessings.

My last point concerns the special Christian sense of dignity. A sense of dignity that requires self-sufficiency, self-generated merit, and perhaps even superiority to most other human beings in one's environment, can be a major obstacle to gratitude. Something like this is perhaps the default conception of dignity among sinful human beings, the kind that people insist on in "ideal" conditions if they have not undergone cultivation in a more gratitude-friendly sense of dignity. By contrast, the sense of dignity that goes with gratitude, the kind cultivated in Christian spirituality, is *dignity as a creature and as a fellow-creature.* It is the sense of one's own importance that derives from and is qualified by thinking of oneself as *fundamentally* a recipient of grace — not just now and then, in the special circumstances that may call for the status of recipient, but from the foundations of one's life, in one's very nature as created by a gracious God. When this sense of being a creature has become implicit in one's bones, then one acts with confidence, with self-respect, both as one gives and as one receives. To someone unacquainted with this spiritual sense of self, it may seem to be a form of slavish humiliation, but to its inhabitant it is just a sense of being human. This is the feeling of dignity that I think we see in Esther Summerson.

CHAPTER TEN

Hope

HOPE AND RESIGNATION

Hope is a construal of one's future as holding good prospects. Like other emotions, hope is not possible unless an appropriate concern is in place; the object of hope is not just something good, but something the subject *perceives* as good, something that seems good *to the subject,* and thus it is always something the individual wants, whether the object be a trivial hope like sunshine for tomorrow's picnic, an important but finite one like the recovery of a loved one from an illness, or the psychologically ultimate one of sharing the glory of God. In hoping, a person delights in the future, welcomes it with enthusiasm, tastes it with the pleasure of anticipation, because he sees excellent prospects of having what he wants.

But we don't always construe as promising the prospect of what we want. Sometimes we construe the probability of fulfillment as poor, while still wanting the outcome very much. If I am "absolutely set on" the picnic and the very reliable weatherwoman announces a 100 percent chance of dark skies and deluge tomorrow, I will be in *despair.* It seems a bit comical to speak of despair here, because mature people don't set themselves absolutely on things like picnics. Yet, if the picnic is in fact everything to me, and I see the prospect of it to be hopeless, then "despair" is the right word. If I am visited by a fit of maturity, I can cure myself of this despair by *resignation.* What is resignation? It is a downward adjustment of the concern. Seeing that the prospect of a sunny picnic tomorrow is almost nil, I adjust my desire for the picnic: sure, I would still love to have the picnic, but I can live without it; I'll plan something else. So now I'm no longer in despair. Resignation, then, is a sort of halfway house between hope and despair. If I completely cease to care about the thing I once hoped for, I neither hope for it nor am resigned with respect to it. If I continue to want it with my whole heart but see my prospects as nil, then I am in despair. To be resigned with respect to something in the future, I must continue to care about it, but in a mitigated way that makes me able to "live with" the poor prospect.

Some of our desires with regard to the future are easier to adjust downward than others. The picnic is an easy case for most of us, but the recovery of our loved one from an illness is difficult. However, here too resignation can rescue us from despair. My loved one may never be the same again; maybe she will die. After a while I learn to live with this possible future. Resignation doesn't yield the delicious happiness of hope, but I am not quite in despair. But according to Christian psychology there is one object for which it is never healthy to mitigate our desire, namely that of sharing the glory of God, the prospect of the heavenly kingdom, of the eternal realm of perfect righteousness and peace. We can resign small hopes without damaging ourselves spiritually: I can resign the desire of my youth to be one of the greatest philosophers of my age without spoiling anything really noble in myself. I adjust the desire downward to fit the prospects as I have come to see them. But to give up the yearning for the eternal order of perfect righteousness is a kind of spiritual suicide. And since the glory of God ultimately encloses the well-being of our loved one, this other prospect comes back too, in an eschatological way. Our resignation to her death or "permanent" disability is not absolute, but we hope for her too that she will share the glory of God in perfect health.

Resignation is a way of tolerating the future, hope a way of welcoming it. Resignation is a healthy option in the case of most of the things we hope for, but it will not be healthy if applied to the most fundamental of our concerns, the one that, according to Christian psychology, is essential to our nature as persons. To dull or downgrade the concern for the eternal kingdom, for a perfect relationship with God and neighbor, is to compromise one's status as a person, to live a damaged life; it is a sort of spiritual crippling. Bertrand Russell's most famous essay, and one of the most widely read manifestos of naturalist humanism of the twentieth century, concludes with the words,

Brief and powerless is Man's life; on him and all his race the slow, sure doom falls pitiless and dark. Blind to good and evil, reckless of destruction, omnipotent matter rolls on its relentless way; for Man, condemned to-day to lose his dearest, to-morrow himself to pass through the gate of darkness, it remains only to cherish, ere yet the blow falls, the lofty thoughts that ennoble his little day; disdaining the coward terrors of the slave of Fate, to worship at the shrine that his own hands have built; undismayed by the empire of chance, to preserve a mind free from the wanton tyranny that rules his outward life; proudly defiant of the irresistible forces that tolerate, for a moment, his knowledge and his condemnation, to sustain alone, a weary but unyielding Atlas, the world that his own ideals have fashioned despite the trampling march of unconscious power. ("A Free Man's Worship," p. 59)

Naturalism is the view that nature with all its processes is all there is, that there is nothing beyond it, nothing eternal, and that moral and spiritual values are inventions of the human mind, doomed to perish like everything else. Russell tries hard to keep his chin up in this essay, despite presenting very clearly the spiritual predicament of the naturalist with regard to the future, and despite calling this pessimism "the firm foundation of unyielding despair" (p. 51). He proposes that in this meaningless, crushing physical universe where our bodies are trapped and doomed, we can satisfy our yearning for something eternal by worshiping the products of our own minds — our art, science, and philosophy, and above all, the art of tragedy. But the brave, forlorn tone of the essay suggests that Russell himself feels that our deepest longing is compromised in what he proposes. The "happiness" he envisions really is resignation.

The apostle says, "May the God of hope fill you with all joy and peace as you trust in him, so that you may overflow with hope by the power of the Holy Spirit" (Romans 15:13). If Paul had been a naturalist, he might have said, "May the god of resignation fill you with tolerance for your destiny," or "May the benign Void enable you to quell your yearnings for eternity," or "May the god of cosmic process make you magnanimous enough to accept your absorption into his consequential nature." But he would not have talked about joy and peace and hope. It is very difficult, if not impossible, both to love life as something wonderful, as Russell wants to do, and at the same time face with utter clarity the cruel pointlessness of the universe as he depicts it. The naturalist seems to buy peace, if one wants to call it that, at the cost of either vitality or mental clarity. Resignation either dulls the enthusiasm for life, or remains incomplete and thus incompatible with the naturalist's dismal picture of our future. Russell's essay is an unstable expression of aspiration and despair, but it is, in its own way, an impressive piece of honest thought and a valiant effort to find a way to cultivate honest despair and noble aspiration in the selfsame human breast.

As our earlier discussions have suggested, the usual substitute for hope (even among us churchgoers) is not a courageous and lucid resignation in the face of oblivion and unrighteousness, but a cowardly self-darkening about ourselves and a dulling of concern. To the unnerving deliverances of our surveying imagination we respond by resigning our hearts in finite hopes. We send our eternal selves out prospecting on earth, where moth and rust and time consume and bad fortune breaks in and steals our hopes away. And as long as reality does not crash in to destroy the houses of cards in which we dwell, we find here just enough satisfaction of our need for hope to keep us from feeling despair — and also from enjoying faith.

Or we make a compromise like the following: "I shall give myself without reservation to the projects and prospects of this earthly life, but just in case something goes wrong, I'll make my peace with Jesus. Religion is, after all, supposed to be a comfort in times of trouble, and let's be realistic: troubles don't always happen to the other guy. I may croak before my projects are all complete, and it would be a pity if I had nothing to fall back on." As a passion for the kingdom of God, this attitude leaves something to be desired. For the mature Christian the kingdom hoped for is the focusing goal of life, to which everything else is subsidiary. In the attitude I have just described the kingdom is not the pearl of great price, the crown of life, the one thing needful, but a sort of consolation prize for those who do poorly in the race. The person I have described does not have the joy and peace of Christian hope; rather, he combines a comically mild form of resignation with a false conception of the kingdom.

Three Advantages of the Christian Hope

What devastates the eternal self is not that it has earthly hopes, but that it ascribes to them a significance they can't bear. Earthly hopes will not let a person down if she does not overinvest in them. But such is human passion that if it lacks a relationship with God it has a strong (if not irresistible) tendency to invest so much of itself in its earthly projects that their unreliability and fundamental unsatisfactoriness become the ground of despair. It becomes clear even to many who believe in nothing eternal — neither God nor his kingdom — that "salvation" is to be found in some kind of detachment from the objects of such hopes. Thus the attempt at peace that the lucid secularist makes through resignation.

But the resignation of the nonbeliever is made problematic by his having no satisfactory future to put in place of the obviously unsatisfactory future of the earth. He needs hope, with its joy, but has to settle for resignation, with its sullen tranquility. This lack of happiness in resignation makes it difficult, if not impossible, for the resignation of these earthly hopes to be very successful. The individual resigns himself to his death, but still finds a secret (desperate) joy in the future of his children or in the thought that his reputation will live on after his death. So his peace is fragile. The Christian, by contrast, has a hope that may be able to fill her with joy and thus to fill the gap that is left when she sees through earthly hopes. Let us not underestimate, however, the difficulty the Christian too will have in detaching herself from earthly hopes. Even if she is very serious, she will find that unhealthy attachments to finite prospects sully her happiness until the end of life, not to mention the difficulties that may beset her believing in her eternal hope. But assuming that she has the courage to believe with some steadiness, she who is resigning only her finite hopes would seem to have a better prospect of success that he whose finite hopes are the only ones he has.

So the Christian who would hope in God must draw back from her investments in finite hopes — because these are bound to let her down, but even more because she finds they are in competition with her hope of sharing the glory of God. She, like sinners generally, is embedded in this passing world, so deeply committed to it that its transitoriness is her despair. But as a Christian she knows that this despair is a rejection of her relationship with God. To become free from it she must invest the ultimate prospects of her life in God alone; and that means a serious alteration of her attachment to her earthly hopes.

So far we have seen two advantages of the Christian over the lucid secularist. First, since she is in a position to have real hope transcending all her finite hopes, she is capable of an honest joy in life. Second, her hope gives her a better prospect of detaching herself from her finite hopes. A third advantage is that the Christian is able to be less wary of her finite hopes than the lucid secularist. In gratitude she receives from the hand of the God of hope the happy prospects that come to her in this earthly life. This means she can rejoice in these exactly as befits limited hopes. Of course she cares whether they are fulfilled, and may care very deeply; but if they are not fulfilled, her eternal hope gives her a healthy perspective on her disappointments, and sustains her in joy and peace. The Christian (I am speaking of the ideal) neither over- nor underestimates the earthly prospects. Not only does the hope of glory enable her honestly to resign all earthly prospects; it also empowers her to take these prospects up again and appreciate them for what they are. Reconciled to their ultimate unsatisfactoriness, and protected against despair over them, she can rejoice and grieve, as is fitting, in the hopes and disappointments encompassed by her short earthly years. As she hopes, she is in a state of health with respect to earthly things. Unlike the tepid pew-sitter, she sees them as they are; unlike the lucid secularist, the resignation by which she sees them as they are does not verge constantly on despair.

EMOTIONS, SENSATIONS, AND MOODS

Now I want to look at our subject from another angle and to think with you about the relations between hope as an emotion and two things that are closely tied to it, namely, the mood of hoping and hopefulness as a character trait.

You have perhaps felt that my claim that emotions are construals is not true to emotions as we feel them. After all, are not emotions in some sense to be *contrasted* with thoughts? What about the old distinction between the mind and the heart, between the "cognitive" and the "emotive"? Have I not committed the philosopher's arrogant mistake of subsuming the heart under the mind, thus really denying the heart altogether? In making emotions ways of "seeing," have I not made them just a species of thought?

I admit to making emotions a species of thought, in some broad sense of that word, but not to denying the heart. As you will remember, emotions are not just any kind of construal; they are *concern-based* construals. But this answer may not quite satisfy you, for even concern-based construals are capable of being declared right or wrong by the kind of standards to which we subject judgments. If I judge that the people in the car behind me are following me with some sinister intent, I may be right or I may be wrong, and the basis on which I judge may be rational or irrational. But that judgment may also be the basis of the construal that constitutes anger or fear or indignation, and if so, then the emotion itself is either right or wrong, either rational or irrational. But, you will say, emotions are not either right or wrong, either rational or irrational; they are not subject to this kind of evaluation. So my view that emotions are construals must be wrong.

People who think that emotions are not subject to rational adjudication are usually confusing them with either sensations or moods. If you have a bodily sensation, such as an itch on your back or a fluttery feeling in your diaphragm, of course it makes no sense to ask whether your itch or flutter are true or false, or based on good evidence or valid reasoning. An emotion cannot be a bodily sensation precisely because it can, like an opinion, be justified or unjustified. I can criticize your anger or your hope for being unjustified. I can say, "You have no reason to be angry; she was trying to help you," or "Your hope is just based on wishful thinking and you ought to give it up." But if I criticize your itch or flutter by saying that you don't have good reasons for them, you will not know what to make of me. Hope, anger, envy, embarrassment, grief, and gratitude can be rational or irrational, and if so, it follows that they can't be bodily sensations. Some emotions are *associated with* typical bodily states, such as dryness in the mouth, blushing, erection of the hair, a burning sensation in the abdominal or chest region, and trembling of the extremities. But these cannot be more than accompaniments of emotion, for the reason given above.

Emotions also get confused with moods. This is a less egregious confusion, because of the closer connection between emotions and moods. Moods, like sensations, are not subject to rational adjudication. Of course, they may be pleasant or unpleasant, and so may be good or bad, and a person may be irrational if he knowingly does something (like take some drug) that will put him in an inappropriate mood. But the mood itself cannot be correct or incorrect or based on good or bad reasoning. Moods are such states as being elated or cheerful, depressed or blue, and grumpy or irritable. If I ask, "Why do you have that itch?" you will answer not with a reason but a cause: "Because I wash my clothes in hard water." Similarly if we ask, "Why is Daddy grumpy?" we are not asking for his reasons (reasonable or unreasonable), but for the causes of his state: "He hasn't had his dinner yet." Just as itches have various causes, so we are put in moods by various causes. Lack of sleep over a period of time can cause depression; caffeine causes irritability in some people and mild elation in others; deeply repressed factors in a person's psychiatric history influence people's moods and create susceptibilities to them; different kinds of music put people in tranquil, excited, or aggressive moods; cacophonous noises — one baby screaming, another banging on pots and pans, and someone else roaring away on a vacuum sweeper — make some people irritable; jogging long distances makes some people feel "high"; and of course narcotic drugs are notorious mood changers.

Another important cause of moods is emotions. If a person wins the lottery, she will very likely not only feel the emotions of joy and hope in seeing her financial situation changed for the better; very likely the cheerfulness of this emotion will spill over into other contexts. For a few hours, or days, or even weeks, she may have a brighter outlook on everything; her mind may be pervaded by a generalized optimism. Similarly, grief at the death of a loved one can color one's entire outlook on life for a period; the grief, which is clearly an emotion, begets a generalized depression, which is not an emotion but a mood. Thus we can see an important source of our temptation to think that moods are emotions. Sometimes when we ask, "Why is Daddy so grumpy?" we refer to an emotion and say, "Because he lost money on the farm sale." We do not mean that Daddy's reason for being grumpy is that he lost money on the farm sale — at least not if his grumpiness is a mood. What we must mean is that Daddy's financial disappointment (an emotion) has caused him to sink into this grumpy state (a mood). His financial setback, by contrast, is a reason for his disappointment. Moods are not emotions, but since they are sometimes caused by emotions, we are inclined to think they are. And when we think of emotions as moods, it is natural to make the mistake of thinking that they are irrational.

MOODS, FEELINGS, AND VIRTUES

The fact that moods are sometimes caused by emotions is not the only connection between the two. Moods also predispose emotions. I am more likely to dwell on the happy aspects of my future (and thus to experience hope) if I am in an even, optimistic, cheerful mood than if I am depressed. If I am in a severe depression I may not be able to "hear" the gospel at all. I hear it with my ears all right, but do not succeed in construing my future in its terms. But being in an optimistic mood is not the same as hoping; hope is a construal of the future in some terms, and Christian hope is the construal of our future in terms of God's promises of eternal life and righteousness.

One of the main purposes of the ornamental aspects of our worship services is to produce moods that conduce to worshipful states of mind (joy, peace, contrition, hope, gratitude). The high-vaulted ceiling of the building may evoke a mood of exaltation, the colors and quiet of the sanctuary a peaceful mood, the music a variety of moods: melancholia to go with contrition; cheer to go with joy, gratitude, love, and hope; triumph to go with hope. These features of the service are not just aesthetically fitting, but encourage moods in us that foster the Christian emotions. So these aesthetic or ornamental features of the service serve partially as aids to our having the Christian emotions in the midst of the worship service.

However, dangers attend this strategy. First, in highly liturgical services as well as some of the more colorfully "emotional" services such as that of the Baptist church I visited in Chapter 1, the mood setting is so powerful that the worshipers may be inclined to mistake the moods they experience in church for Christian emotions, or to mistake the passing emotional states precipitated by the "aesthetic" aspects of the service for genuine expressions of the Christian emotion-virtues. This is especially true where the worshipers are encouraged to seek religious "experiences." If the minister does a lot of talking about hope and joy in the Lord, and the importance of having these, and at the same time is engineering the service to produce moods of exaltation and triumph, it will not be surprising if the congregation tends to take such moods and feelings for Christian experience. There is nothing peculiarly Christian about moods of exaltation and triumph, or passing feelings of one sort or another; these kinds of change happen just about every time one goes to a movie. The danger in aesthetically rich noncognitive Sunday experiences is that people will be partially immunized against real Christianity by being made complacent about their spirituality. Church leaders do this sort of thing to their congregations quite innocently. But once they learn to distinguish the Christian emotions from the moods and passing feelings a worship service can induce, it could become an important minor part of preaching and Christian education to clarify for their people this danger of sentimentalizing Christian faith.

Let us say an individual goes to church, hears the word of the gospel, and with gladsome mind construes his eternal future in terms of it. Thus he experiences Christian hope. But he also needs to be warned, directly or indirectly, that the educative purpose of the worship service is not just that he should experience hope *in the service,* but that by the experience of hope that he has there, he should be on his way to becoming a hopeful *person.* The hope he experiences in the service should become a deeply etched hopefulness, a character trait that he carries into the most diverse and unconducive situations of his life, situations where the environment, unlike the church, does not at all predispose him to hope, but where he must carry his hopefulness, environmentally unsupported, in his own heart. Hopefulness becomes a toughness, an independence from his environment, a way in which he transcends his immediate situation.

John Calvin gives eloquent expression to the incongruity between the Christian's hope and the Christian's environment:

> To us is given the promise of eternal life — but to us, the dead. A blessed resurrection is proclaimed to us — meantime we are surrounded by decay. We are called righteous — and yet sin lives in us. We hear of ineffable blessedness — but meantime we are here oppressed by infinite misery. We are promised abundance of all good things — yet we are rich only in hunger and thirst. What would become of us if we did not take our stand on hope, and if our heart did not hasten beyond this world through the midst of the darkness upon the path illumined by the word and Spirit of God! (quoted in Jürgen Moltmann, *Theology of Hope,* pp. 18-19)

Thus even in the most intimate confrontation with sin and death, the Christian in whom hope has become a character trait can experience joy and equilibrium. In a letter C. S. Lewis wrote two months before he died, this joyful equilibrium comes out clearly:

> What a pleasant change to get a letter that does not say the conventional things! I was unexpectedly revived from a long coma, and perhaps the almost continuous prayers of my friends did it — but it [would] have been a luxuriously easy passage, and one almost regrets [having] the door shut in one's face. Ought one to honor Lazarus rather than Stephen as a proto-martyr? To be brought back and have all one's dying to do again was rather hard. When you die, and if "prison visiting" is allowed, come down and look me up in Purgatory. It is all rather fun — solemn fun — isn't it? (Quoted in R. T. Herbert, *Paradox and Identity in Theology,* p. 174)

Being able to carry one's hope into situations which to the worldling would appear most contrary to hope; to experience the hope of life in the midst of death and the hope of righteousness amidst the moral degradation of the present world — this seems to be what the apostle Paul has in mind when he connects Christian hope with "endurance" and "character" (Romans 5) and with "steadfastness" (Colossians 1; Romans 15).

HOPE AND OPTIMISM

I turn now to the question of what we can do to nurture hopefulness in ourselves. How can one grow in integral hopefulness? How can one become, not just a liturgical hoper, but a "secularized" one in whom hope has become a tough transcendence for all situations? Why is our hope so weak? Why does the prospect of an eternal happiness seem so dim compared with the prospects of finite happiness? Why does it occur to us, again and again in the Christian life, that this hope of glory is just a fiction, an empty dream?

Perhaps we are inclined to think it's because the hope of sharing the glory of God is just intrinsically improbable. After all, nothing we can observe in nature would tend to support it; the whole "style" of nature seems to be that of finitude and death. Beside the achievements of knowledge in the natural sciences, this hope seems so unsupported. Isn't it just a fantasy woven by the human mind? Didn't Tolstoy describe our life aptly: "In infinite time, in infinite space is formed a bubble-organism, and that bubble lasts a while and bursts; and that bubble is Me."

We have the hints: the resurrection of Jesus (without which it is very difficult to see how the Christian church got going); the testimony, which many deep people have found compelling, of the Holy Spirit; the congruency that the promise of the kingdom has with the deepest yearnings of some of the most intelligent human spirits. But alternative explanations can be offered of all these things; all can be construed in purely naturalistic terms. So in the last analysis the hope of glory is what the church has (almost) always said it is, a matter of venturesome faith. Objectively we are given, at most, ambiguous clues. The certainty of hope, if such certainty exists, must come from the kind of life we live, the kind of persons we are, the quality of our daily interaction with God and our fellow human beings. We must be people who trust in God and trust in those impulses that put us in touch with him; we must nurture not the naturalistic spirit in us, but the one that whispers to us (much of the time) that our life is more than bubble-organisms in space-time.

It is perhaps not quite true that hope springs eternal in the human breast, but even if we take this saying as a poetic exaggeration, it expresses a truth about human nature. A pre-reflective optimism built into us, and deeply confirmed by a happy childhood, gives us resiliency in the midst of suffering and a tendency to hope in the face of dismal prospects. It is not built on any actual calculation of prospects or even the most cursory reckoning with actual possibilities. This animal hopefulness is present, mixed with pessimism and more or less realistic assessments of the future, in all of us. But it is evident in its purer forms in children and adolescents, and very occasionally in an unreflective or sheltered adult. It is a disposition to look for the happy elements of the future, and not to dwell on the dark side. Like a mood of cheerfulness, it is a predisposition to construe the future in happy terms. But insofar as this disposition finds its concrete hopes within the present mortal life, there is always a dissonance between the pre-reflective optimism and the concrete hopes in which it issues, a dissonance brought out by reflecting on the passing nature of this life. The dissonance is that the hopes in which the optimism becomes an emotion are always equally grounds for pessimism. The optimism that springs almost eternal is one that ill fits earthly hopes, but nicely fits an eternal one. An aim of Christian education is that this pre-reflective, moodlike animal hopefulness be transformed and fulfilled in the solid emotion-virtue of an eternal hope.

So the hope of sharing the glory of God is an enduring hope, tailored to our eternal nature, a hope that will not let us down. But our hoping in its terms is very far from solid and enduring. The object of our hope is eternal, but our hope itself is, in many of us, the very opposite, an up-and-down thing, shifting with our circumstances and our moods, with the company we keep and the books we happen to be reading. After feeling it in church, it sometimes dissolves out in the world. Magnificent resolutions to have our hope in God alone are followed in a few minutes by the old patterns of trusting in our schemes and the probabilities of finite prospects, and doing our best to conceal from ourselves the blatant deception in which we are indulging.

HOPE AND SUFFERING

This is where our sufferings can come in. Paul says that suffering produces endurance, and endurance character, and character a hope that does not disappoint us. Suffering can stabilize the hope of glory in us, giving it that toughness that makes it a secular, non-churchy thing, that delivers it from dependence on organ music and oratory, on pastoral "presence" and weather and comfortable pews and adequate heating and cooling and the last book read, and makes it a principle of our persons that we carry into unsupportive situations. What kind of sufferings can educate us in Christian hope? It is not so much the kind of suffering that is important, but what we do with it. Loneliness, betrayal by family or friends, the triumph of one's enemies, the impotence of disease or old age, the death of a loved one, a disappointment in business or love, hatred and opposition by other people — these all can help to teach us Christian hope, if only we take the right attitude toward them. How shall we construe such sufferings?

A suffering can become a viscerally moving symbol of the present world's unfitness to satisfy my deepest needs. It can become a reminder, more vivid than any mere word of truth, that the present passing world is not my final home — that I am a sojourner, a passer-through. And so sufferings can become a powerful aid in getting the right perspective on the prospects the world offers. The Christian does not despise those prospects, as one might who did not believe that God created this present world; but he learns from his sufferings not to put his deepest heart into those prospects, and to reserve it instead for what is promised in the gospel.

I can meditate for weeks or months on the futility of life apart from God's kingdom. But if my own life is progressing gloriously and veritably glowing with earthly hopes, if nothing in it makes a strong impression on me of that futility, then meditation may not have the power to detach me significantly from my earthly prospects. While I may know that such prospects don't deserve an ultimate trust, this "knowledge" remains mostly "intellectual." But a suffering, rightly construed, can bring that knowledge into my heart, fostering the hope of glory as an enduring trait of my character. And a Christian who sees how his sufferings are training him in a hope that does not disappoint learns to rejoice in them.

It takes vigilance to make these sufferings into teachers of hope. When a suffering comes on me, my first inclination is not to take it as an ally in my struggle to detach myself from earthly hopes, but instead to see it in one of two ways. First, I may see it as something to rid myself of as quickly as possible, so as to get back to my normal, happy, worldly state of mind. This is worldliness pure and simple. The Christian too will welcome relief from her sufferings (they are, after all, sufferings), but she is willing to dwell in them for a while, draw them into herself, recognize them as a normal part of earthly existence and not something to be surprised or enraged about. She lets them sink in and become part of her worldview; and afterwards, if they pass, she does not reject them as something alien to herself, but remembers thoughtfully that this too is the sort of thing that makes up our present existence.

The second worldly way is to wallow in sufferings. This is perhaps not so obviously worldliness, since I do take a certain joy in the sufferings, and do not dissociate myself from them as in the first way. But it is still worldliness, since the sufferings don't become a means of relating myself happily to God and his kingdom. Wallowing admits of several forms, the chief among which are dragging others into the muck, turning the muck into a ground of superiority, and getting the universe into one's debt. Some people turn their suffering to a morbid sort of rejoicing by groaning and complaining and palling social gaieties with gloomy dicta. They try to ensure that others will feel miserable along with them. Masochism becomes a cover for sadism. Still others derive from their sufferings a sense of superiority over the happy people in the world, as though suffering *per se* somehow qualified them as more deeply human than the uninitiated. Still others get a sense of ascendancy by thinking roughly along these lines: "I have been wronged by the universe. It clearly owes me something for the suffering I am going through, and I can at least rejoice in that. And if unjustly (O cruel injustice of Being itself!) it does not pay off with happiness hereafter — well, that's fine too, because it is thus all the more indebted, indeed perhaps eternally indebted, to me."

The Christian, by contrast, does not rejoice in her sufferings out of sadism or any sense of superiority, but because they bring her into closer communion with God. However, two kinds of sufferings seem incapable of this educational value. One is the sense of abandonment by God, and the other is intense physical pain.

People who are disposed to communion with God sometimes have periods in which God seems cruelly absent. The warmth of fellowship with him, the satisfactions of prayer, and the comfort and joy of faith have disappeared; the person experiences dull anxiety, depression, and a kind of guilty grief. This is not just the absence of faith. Many people lack faith, yet experience no suffering over it. It is the more intense feeling of abandonment. It seems odd that a person should take this suffering as indicating the necessity of hoping in God alone. Her suffering is her inability to hope in God, if we mean by "hope" to feel hopeful in him, to construe him as the ground of her ultimate prospects. Being not a worldly suffering, it cannot become a symbol of the inadequacy of the world; it is a spiritual suffering, and so if it is to be a symbol, it must be a symbol of ultimate disappointment: even God cannot be trusted.

This kind of suffering does not educate in the way that more ordinary sufferings can, and yet it too can have an educational effect. One of the distortions into which the believer is likely to fall if she becomes too athletic in the spiritual use of worldly sufferings is to think herself too much the author and controller of her faith and hope. But faith and hope, like every good and perfect gift, come down from above, and to be perfect they must also be so understood. St. Paul says that hope does not disappoint us, because God's love has been poured into our hearts through the Holy Spirit. And this pouring of God's love into the thirsty heart of the sufferer is a typical, if not very frequent, experience of Christians. A woman is praying in the darkness of abandonment, praying more out of a sense that she ought to be doing so than out of any sense of genuine encouragement. She has been in this state for weeks or months. Though she continues her religious exercises, it has occurred to her more than once that she has become an unbeliever. And then suddenly, out of the spiritual darkness, God's love floods in on her, and her joy and hope are renewed more powerfully and deliciously than she could ever have thought possible. It is as though God is saying, "*I* am your hope and your salvation; in me alone you will trust, and not alone for your salvation but even for the faith by which you grasp it."

The other kind of suffering about which we may have doubts is intense physical pain. Otherwise faithful people, for whom mental sufferings are spiritually usable, sometimes find that physical sufferings obliterate their consciousness of God and their concern for anything other than the pain. I find this to be my own case, but am not convinced I ought to be complacent about this spiritual state. More mature people are able to turn physical pain to spiritual advantage. Physical self-torture abounds in the history of ascetical spirituality, though the attitude toward pain is not always healthy in that context. A healthy attitude is evinced by a remarkable English woman, Edith Barfoot of Oxford, who turned relentless physical suffering into a "vocation" of service to God and man that made her one of the most joyful Christians of her time. Her own account, along with the witness of a number of her friends, has been edited and published by Sir Basil Blackwell as *The Witness of Edith Barfoot*.

WORSHIP SERVICES AGAIN

So far in this chapter we have found more grounds to be suspicious of worship services than we have to be hopeful about their effect on our spiritual development. The preoccupation with what happens in the service and the engineering of the service to affect people by the architecture, the music, the decoration of the sanctuary, and the voice, diction, and rhetorical powers of the preacher skew the emphasis away from character building and toward "experiences." I have tried to correct that emphasis a bit by talking about the connection between suffering and the steadfast or enduring character of the Christian emotion-virtues. These emotions begin to count spiritually only when they become ingrained as character traits, only when the individual becomes steadfastly disposed to see the world in their terms. But we have also seen that hope, as conceived in Christianity as well as in ordinary life, is more than a mood and more than a pre-reflective optimism. It is a construal, a way of "taking" or "seeing" the future. As such it is a way of focusing attention, of dwelling on the future, a way, we might even say, of experiencing the future. And as such it has to be something that happens at this or that particular moment of the day when our mind turns to our eternal future. So it is fitting to have a regular context in which to dwell on the mercies of God and turn our attention to the future he has prepared for us.

The idea of an *act* of gratitude is quite natural. Christians and non-Christians alike daily perform acts of gratitude whenever they say thank you to one another, write thank you notes, and return favors. Such acts can of course be perfunctory or insincere, but equally they may be occasions for focusing grateful attention on the giver, the gift, or oneself as beneficiary. For the Christian, prayers of thanksgiving, as well as acts of neighbor-love, are not just expressions of thanksgiving to God but are also exercises of it, in both senses of the word: they are the *performance* of construing things gratefully and the *discipline* of learning to do so with greater regularity, naturalness, and profundity.

The idea of an analogous act of hope seems less natural. In general human life, no act or family of acts seems to qualify as acts of hope. But Christians have such an act in the service of Holy Communion. Rightly used, the Eucharist becomes at the same time an act of remembrance and an act of anticipation: remembrance of the suffering of Jesus through which we have been declared fit to enter into God's presence and start our long trek of sanctification in his fellowship; and anticipation of the perfection in which that process will one day issue. The Eucharist is a stated time for dwelling on the future that God has promised us in Christ. And so it is fully as much an exercise of hope as prayers of thanksgiving are an exercise of gratitude.

The Christian's life is punctuated and buoyed up by the acts of hope that are his celebrations of the Lord's Supper; over a lifetime, rightly used, such services play their part in etching hope into his consciousness. But they will be able to play that part only if he also dwells on his hope in the difficult circumstances of the daily struggle, only if his hope has been secularized and toughened by reflection on the hopelessness of all those earthly hopes that beckon so alluringly to his heart.

CHAPTER ELEVEN

Peace

PEACE OF MIND?

A major attraction of religions, philosophies of life, and psychotherapies is the hope of mental tranquility, of relief from anxieties, fears and griefs, anger, guilt, and a sense of inadequacy. Such "negative" emotions are not only distressing; they often diminish our work, our relations with our fellows, and even our bodily well-being. From the ancient psychotherapies of Epicureanism, Stoicism, and Skepticism to our contemporary anti-anxiety and anti-depressant drugs, systematic desensitization, anger- and grief-counseling, and all the rest, a driving question has been, "Whence comes my peace?" The question may be almost generically human, but the answers to it offered by the various religions, therapies, and philosophies of life differ markedly, and the traits they engender in their adherents, when successful, are also diverse. This chapter will sketch the distinctive contours of Christian peace as a state of mind. I will compare it with just two of its many rivals in the history of philosophy, religion, and therapy.

During his ministry, Jesus was forever meeting distraught, troubled, anxious, worried, fearful, disturbed people. The encounter with him seems sometimes to have brought a reduction in this "upset," a sense of equilibrium and comfort. Often the peace followed on some physical improvement, but sometimes it was wrought simply by Jesus' acceptance: "Your faith has saved you; go in peace" (Luke 7:50). He taught calm: "So do not worry, saying, 'What shall we eat?' or 'What shall we drink?' or 'What shall we wear?' For the pagans run after all these things, and your heavenly Father knows that you need them. But seek first his kingdom and his righteousness, and all these things will be given to you as well" (Matthew 6:31-

33). "Take my yoke upon you, and learn from me; for I am gentle and humble in heart, and you will find rest for your souls" (Matthew 11:29). Before he went to the cross, Jesus said to his disciples, "Do not let your hearts be troubled. Trust in God; trust also in me" (John 14:1), and "Peace I leave with you; my peace I give you. I do not give to you as the world gives. Do not let your hearts be troubled and do not be afraid" (John. 14:27). In the opening to his second letter to the Corinthians, the apostle Paul writes, "Praise be to the God and Father of our Lord Jesus Christ, the Father of compassion and the God of all comfort, who comforts us in all our troubles, so that we can comfort those in any trouble with the comfort we ourselves have received from God. For just as the sufferings of Christ flow over into our lives, so also through Christ our comfort overflows. If we are distressed, it is for your comfort and salvation; if we are comforted, it is for your comfort, which produces in you patient endurance of the same sufferings we suffer. And our hope for you is firm, because we know that just as you share in our sufferings, so also you share in our comfort" (II Corinthians 1:3-7).

'Tranquility' or 'contentment' or 'calm' is not quite the word for the peace that people typically experienced in response to Jesus' words and actions. The peace that Zacchaeus found was an excited peace, a joyful, grateful state that led to action in the style of God's kingdom (Luke 19:1-10). Paul begins each of his letters by wishing his readers peace: "Grace and peace to you from God our Father and the Lord Jesus Christ." But Paul is not wishing his readers a state of mental quiescence or indifference such as Buddhist or Stoic practices aim at, or the self-complacency that Rogerian psychotherapy seems to promote. To the morally and spiritually complacent, Jesus brought not calm, but upset: "Do you think I came to bring peace on earth? No, I tell you, but division" (Luke 12:51). It's a safe guess that he raised the anxiety level of the rich ruler (Luke 18:18-30) and some who listened nearby. Many of his parables aim to disturb the religious, and Jesus certainly did not promote feelings of peace in the money changers he drove with a whip from the Temple courtyard (John 2:14-16). We see a holy upset in this anger of Jesus, in Paul's "great sorrow and unceasing anguish in [his] heart" (Romans 9:2) over the Jews' rejection of the gospel, in Paul's distress over his bondage to sin (Romans 7:24), and in the ancient prophets' wrath at the injustice and idolatry of Israel. Ideal biblical personality is not monolithically calm, as the Stoic personality is. Yet a kind of calm has its place in this personality; emotional peace is a Christian virtue. In this chapter I will examine this vir-

tue, display its structure, and try to understand how peace is achieved and
how it relates to the various kinds of emotional upset that it addresses.

TWO APPROACHES TO EMOTIONAL UPSET

The emotions of upset are kinds of frustration; that is, the upset person
wishes something to be the case and perceives it to be not so, or wishes
something not to be the case and perceives that it is so. The impression of
the contravention of the wish is the emotion. In anxiety, a person wishes to
be secure in some way (e.g., financially secure, or able to answer the questions that will be posed to him in an interview); but he perceives — perhaps
subliminally — that he is not secure in the desired way. In grief the individual wishes to retain something to which she is strongly attached —
paradigmatically a person, but it may be something non-personal — and
perceives this object as lost to her. In anger one wishes to be treated fairly or
respectfully by agents, or one wishes this for some other party with whom
one identifies, but somebody or some quasi-personal agency frustrates this
wish with an offense. In feeling guilty, a person wishes to be morally upright, but perceives himself as morally defective. I am not saying that, to
have an upsetting emotion, a person must *first* have a *conscious* wish for
some state of affairs. The wish may be purely dispositional, or unconscious
in some other way, becoming actualized and/or conscious only in the emotion that characterizes its frustration.

    The frustration-analysis of the emotions of upset suggests two strate-
gies for emotional peace. The one that comes most spontaneously to mind
is that if emotional upset is frustration of wishes, then peace is their satisfaction. Peace from anxiety is to be won by finding adequate security; from
grief, by getting back the object of attachment; from anger, by getting revenge (a sort of satisfaction of the desire that justice be done); from guilt, by
living righteously. The problem with this naïve strategy is that the object of
the wish cannot be attained, at least not over the long haul, in the direct,
simple-minded way envisioned. This is perhaps most obvious in the case of
grief over some irreparable loss, but a little experience with life shows us
that we are never really safe in the ways the anxious person would like to be,
that it is not workable either to avoid being offended against or always to
take revenge against our offenders, and that efforts to be righteous by simply living righteously cannot be sustained or (depending on our moral tra-

dition) even begun. We can, in the short term, sometimes contrive to satisfy some of the wishes that lie at the base of the upsetting emotions, or if not to satisfy them fully, to deceive ourselves into thinking we have done so. But it is the wisdom of the more systematic approaches to emotional peace to eschew the direct satisfaction of these wishes, and instead, in one way or another, to eradicate, mitigate, or sublimate them.

A BUDDHIST APPROACH

A striking example of this is the Theravada Buddhist pursuit of the state known as "the attainment of cessation" *(nirodhasamapatti).* The practitioner traverses a series of meditations designed to attenuate the contents of consciousness until consciousness (and, in Buddhist doctrine, even mind) ceases altogether. First, he meditates on the infinity of space, so as to become unaware of distinctions among things. Next, he transcends the infinity of space, meditating on the infinity of consciousness, so as to become unaware even of space. Then he meditates on the proposition, "there is nothing," so as to become unaware even of contentless consciousness. Having become unaware of consciousness, he transcends the sphere of nothing at all, entering the sphere of neither conceptualization nor non-conceptualization. This stage seems to differ from the preceding three in not focusing on any proposition; its point is to get beyond conceptualization, but not in such a way as to *think* of non-conceptualization (since, presumably, that would itself be a sort of conceptualization). Last, as the practitioner transcends even the sphere of neither conceptualization nor non-conceptualization, he reaches the attainment of cessation. He enters a cataleptic trance, which may last a week, in which he neither reacts to any stimuli nor performs any action, mental or otherwise. In the practitioner's body, respiration ceases and metabolic processes slow to a minimum comparable to those of an animal in the deepest hibernation. The story is told of Mahanaga, a monk who was in the attainment of cessation when the meditation hall caught fire. Everyone fled except him, who sat unaware amidst the flames. The villagers brought water, put out the fire, repaired the building, and scattered flowers around Mahanaga, who did not emerge from his trance until the appointed time. (Information in this paragraph comes from Paul J. Griffiths, *On Being Mindless: Buddhist Meditation and the Mind-Body Problem,* chapter 1.)

Tranquility is here achieved in an uncompromising way, by liquidating the mind altogether, by eradicating the desires that are at the basis of the emotions of upset, yes, but at the same time canceling all other principles of individuation and agency: consciousness, thought, motivation. This radical approach serves to highlight, by contrast, some of the conditions that must be met in the Christian virtue of peace. Christian peace must be achieved within the parameters of selfhood, because only selves — individuated persons — can love, serve, obey, trust, praise, thank, and act in any of the other ways that Christians are called to do in this world and expect to continue to do with incomparably greater potency and perfection in the coming kingdom. This kind of Buddhist peace shuts down the activities of life that are, by Christian lights, its central goods. Because of the importance of emotions in the Christian life, it will not do to undercut the personality's capacity for emotions *in general* by eradicating all desire. The Christian is encouraged to hunger and thirst for righteousness, to seek God's kingdom, to love God and neighbor. These are just the sort of concerns that ground the distinctively Christian emotions and actions, and center the flourishing person: "Where your treasure [what you desire or are concerned about] is, there your heart [that is, the real you] will be also" (Matthew 6:21). In Christianity, selfhood is a good thing, and a central feature of it is interest, concern, passion for the right things.

Stoic Tranquility

A less radical approach, one that preserves some individuality and agency while still undercutting the concerns basic to the emotions of upset, is found in Stoicism. According to Marcus Aurelius, peace is achieved by construing all events from the point of view of the universe, thus transcending one's private passions. The tranquilization is achieved by taking an objective, impersonal view of things; for it is the personal, individual point of view that engages the desires on which the emotions of upset are founded. The *individual* learns to take an impersonal view of the situations of his life.

> Just as we say that Asclepius prescribed horseback riding for someone, or cold baths, or walking barefoot, so we say that the nature of the Whole has prescribed disease for someone, or lameness, or loss of limb, or anything else of the same kind. In the first statement the word "prescribed"

is used with much the same meaning as in the second. Asclepius orders something as contributing to health, and what happens to every individual is somehow ordered for him as contributing to his destiny. . . . You must consider the doing and perfecting of what the universal Nature decrees in the same light as your health, and welcome all that happens, even if it seems harsh, because it leads to the health of the universe, the welfare and well-being of Zeus. For he would not have allotted this to anyone if it were not beneficial to the Whole. (*Meditations,* V, 8)

Subjectively speaking, misfortunes are frustrations: getting what you don't want, or not getting what you do want. If we were always willing to accept whatever comes our way, nothing would be a misfortune for us. What would appear, from the naïve, personal perspective, to be misfortune — say, loss of one's financial security, or the death of a friend, or a moral offense against oneself — is not really a bad thing, according to Marcus, from the universe's point of view, because such private "misfortunes" are just part of the mosaic making up the beautiful whole that is the universe. Through the Stoic disciplines in which one comes to see all the events of one's life as contributions to the beauty of the whole, one attenuates the desires for individual security, for the continuing presence of one's friend, for freedom from moral offenses against oneself, for the well-being of one's children, that form the basis of the emotions of upset. One's only real wish is that the universe should proceed just as in fact it proceeds, along with the second-order wish that one should wish just this; so none of one's wishes is contravened.

The Stoic sage in the height of detachment does not, like the Buddhist in the attainment of cessation, lose consciousness or agency: *he,* Marcus Aurelius (or whoever), is conscious of the events of *his* life from this non-personal perspective; it is he who actively undertakes to identify himself with the perspective of the universe. Being an agent, he can take Stoic pride in his virtue and hold himself responsible for lapses. And yet when we Christians assess him, we see that the Stoic has emaciated his self. For tranquility's sake he has learned to be dispassionate about some things for which we should be passionate, if our persons are to have "substance." A woman who has so little personal stake in moral offenses against herself that she cannot be angered by them also has, in Christian perspective, too little sense of who she is (a child of God, with the dignity that entails), too little self-respect. The Stoic too has self-respect, but unlike Christian self-respect, his makes no demands on the world, because socially it is completely thin, not related to the attitudes of others in the robust brotherly/sisterly ways that Christian self-respect is. A man who can regard his child's illness as just one more of the devices by which the universe as a whole prescribes health for it-self has a hollow soul, however intentionally, and in a sense heroically, he has brought himself to this state. That child is rightfully a *particular* object of the father's love, an "attached" part of the father's self, and the Stoic strat-egy denies this. Stoic detachment seems to excise the attitudes basic to friendship. To the man who meets another who is weeping for grief Epictetus says, "As far as conversation goes . . . do not disdain to accommo-date yourself to him and, if need be, to groan with him. Take heed, however, not to groan inwardly, too" (*Enchiridion,* XVI). By contrast, the Christian is instructed to "Rejoice with those who rejoice, mourn with those who mourn" (Romans 12:15), and there is no appended warning to protect one-self from the emotional pains that attend such attachment. Jesus laments over Jerusalem, his people (Matthew 23:37-39); and his attitude to the pros-pect of his final suffering is not detachment, but that of one who feels the full brunt of it as a violation of his person and a violation of what he most deeply cherishes (Matthew 26:36-42). The Stoic's person, reduced as it is to the love of his own virtue, is inviolable. Not so Jesus' person.

THE CHRISTIAN CONCEPT OF PEACE

'Peace' *(eirēnē)* in the New Testament does not always denote a psychologi-cal state. The word sometimes refers to a relationship with God (Romans 5:1, Ephesians 2:14-17), sometimes to concord in human relationships (Ephesians 4:3, James 3:18); third and most centrally, it is a synonym for the comprehensive state of salvation, the state of final fulfillment of God's will for the creation (Luke 1:79; 2:14), which has been signaled and proleptically brought about in the death and resurrection of Jesus Christ. It is the shalom of God, that state of righteousness and prosperity and harmony and wellness of all things, to which the prophets of the Old Testament had looked forward (Ezekiel 37:26ff, Isaiah 48:17-19; 66:12-14), which is to be enjoyed when God is fully recognized and obeyed as Lord. And fourth, as in Romans 15:13, Colossians 3:15, and Philippians 4:6-7, 'peace' refers to a state of the believer's soul.

It is easy to see how these elements constitute a single concept, with the third element at the center. Although peace involves an end to the groaning of the entire creation (Romans 8:22), the New Testament is interested chiefly in human beings in their relationship with God. Thus shalom is constituted, most centrally, by human beings living before God's face as he has ordained them to do and by God's looking on them with approving joy and blessing them with the fruits of righteousness. This God-human relationship is fittingly called peace because it is the antithesis of the opposition and hostility between God and humanity that Christ's incarnation, ministry, death, and resurrection are intended to overcome. Shalom is also characterized by relationships of love and respect and mutual helpfulness among human beings that reflect their being all children of one Father, the opposite of the hostility and division from which Christ came to save us. This reconciling work of Christ is expressed succinctly in Ephesians 2:14-16: "For he himself is our peace, who has made the two one and has destroyed the barrier, the dividing wall of hostility, by abolishing in his flesh the law with its commandments and regulations. His purpose was to create in himself one new man out of the two, thus making peace, and in this one body to reconcile both of them to God through the cross, by which he put to death their hostility."

But it is integral to the working of this salvation, the actualization of this peace, that people hear what has been accomplished in Christ: "He came and preached peace to you who were far away and peace to those who were near. For through him we both have access to the Father by one Spirit" (v. 17). Through preaching and hearing and believing (Romans 10), the peace that God has wrought in Christ can take up residence in the souls of people. This fourth element, the peace of Christ ruling in the hearts of believers (Colossians 3:15), is not an incidental addition to the concept. If peace as the fulfillment of God's purpose in creation is to be explicated in terms of peace as fitting relationship to God and fellow humans, then, on the assumption that personal relationships are a matter of attitudes, emotions, and intentional actions that require self-understanding and understanding of one's situation, a mental assimilation of what Christ has accomplished (peace as a state of the soul) is necessary for peace itself. To the extent that *we* are not *filled* with peace as we trust God (Romans 15:13), the peace aimed at in Christ's work is not accomplished.

We are here interested in peace as a state of the soul, and especially in how Christian peace, so understood, overcomes the emotions of upset. The question arises, what kind of state of mind peace is; two possible answers are "an *absence* of the emotions of upset" and "an *emotion* that overcomes the upsets."

It is clear that the Buddhist attainment of cessation is a sheer absence of emotion, as it is of every other conscious state. This is less clear of the tranquility experienced by the Stoic. Official Stoic doctrine identifies virtue with an extirpation of the passions, but anyone who reads the letters and essays of Seneca gets the impression that there is still room for quite a bit of emotion, at least of a genteel and calm kind, in a well-ordered Stoic personality (see, for example, Seneca's essay "On Favors," in which he talks very sensitively and even passionately about gratitude). The Stoic sage is conscious of his tranquility, and thus can feel it, in some sense of the word. Besides this, Stoic tranquility goes some distance toward matching the view of emotions taken in this book. An emotion is a concern-based construal, a sort of seeing-as, or more broadly an experiencing-as or perceiving-as in which the construal impinges on and takes up some concern of the subject. Marcus Aurelius urges the reader to construe the "harsh" things that happen to him — lameness, loss of loved ones, etc. — as contributions to the universe's being a harmonious, law-governed, admirable whole. They are to be so construed as not to be experienced as impinging on the typical individual personal concerns that are the basis of the emotions of upset. If someone succeeds in this, he will not have the emotions of upset, but since he is construing those events in *some* way, perhaps he is still in a state of emotion, if only the construal impinges on *some* concern of his.

The Stoics tell us that, while most of the things that people think are good and bad are in fact neither good nor bad, virtue *is* good and vice *is* bad. The wise person, then, does seem to have the concern to be wise, that is, the desire to have the Stoic attitude about everything that happens. If so, then the Stoic can have a kind of joy in his status as a wise and tranquil person: as a result of construing the harsh events of his life as contributing to the Whole, he can now construe himself as having the virtue that he is concerned to have. One might think that this double construal — construing himself as construing the universe as . . . — is a rather roundabout way of getting joy. But reflexive joy is a perfectly common and legitimate kind of joy, and the Stoics were certainly reflexive (that is, *self*-attentive, *self*-concerned). There is, however, also a more direct Stoic joy: if the Stoic also regards the harmonious whole that the universe is as a good and admirable thing, then he seems to be concerned, or to care, that the universe be as it is; so when he construes it as a harmonious whole, he takes a certain impersonal joy in *it*.

Christian peace resembles that of the Stoic in being a willingness for the universe to be just the way it is. But Christianity has a different understanding of how the universe is. The universe is not just what it appears, to secular eyes, to be; it is a place that has been visited by God in an extraordinary way. The Christian experiences the emotion of peace when she is "moved" by the vision of herself as no longer at enmity with God because of Christ's reconciling work. She feels peace when she construes God as no longer an adversary, but now a friend with whom she can "work." She feels the peace of God, which passes understanding, when she construes a neighbor, with whom she was at enmity, as a brother or sister because of Christ. In each case, the construal touches a concern, perhaps previously latent or unconscious, a desire that the enmity come to an end. This concern would be a corollary of the desire for the kingdom of God that I discussed in Chapters 3–6.

The construal of self, God, and neighbor in terms of *former enmity* is what distinguishes peace from other Christian emotions, such as joy and hope and gratitude. If one thinks of God's love and fellowship without setting it in the context of a former enmity, then it is perhaps more fitting to call one's emotion joy than peace. If what is salient about God's shalom is its status as a gift, then the emotion should be called gratitude; and if its futurity is salient, then it is hope. Since the shalom of God has all these features — goodness, gift, futurity, and end of enmity — the difference between these emotions is determined by which of these features is salient at a given moment, and in the course of Christian experience they trade places, fading into one another in ways that no one could, or should particularly want to, keep track of. In the old Hebrew way of thinking, peace was a very broad concept, encompassing all well-being and not *requiring* the suggestion of a former enmity. But if peace is to be distinct from the other Christian emotions, something in its character needs to mark it off, and the strong New Testament emphasis on reconciliation in God's work of salvation — the overcoming of alienation and of the divine-human and human-human strife that characterize it — justifies this way of doing so.

So far, it is perhaps not clear how Christian peace is analogous to the two other kinds of mental peace that we considered at the beginning of this chapter. How does it achieve what the Buddhist and Stoic strategies seem centrally designed to achieve: to overcome emotions of upset such as anxiety, grief, anger, and guilt?

CHRISTIAN PEACE AND THE EMOTIONS OF UPSET

Anxiety is a construal of oneself or something one cares about as under dull threat. Jesus tells us not to be anxious about what we eat or drink or put on, and so speaks to those of us who perceive ourselves as under threat of some such lack. If, instead of setting our minds and hearts on the satisfaction of these needs, we seek his kingdom, our anxiety will be quieted. When Jesus says, "seek first his kingdom and his righteousness, and all these things will be given to you as well" (Matthew 6:33), he is not commending such seeking as a means to getting food and clothing. He is instead urging that we focus our minds on God's shalom *rather than* on the details of our survival. If we do, we will experience God's goodness to us, his Fatherly providential care; we will perceive ourselves as secure in him even if, as may happen, there is a shortage of food and clothing. This is a little bit like the Stoic strategy of seeing one's situation in terms of the larger picture, but the difference is that this picture is not impersonal. The universe doesn't care whether I flourish as an individual, as long as my flourishing or failing to do so contributes to the beauty of the Whole. But God cares for our individual flourishing, though he does not always provide for it in just the way we would prefer to be cared for. Since this security is intrinsic to the shalom that the Christian experiencing the emotion of peace perceives — the doctrine of shalom being the doctrine of our security in God through the work of Jesus Christ — this emotion cancels the perception of insecurity that is anxiety.

The apostle says, "Have no anxiety about anything, but in everything by prayer and supplication with thanksgiving let your requests be made known to God. And the peace of God, which passes all understanding, will keep your hearts and your minds in Christ Jesus" (Philippians 4:6-7, RSV). The peace of God is the currently invisible state of the universe that has been brought about through Jesus Christ. Prayer and supplication with thanksgiving can overrule anxiety because they are knowingly addressed to the God of peace, the Author of shalom. They are in part exercises of attention to God under the aspect of his being the rock of our salvation, the mother hen who covers us with the security of her everlasting wings in the cross and resurrection of Jesus. The construal of our situation in terms of God's shalom is peace as an emotion, and it mitigates anxiety.

Grief is a construal of some great good as lost to oneself (or perhaps to those one loves). Thus one may grieve over a lost lover, lost opportunities of youth, a home of long residence, a dead child, one's kinsmen who have rejected Christ, or a permanently (as it seems) destroyed valley. Peace over-comes or mitigates different griefs in different ways. In the Christian vision of well-being in Christ, the lover, the opportunities, the home, may simply be swamped in goodness; one may cease to grieve over them because in com-parison with the kingdom of God they hardly seem to be goods: we may even count them as refuse (Philippians 3:8). Grief for the dead child is miti-gated by the hope that in God's mercy she may one day be restored, as is Paul's grief over his beloved kinsmen's hardheartedness (Romans 11:25-36). We speak of hope here, but this hope may also be the emotion of peace, if the cessation of enmity is in view, as it certainly is in the Romans passage.

Anger is a construal of someone as an offender, as morally bad and de-serving punishment. It is a construal of him or her as opposed to oneself (in case the supposed offense is against oneself) or to somebody one loves. Since the angry person judges by standards with which he affectively identi-fies, he "looks down" from a position of righteousness on the offender. This is not to say that the offender is construed as *in all respects* opposed to the good, or as in all respects morally inferior to the angry one. Nor is it to say that the angry person *believes* the "offender" to be morally bad and deserv-ing punishment; a construal is an appearance that may be at odds with the same subject's beliefs. Anger tends to compromise and spoil love, even though it is possible to be angry at somebody one loves, and some anger even expresses love (for example, a parent's anger at her anorexic child). (For more on anger, see my *Emotions,* pp. 202-21.) The emotion of peace, as we have seen, is a construal of oneself, nature, God, or one's fellow human beings, in terms of the shalom that God has wrought in Jesus Christ. In this vision the neighbor (in this case he is an offender) is construed as a fellow sinner, one for whom Christ died, as he died for oneself, that we might be reconciled to God and to one another. In owning one's own reconciliation to God in the emotion of peace, a person owns his brother- or sisterhood with this offender. As a heartfelt vision of reconciliation on all sides, Chris-tian peace is at odds with the alienation involved in the grammar of anger. This is why Christian peace, when one really feels it, dispels anger and tends to bring conflict to an end and fellowship to a beginning.

Guilt is a construal of oneself as sullied by one's own misdeeds or omis-sions, as deserving punishment and alienated from the standard of righ-teousness and the person(s) one has offended against. If peace is the construal of oneself as loved, forgiven, washed clean, reconciled to God and neighbor, and destined for moral and communal perfection, it is clear enough how peace (like the other emotions that have the various aspects of God's shalom in perceptual view) overcomes this emotion of upset — how it is, in its own very different way, the Christian counterpart of Buddhist attainment of cessation and Stoic tranquility. Like Stoic tranquility (and unlike the attainment of cessation), it overrules the guilt by calling into play a gestalt on the world (God, neighbor, and self) that replaces the frustrating gestalt with one that satisfies one's concern for moral purity. Christian peace differs vastly from Stoic detachment in the particular view of the world on which its therapy for the emotions of upset is based, and in the concerns that properly correlate with that view of the world.

Christian peace mitigates — even eradicates — some of the trouble-emotions. But it does not aim to banish them wholesale, as do the Buddhism and Stoicism we have considered for comparison. Paul speaks of his "great sorrow and unceasing anguish" (Romans 9.2) over his kinsmen's resistance to the gospel, and of his anxiety for all the churches (II Corinthians 11:28). Some people were looking for a reason to accuse Jesus, and saw an opportunity in his willingness to heal a man with a withered hand on the Sabbath. Noticing this, Jesus "looked around at them in anger and, deeply distressed at their stubborn hearts, said to the man, 'Stretch out your hand'" (Mark 3:5). When Jesus saw Mary, the sister of Lazarus, weeping for her dead brother, "he was deeply moved in spirit and troubled" (John 11:33) and then he himself wept for Lazarus; he lamented the moral state of Jerusalem (Matthew 23:37-39), and on the night before his death he said, "My soul is overwhelmed with sorrow to the point of death" (Matthew 26:38).

Christianity is not a therapy for those who wish never to be upset. The mature Christian knows about the shalom of God and has it within his emotional repertoire to feel it, but he also acknowledges, and sometimes perceives with the eyes of his heart, the real evil that exists in his world. Not to be able to recognize this evil and perceive it emotionally is from a Christian point of view an unacceptable blindness and fault of character. So, unlike the perfect Stoic or the perfect Buddhist, the mature Christian does sometimes become anxious or angry, does sometimes grieve, does feel the painful perturbation that is part of contrition or compassion. Because the passion that Christianity cultivates is from above, yet engaged with the world of contingencies, it represents the possibility of negative emotions unknown among the pagans.

But it does mitigate many of the upsetting emotions of everyday life, and it provides a perspective of hope and peace and joy that are equally unknown in paganism. The well-developed Christian is like the Stoic in having undergone a transformation of his natural concerns. While he grieves some losses, he does not grieve, for example, the loss of wealth or prestige, except perhaps in some rare case in which such loss affects his work for the kingdom; and even then he supposes that God is inventive enough to find some way of getting the work done, and so the grief is mitigated. While he does sometimes get angry, he does not much get angry at purely personal offenses against himself, since his concern for self-respect (and he *does* have such a concern) has been sublimated in kingdom terms and thus he has become less vulnerable to ordinary insults. While he may be anxious about some things, he is not anxious to secure himself once and for all in a comfortable retirement with an assured supply of food and clothing. The constitution of his cares being more spare and indeed detached than that of the heathen because of the disciplines by which, for the sake of God's shalom, the Christian has mortified his "flesh," he is made invulnerable to some of the major emotional upsets that torment the heathen. But the main source of the Christian's calm is not this privative strategy, but the positive vision of what God has done and will do for us and for the whole creation in Jesus Christ. When this vision is seen with the eyes of the heart, it is the Christian emotion of peace.

CHAPTER TWELVE

Compassion

WHAT COMPASSION IS

One of the most terrible things about dying, as Ivan Ilych experienced it, was that his family and friends made him feel so utterly alone in it. They were in the bloom of health and pleasure, in the midst of social hilarity and vigorous activity. He, in his disgusting misery, weakness, and despair, was an alien to them. Only one person, a servant boy, took a different attitude:

> [Ivan Ilych] saw that no one felt for him, because no one even wished to grasp his position. Only Gerasim recognized it and pitied him. And so Ivan Ilych felt at ease only with him. He felt comforted when Gerasim supported his legs (sometimes all night long) and refused to go to bed, saying: "Don't you worry, Ivan Ilych, I'll get sleep enough later on," or when he suddenly became familiar and exclaimed: "If you weren't sick it would be another matter, but as it is, why should I grudge a little trouble?" Gerasim alone did not lie; everything showed that he alone understood the facts of the case and did not consider it necessary to disguise them, but simply felt sorry for his emaciated and enfeebled master. Once when Ivan Ilych was sending him away he even said straight out: "We shall all of us die, so why should I grudge a little trouble?" — expressing the fact that he did not think his work burdensome, because he was doing it for a dying man and hoped someone would do the same for him when his time came. (Tolstoy, *The Death of Ivan Ilych*, p. 138)

Compassion is the construal of a suffering or deficient person as a cherished fellow. Like other emotions, it is not a disinterested construal. Compassion is a form of love, but distinguishable from other forms of love by the terms of its fellowship. Friendship, family affection, love of spouse, and love for fellow believers all differ from compassion in that the terms of this latter fellowship are suffering or deficiency: the beloved is viewed in terms of a fellow-suffering (actual or potential) or a fellow-deficiency. When I perceive someone compassionately, the weakness or suffering or dysfunction I see in him is a quality I see also in myself. Of course I can have compassion for someone I love as a friend, a family member, a spouse, or a fellow believer; my point is just that compassion is not the same as these other forms of love, and that the difference lies in how the beloved is viewed. It is not *as a fellow sufferer* that I (usually) love Elizabeth my wife, but it is *as a fellow sufferer* that Gerasim loves Ivan Ilych.

From the fact that compassion is a form of love based in the fellowship of suffering and deficiency, it follows that it is a form of neighbor-love. By "neighbor" the Christian means anybody we come in contact with. Not just anybody is my friend, a member of my family, my spouse, or a fellow Christian. These bonds of fellowship are limited by qualifications that not everybody has or can have, and so they are not forms of neighbor-love. But a vulnerability to suffering, weakness, and death and a participation in dysfunction are things I have in common with every human being, and a fellowship based on this feature is one I can have with anybody who comes along. Gerasim's willingness to devote so much of himself to Ivan Ilych is not a function of any special tie of family or friendship; he simply sees another mortal, like himself, in need. And in this vision of community his heart goes out. And then his shoulders.

There are sentimental people whose hearts seem to go out to the suffering while their legs and arms and shoulders remain inert. But where compassion is strong enough to be called a character trait, it typically results in an action congruent with viewing the other as a sufferer much like oneself. If the suffering is physical or mental, the action will probably be some effort to alleviate it. If it is a deficiency, such as some weakness of will, body, or mind, forbearance is often in order. If the deficiency is ethical, compassion will typically move to forgiveness, gentleness, and mercy, with the indescribably many forms of behavior typical of these. I too am susceptible to the suffering I see in this other, I too am weak and deficient in many ways, I too will soon die. I too am a sinner in need of forgiveness — when these considerations issue in helpfulness, patience, mercy, and gentleness, compassion has prevailed.

ALOOFNESS

The vice corresponding to compassion can be called "aloofness." Aloofness is the disinclination to see the commonality between myself and the sufferer I meet, the inclination to dwell on differences between myself and the deficient one — differences that create a distance between him and me. Aloofness is either a matter of denying an obvious similarity between myself and another or of accepting the appearance of difference between myself and some deficient person.

The Pharisee who prays "I thank thee God that I am not like that publican" accepts the appearance of his own righteousness and the appearance of sinfulness in the publican, and misses the commonality. After all, it is well known what a despicable thing it is to take money from one's own people for the maintenance of the foreign occupation. And as for the Pharisee himself, it is clear for all to see that he fastidiously meets his religious obligations. He is the willing victim of standardized, unspiritual, public ways of seeing: being spiritually blind to himself, he cannot see others as they really are. And thus an illusion of distance is created: because he does not know himself, others look so very different to him. But why does he not know himself? Because in an important sense he has not become serious about his standing before God. He has not passionately undertaken the project of becoming inwardly fit for the kingdom, pure in heart before the Father who sees in secret. He is a nice person with a conveniently external moral standard, who does not want to apply any other standard. He has undertaken the task of becoming pure in action, but has neglected becoming ethically good. Were he to undertake this most deeply human of projects, he would soon see that even this supercilious attitude toward the publicans was enough to render him roughly equal to them in moral status. (Jesus seems to imply that whatever difference might be left would not be to the Pharisee's advantage.) And with this awareness of his own failure of the heart, he could begin to take that gentle, nurturing attitude toward publicans and prostitutes that is compassion.

The aloofness of the Pharisee is shocking and proverbial, of course, and he is hardly lacking in fellow travelers. We all know, and are or have been, such moral oafs: "No, I must say, I make it a policy not to visit hospitals. It is just too depressing, all those people lying in beds, sick and hurt, with the smell of disinfectant and medicine (and sometimes worse things) in the air. Of course I feel sorry for them, but I just can't take it. And for the past ten years I've made it a strict policy not to go to funerals. I've found that when I do go, I wake with bad dreams and terror in the middle of the night; I guess I'm just sensitive, but I find it even spoils my bridge sometimes, and I get to drinking more, which is so distressing. My daughter has fallen in with a bunch who meet in an old store building in the rough section of town, where they sing hymns and feed the bums and try to get jobs for teenagers. It's a sweet thought, but completely unrealistic; and I have to admit it strikes me as a little bit *indecent,* for a nice girl like my Judy. Those people are so *different,* and so unpredictable. As for me, when I drive through that section of town, I keep the windows rolled up tight."

Ivan Ilych's family and the Pharisee and the nice upper middle class person whose heart I just bared to you are the sort of people who dismay us Christians. Indignation is what we feel, indignation on behalf of injured humanity. They probably think that prostitutes and dope addicts and bums and people on welfare are the ones who are going to hell, and quite naturally too, if you think of hell as a kind of trash barrel. But we, being radical Christians (or at least sort of radical — we read *Sojourners* and think it's the greatest thing to come down the pike since Dorothy Day), have a deeper insight. We know what real trash looks like. And it ain't prostitutes and welfare recipients.

But even to us cognoscenti there perhaps cleaves a stubborn stain of aloofness. A young pastor glances at the clock and sees he must put down a moving and fascinating article on St. Francis of Assisi that has appeared in the December issue of *Sojourners.* It is time to make the hospital rounds. He leaves the plush office provided by his affluent congregation and goes down and cranks up his symbolic 1985 Chevy. Everything goes well as he visits a young wife who has just delivered a healthy girl baby and a teenager who broke his leg in football practice. But the last visit of the day is more difficult: a fifty-year-old woman dying of lung cancer. He wants very much to be a good pastor and to sympathize with her and thinks to himself in the midst of the visit that he is not doing too badly. She seems to be deriving comfort from the visit, and he hasn't made any obvious blunders so far. The patient, shriveled and unable to leave the bed, asks him to lift her head and put another pillow under it. As he does so, the muscles that fill his shirt strain against his sport jacket. Then he says a moving prayer with her and leaves. As he walks out into the balmy air of a spring evening in the city, he can't resist a certain sense of exaltation at being away from the hospital room and out among his own kind once more. What an alien being that sufferer seemed, lying so weak and helpless at death's door! He glances at his watch, and is glad to see that he has time to stop at the office on his way home, and finish that article on St. Francis.

ACCEPTING ONE'S VULNERABILITY

Young people are often short of compassion. Even the nicest of high school students may think that treating a "nerd" as a fellow human being is inconceivably beyond the call of duty — roughly similar to respecting the rights of cockroaches to hospitable treatment in one's home. Nerds, homosexuals, cripples, people over thirty, and other sufferers are occasions for hilarious (and almost innocent) jokes rather than objects of human concern. One possible reason for this character deficiency in young people is that they haven't suffered enough to identify readily with sufferers. Because of narrow experience, their hearts do not go out to people who are "different," but remain enclosed within their own skins. It is not that they fail to recognize that the other is suffering or deficient: their jokes at his expense show that they do. They lack a recognition of themselves in that suffering, a visceral impression of the connection between themselves (their weakness, vulnerability, sinfulness) and the suffering or deficiency of the other.

But merely having suffered does not guarantee compassion. Some who have suffered deeply become embittered about life or consumed with the project of self-protection. Compassion means that one's heart goes out to someone else, but people sometimes respond to suffering by turning their heart inward. Suffering becomes for them a reason for increased self-preoccupation, in the form of efforts to get relief for themselves or to avoid a recurrence of their suffering or to indulge in self-pity over it.

What makes the difference? How can a person turn his sufferings to his spiritual benefit and the blessing of others through compassion? Let me take a stab at a partial and rough answer. Suffering can become the basis of compassion only if the person in some way comes to an acceptance of it. If I dissociate myself from my own death, sufferings, sins, and inadequacies — denying that they are really part of me and part of my condition in this life — then it is natural that I will keep my emotional distance from sufferers. If in my secret heart the answer to the question "Who am I?" comes back entirely in terms of shining success, strength, health, pleasure, and being a good guy, then of course I am quite a different sort of being from these sufferers, these sinners, these unfortunate or even dying people. To be sure, I will have to acknowledge that they are human beings, and to that extent bear an unsettling resemblance to myself; but it would be going too far to think of them as fellows on the road of human life. If I refuse to accept my sufferings and deficiencies, no amount of them will make me a compassionate person.

For this reason the process of becoming transparent to oneself that we discussed in Chapters 3–6 is an important ground of compassion. That process forces me to come to terms with my vulnerability and weakness; I come to know viscerally and steadily that I am destined for death and subject to moral failure, and in one way or another I become reconciled to this fact. I get an emotionally clear view of myself in my darker aspect, and thus lay the groundwork for seeing as fellows those who are walking through the valley of the shadow of death. I have suggested that this process is encouraged by the Christian hope. Those who believe that death is not the last word have a resource for facing death honestly that non-believers lack. So Christian hope is a psychological aid to compassion.

The compassion of the youth Gerasim, Tolstoy seems to be telling us, is grounded in Gerasim's peasant (Christian) acceptance of his own vulnerability and transience. Because he is relatively at peace about the prospect of his own death and about the prospect of his undergoing the humiliating process of bodily degeneration, he is able to be a genuine companion to the stinking and groaning Ivan Ilych. By contrast, for the self-opaque members of Ivan Ilych's family the latter's suffering is nothing but a rather disgusting intrusion into their life, a nasty inconvenience to be avoided if possible, and certainly nothing that suggests an essential kinship with themselves.

ACCEPTANCE IN ANOTHER SENSE

We have seen that the experience of suffering, finitude, and dysfunction is needed in the development of compassion; in addition, one needs an acceptance of these as a part of one's identity. But there are cases in which a person has experienced weakness, and in some sense accepts that fact, and yet is not compassionate. An examination of such a case will help us to see a little more deeply what we must mean by "acceptance." Not just any sort of acceptance will do; what is required is that the individual accept his vulnerability as part of his present self.

The early chapters of Gordon Liddy's autobiography, *Will,* recount the extreme measures he took as a boy to overcome his excessive fears. In each case the cure takes the form of confronting the fear: afraid of rats, he eats one; afraid of electrical storms, he lashes himself sixty feet up a seventy-five foot pin oak in the midst of violent wind and lightning. He also overcomes his fear of pain by suffering it. At one point, he takes the position of catcher on the baseball team because it involves getting hit by bats and big boys bound for home plate, and nobody else wants the position. He reports that he would go back into the play while still hurt, and "with a convert's zeal I became contemptuous of anyone who didn't want to play hurt" (p. 28). Liddy expresses a bit of condescension toward his youthful "convert's zeal," but this story foreshadows the grown-up Liddy's attitude toward weak and cowardly people. With the continuing zeal of a convert, he holds them in contempt: I overcame my weakness and fear, and they could too; but they don't, so they are scum. He is like the rich man who, having made it out of a poverty-stricken youth, does not use his firsthand knowledge of poverty as a basis for sympathizing with the poor, but instead as a reason for dissociating himself still further from them: I made it, and so could they; but the vermin won't work.

In a perfectly good sense of "know," Liddy knows what it's like to be weak and fearful. He has not forgotten it, as his vivid writing about these experiences shows. And in a perfectly good sense of "accept," he accepts this fact about himself: he is not at all trying to cover it up; in fact, he is glorying in it; he enjoys revealing it to others. And yet his aloofness toward cowardly and weak people is especially virulent: he is not just indifferent to their plight, but positively hateful toward them on account of it. I suggest that this violent dissociation of himself from the weak and fearful is possible because he does not identify his present self with the self he was when he was weak and fearful. He has contempt not only for others with these traits, but also for himself — that is, for the person he once was. In some sense he is the same person who was once weak and fearful, but emotionally he does not look on that boy as being himself; he does not "identify" with him. Since he dissociates himself from himself insofar as he is weak, his "self-knowledge" does not become the ground for appreciating the commonality between himself and those others. And note the propriety of the quotation marks I just put around 'self-knowledge': in one sense, this is not self-knowledge. What Liddy knows in remembering the boy he was before his courageous acts is an alien self, a self he no longer owns to be himself, a self he has rejected.

Why is Liddy unwilling to identify with the cowardly boy he once was? His upbringing seems to have predisposed an obsession with strength, and his autobiography expresses this obsession. His passion for being personally strong is not balanced by other passions that might mitigate his fear of weakness. His book implies that Liddy is still suffering from a certain lack of self-confidence, that he still needs to "prove" himself; and he proves himself again and again by being a tough guy. (I am not saying he was any less confident at the time of writing the autobiography than most of us are.) If Liddy were cooler about himself, just a little less afraid of being caught in some weakness (that is, if he had more of the deep liking of himself that I talked about in Chapters 6 and 9), he might find it in his heart to reach out to that fearful boy who grew up in the '30s — and hug him emotionally to himself. And that would be the beginning of a new attitude to others who are weak and fearful. Also, having given up Catholicism, Liddy perhaps has no conceptual framework pressing him to understand himself in any other way than as the self he obviously seems at the time to be — a man in the strength of maturity with certain mental, emotional, and physical powers.

Liddy's failure to identify with the weak person he once was and the weak person he will someday again become (if he lives long enough) does not result from lack of information or a bad memory. It is not as though he has forgotten what he once was or has failed to reckon with what he will probably sometime be. One is not under any logical compulsion, after noting the normal career of the human organism from weakness to strength to weakness again, to identify one's present self with all stages in that career. It may seem to us a little narrow-minded, and maybe psychologically imprudent, to refuse to admit as part of his personal identity the features he once had and may someday again have but which he has succeeded in chasing away; but he cannot be accused of being uninformed or absentminded or illogical for doing so.

Self-knowledge involves an element of choice at this point. We have to make some decisions about what we are going to accept as part of ourselves. Shall I accept as part of me the self that was crude and cruel at the age of fourteen? That was weak and cowardly at the age of ten? Or shall I deny that earlier self, identifying myself narrowly in terms of the traits I currently possess? Shall I accept as part of me the condition I may one day be in — of poverty, disease, weakness, senility — or shall I accept only what I more or less obviously now am? And when it comes to looking at others, the question will be, Shall I see in a weak and cowardly person, or an old, confused person, or a crude and arrogant person, a fellow human, dear to me? Or shall I see in such a person a member of a different class than mine, a class I did or will, admittedly, belong to, but which I do not accept as part of my present self?

COMPASSION AND INNOCENCE

In Martha Nussbaum's excellent discussion in *Upheavals of Thought,* she points out that compassion, as it was understood in the tradition of the Greek tragedians and by Aristotle, as well as in much of modern popular culture, requires that the recipient of compassion be innocent of his own suffering. Thus, if a person like the prodigal son in Jesus' parable has brought his misery on himself by his own foolish or immoral action, then he is not worthy of compassion and we should neither feel sorry for him nor treat him in the ways characteristic of compassion. Had the father of the prodigal son been an adherent of the tragic tradition, he would have waited for his son to come to the house, and when he came with his repentance and his tale of woe the father would have listened and looked stern and said (because he was merciful), "I will accept your offer to become one of my hired servants; I will pay you a fair wage, and you can live on the farm." As we know, the father in the parable, who is God our Father, did not act in this way, but, violating the standards of tragic compassion, "saw him and was filled with compassion for him; he ran to his son, threw his arms around him and kissed him" (Luke 15:20) and treated him in every way like a son. This is a striking case of Christianity's departure from worldly wisdom. I think it is because of Christianity's strong association of compassion with forgiveness. After all, the parable provides a paradigm, not only for compassion, but also for forgiveness. In the Christian ethic, psychology and spirituality, compassion is a major motivator of forgiveness, and forgiveness frees one to be compassionate. The Greek tragedians did not know much about forgiveness.

The father in the parable is God. The parable is about God's compassion, but it is also a model for our compassion toward one another. "Be perfect, therefore, as your heavenly Father is perfect" (Matthew 5:48). A major theme of this chapter is that compassion involves a cultivated acknowledgment and perception of our own vulnerability, weakness, finitude, and dysfunction. In a sense, we have a reason for compassion that is unavailable to

God. He shows compassion without being weak, finite, or dysfunctional. In a sense, compassion should be easier for us than it is for God. But to exploit this reason for compassion, we must be honest, and we must be willing to stress, in our relations with others, our own fallibility.

A SELF-CONCEPT STRETCHED

The Christian is under pressure to stretch her self-concept (but not beyond the truth), rather than shrink or restrict it. She is encouraged to pick up analogs of weakness in her past and possible future as well as her present and, using these as points of departure, to see commonalities between herself and her weak neighbor. She is under the pressure of God's love to include in her self-understanding many features that to a prosaic and unspiritual eye would seem obvious candidates for exclusion. In the bloom of health she can identify with the sick and dying. In the strength of her maturity the weakness of a child does not seem alien to her. In the fullness of sainthood she can see herself in a criminal who has committed the most outrageous crimes. All this may seem paradoxical and impossible to the non-Christian. But to the Christian it is the glory of her life, the imperative imitation of God, and an exercise in truthfulness.

The Christian story is that of Emmanuel, God with us. In it God is not just near us, or beside us; he is one of us. It is the story of his "identifying" with us in the most literal sense — of his altering his identity in our direction and for our sakes. He did not just sympathize with us from a close proximity, stand beside our hospital bed as it were. He took on human nature, including bodiliness, susceptibility to pain and death, the whole range of human sadness and joy, and even, mysteriously, sin. Paul exhorts the Christians at Philippi to imitate God's compassionate seeing: "Have this mind among yourselves, which is yours in Christ Jesus, who, though he was in the form of God, did not count equality with God a thing to be grasped, but emptied himself, taking the form of a servant, being born in the likeness of men" (Philippians 2:5-7, RSV). And to the Corinthian church Paul writes, "for our sake he made him to be sin who knew no sin, so that in him we might become the righteousness of God" (II Corinthians 5:21, RSV). In Jesus, God the Son chooses to extend his identity to encompass our condition. God is "broad-minded," even about sin. He spreads his mind as a hen spreads her wings to cover every last chick, down to the weakest and most obstreperous in the brood. But he is not like people who are sometimes called broad-minded, when in fact they are short on moral passion and understanding. In such people broadmindedness about sin is just a deficiency of concern about sin and its consequences. God's broad-mindedness means that, however much he abhors sin, he is willing not to dissociate himself from us, even on this account — indeed, he takes the initiative in associating himself with us as closely as possible, precisely on this account. In God's compassion the Christian has the warrant and charge to go and do likewise. The difference is that in us, the identification with the weak and sinful is more a matter of honest acknowledgment than of self-transformation.

In the first four sections of this chapter I have spoken of human compassion as recognizing in someone else's lowliness an analog of the same lowliness that I can find, at least potentially, in myself. But ideologically narrow-minded people raise for us the question about how far I must go in drawing into my self-understanding human features that are not actually my features now. I have admitted that a reasonable person is not compelled by either facts or logic to understand herself in such a way that she sees others compassionately. A choice confronts us. Non-Christians who are compassionate, and indeed most Christians who have not received explicit teaching on this matter, make such choices without much reflection. They make them instinctively. They do what comes naturally. And what comes naturally is choosing to understand ourselves in such a way that we have a certain degree of compassion for others. The philosopher David Hume even held that "sympathy" is a universal human trait. People vary greatly in the amount and kind of sympathy they have for one another, but it is surely true that there are tendencies in the human breast to identify with others when they are suffering, and the upbringing of many people makes them at least somewhat broad-minded.

But the absolute center of the Christian faith, the model for all Christian seeing and behaving, is the compassionate incarnation of God in Jesus Christ. The idea of a narrow-minded Christian is a contradiction. Broadmindedness is a choice, but for the Christian the choice has already been made; to accept God's mercy in Jesus is to place oneself under constraint to strive for a broadness in one's self-concept and in one's mercy. When a person comes to acknowledge that Jesus is the Lord, she no longer has any choice about how far to go in identifying herself with weak, suffering, or sinful people. Because no person is too lowly for her Lord, none is too lowly for her, either. For this reason the Christian community does not settle for whatever compassion comes naturally, but educates for it. It holds constantly before itself the tender stooping love of God and by so doing constantly seeks to stretch the self-concepts of its individual members into a broad-mindedness imitative of its Lord's.

From the Christian point of view, only God chooses to identify with the weak and sinful. For in his case he who was not weak and not sinful became weak and became like a sinner for the sake of the weak and sinful. In compassion the Christian does not *become* weak and sinful for the sake of some fellow human being; instead she acknowledges a commonality between herself and this sufferer, a commonality of which there is abundant evidence for anyone with eyes to see. For a sinner to be Christianly merciful is not for her to be first a judge, honorable and wise and just, and then secondly, to stoop in generous condescension to pronounce a milder sentence than the sinner deserves, or even to let him off scot free. No, Christians do not stoop when they are compassionate; only God stoops. To be merciful as a Christian is not in any way to be merciful as a judge (even if by some social necessity a Christian happens to be cast in the role of judge). It is, instead, to see that sinner as a fellow sinner. And in the face of the moral hierarchies suggested to us by human standards of discrimination, by the differences so obvious between us upright citizens and the murderers, rapists, thieves, and cheats who fill our prisons, it is an ongoing task of Christian education to keep ourselves aware of our full membership in the universal brotherhood of miscreants.

Compassion and the Gospel of Christ

The story of God's incarnation provides a model of compassion for the Christian to imitate and an imperative for him to do so. But the gospel is not just a model and imperative. It is also, and primarily, good news. It is the news of our redemption from sin and death, information about a new status, hitherto unknown to us, that we enjoy before God. It is the declaration that we have been washed clean and are destined to live in his eternal kingdom. The accomplishment of this new status is closely, though mysteriously, tied up with God's humbling himself and identifying with us in the life and death of Jesus of Nazareth. I want now to say a little about how believing this declaration engenders compassion. And I shall do this by relating compassion to two other virtues that we have discussed, gratitude and hope.

If I believe the gospel in a spiritual way, then I see myself very gladly as the recipient of this undeserved gift of eternal life, and I see God as my absolute benefactor. This is Christian gratitude, and it has two consequences relevant to compassion: a sense of absolute dependency and a sense of blessing.

The earning mentality that is so often the basis of aloofness is eradicated to the extent that a person is grateful in a spiritual way. If I know myself to be absolutely dependent on God for the most important thing in life, then any accomplishments I may have to my credit are swamped in this dependency that I share with all others, and so are prevented from becoming the basis for dissociating myself from those who are weak or needy or sinful. In this manner, Christian gratitude clears the way for that sense of identification with others that is so basic to compassion.

But Christian gratitude is much more than a sense of absolute dependency. That by itself would not motivate compassion. If I am grateful to God in Jesus Christ, I see myself as perfectly and radically blessed, as accepted and important in the universe, as one on whom God's love has been showered, as a worthy one. Perfect Christian gratitude is not just a sense of absolute dependency, but also a sense of spiritual well-being. It unites being bowed down with being exalted. So gratitude involves the self-confidence that is also necessary to compassion. To be grateful is to have the self-possession to be unselfish, to be sufficiently secure at the center not to be self-centered. Gratitude is the self-accepting acceptance of God's gift; it is the healthy being-at-one with myself as poor and weak and unworthy. And so genuine gratitude to God practically guarantees compassion. To the person who is filled with thankfulness to God in Jesus Christ, compassion is not a duty to which he forces himself more or less against his will; being outgoing, self-giving, is "natural."

Christian hope is the construal of our future as life without death in a state of perfect obedience to God and perfect fellowship with all others. Like gratitude, it predisposes or enables compassion in at least two ways. First, it can dispel a basic cause of our faltering in compassion. When a person we are trying to help is obtuse to our graces or makes no progress, we may lose enthusiasm and tend to go our own more selfish way, thinking the situation hopeless. And there may *be* little or no hope, by worldly ways of reckoning, for a person who is ill, or mutilated by a perverse upbringing, or deficient mentally. And sin seems so intractable. Furthermore, from the purely secular standpoint there isn't any ultimate hope for any of us. As

Bertrand Russell declares, ". . . that no fire, no heroism, no intensity of thought and feeling, can preserve an individual life beyond the grave; that all the labours of the ages, all the devotion, all the inspiration, all the noon-day brightness of human genius, are destined to extinction in the vast death of the solar system" (*Mysticism and Logic,* p. 51), is a fact that must underlie our entire outlook on ourselves and others, if we are lucid secularists. It is al-most a tautology that hopelessness, whether particularized or cosmic, tends to discourage. What is the use of going on, if in the end I will inevitably be foiled? If all is vanity, why should I bother with the unnatural project of identifying with the poor and weak when I am rich and strong? Why should I not accept the advice of Solomon, that "a man can do nothing better than to eat and drink and find satisfaction in his work" (Ecclesiastes 2:24)? But in hope the Christian dares to believe that the things he does in imitation of Jesus are not destined to be foiled. Much of human endeavor will be brought to nothing, but these imitative acts will count; they will somehow be taken up and preserved in the kingdom (I Corinthians 15:58). And so in the face of the many appearances that discourage compassion, the Christian's hope is a source of strength.

Christian hope not only defends our compassion against the discour-agement of hopelessness; also, something about the thing Christians hope for presses us toward compassion. We hope for the kingdom of God, the kingdom that began to break in on the world in the life and death of Jesus. We hope for a social condition in which our own identification with one another will reflect Christ's identification with each of us. A sharp example of the way the Christian vision of the kingdom determines compassion is found in Malcolm Muggeridge's book on Mother Teresa of Calcutta, *Something Beautiful for God:*

> Accompanying Mother Teresa, as we did, to these different activities for the purpose of filming them — to the Home for the Dying, to the lepers and unwanted children, I found I went through three phases. The first was horror mixed with pity, the second compassion pure and simple, and the third, reaching far beyond compassion, something I had never expe-rienced before — an awareness that these dying and derelict men and women, these lepers with stumps instead of hands, these unwanted chil-dren, were not pitiable, repulsive or forlorn, but rather dear and delight-ful; as it might be, friends of long standing, brothers and sisters. How is it to be explained, the very heart and mystery of the Christian faith? To

soothe those battered old heads, to grasp those poor stumps, to take in one's arms those children consigned to dustbins, because it is his head, as they are his stumps and his children, of whom he said that whosoever received one such child in his name received Him. (p. 38)

Jesus called himself the light of the world, and this incident is a vivid instance of his shedding light. The third phase of Muggeridge's consciousness of the people to whom Teresa was ministering is what I have been calling compassion: in these weak and suffering ones, Muggeridge sees "dear and delightful . . . friends of long standing, brothers and sisters." But he sees them as his brothers and sisters because he sees them as ones whom Christ first identified with, owning them as his brothers and sisters. Christ's identification with ones like these was so complete that he could say that whoever received one of these in his name received himself. So Jesus is the light that shines on these derelicts and lepers and unwanted children and reveals, to those who have eyes to see, that they are dear brothers and sisters, fellow members of the kingdom of God. This is Christian compassion.

Jesus called not only himself but also his disciples the light of the world. Teresa was in fact functioning as such a light to the eyes of Muggeridge that day. Perhaps he would never have seen those people as they were, would never have got beyond his "horror mixed with pity" and his "compassion pure and simple," had he not been introduced to them by that holy woman. She was a derivative light for lighting up blind eyes and letting them see with compassion — derivative from her Lord. Just as he created, by his compassion, a miniature and a foretaste of his kingdom on the hills and in the towns of Galilee and Judea, so she created a miniature and foretaste of it in the heart of Calcutta.

COMPASSION FOR WINNERS

Compassion is directed primarily at people who are in some obvious trouble. But I want to say a word or two about the relevance of compassion to people who to all appearances are "winners." Such people, especially if they are arrogant or ruthless, may not seem fit objects of compassion. And yet they very often (always?) are. Sometimes the most powerful and crass person is really a sufferer, a lonely one, a frightened one. It takes resoluteness and a bit of empathetic insight to see through the facade of strength and boasting and arrogance and wealth and power and intelligence and to see one who is in trouble, one of God's lost sheep. Consider the following case, which is partially fictionalized.

On the surface Pastor Q ruled the church with an iron hand, used "political" tactics to consolidate and perpetuate the power of his position, and reserved his attention for the rich and powerful people in the congregation. He centered his "ministry" on things that showed to the lust of the eyes and the pride of life, such as thick new carpets and curtains for the parlor, perpetual paint jobs throughout the building, landscaping, and a smooth and sumptuous Sunday morning service. He tended to undercut the position of his colleagues on the church staff, and not to communicate with them. He knew what the gospel was, because he persuasively included it in five or six sermons during his seven-year tenure in the church. But in retrospect one suspected that those were calculated occasions, the last one being the morning on which the pastoral search committee from a plush church on the West Coast was visiting. To the relief of the more discerning members of the congregation, that committee took the bait.

The church member (let's call him Z) had a stormy relationship with Q during his pastorate. An especially difficult episode occurred when the Consistory was sponsoring the purchase of a rather expensive fence to protect the churchyard from unwelcome feet. In a meeting he raised an objection to this use of the Lord's money, and was told by Q that the proper channel for such an objection was a letter to the Consistory. As he wrote the letter, it bore in on him that the fence folly was not isolated, but was the result of the church's not being given spiritual leadership. So he decided to surround the fence with its spiritual context by including in the letter an analytical critique of two or three of Q's recent sermons, and challenging the members of the Consistory to require Q to teach Christian discipleship, thus warding off future fence follies. When Q recommended a letter to the Consistory, he didn't have this in mind.

When the letter was read before the elders at the next meeting of the Consistory, Q was furious and dismayed. His hand was being called before the very people whose trust and respect he most needed. When Z got wind of how much Q felt personally injured by the letter, he called him up and apologized, as far as he could, and sought reconciliation. The reconciliation was at best grudging and distrustful, but it did mean that the two men saw one another more frequently than hitherto. For a few Sundays after the letter the sermons seemed to have a bit more Christian content, but the effect did not last long, and on the whole the letter seemed only to have made Q still more self-protective and ruthless in his methods.

Z admits that in his naïveté he was surprised to see that the letter caused Q such a sense of personal injury. Q had appeared to him a tough guy who could take anything, a dapper sophisticate in command of the situation, clear about what he wanted and ruthless in getting it. When it appeared how wrought up he became, Z began to see him differently. He now seemed almost like a confused child. Maybe he was desperately grasping after control of others because he felt so powerless and out of control of himself. Throughout his relationship with Q, Z vacillated between an angry view of him and a more compassionate one. Sometimes he wanted to do anything he could to run Q out of town, to get him to stop destroying the church, and to punish him for the damage he had already done. But at times of more penetrating insight, his heart went out to him in the desire to nurture this lost soul. He found himself struggling to see more compassionately and very often, to his discredit, losing the struggle.

I am not saying there is never a time to be angry and hold a person responsible for his misdeeds. But often behind those misdeeds is also a crippled person, who needs not attacking, but help. And even if we decide, after due searching with the eyes of compassion, that strong opposition is called for, the strategy of the opposition will almost always be qualified by the compassion. In the case of Z, if he had had the insight of compassion from the beginning of his tangle with the pastor, he would probably not have written that letter; he would have anticipated the hurt and hardening that it would cause. He might instead have tried to befriend Q, to nurture him toward reform rather than just blast him out of the saddle. To be always poised to address weakness and suffering is the strong and creative compassion of the Christian. To search the situation compassionately (even if, in the unlikely event, one doesn't find any weakness in the offending person) is to soften and humanize one's approach, and probably to make it more effective in changing people for the good. When it comes to improving people, love is stronger than anger, and nurture more effective than injury.

DISCIPLINES OF COMPASSION

Before we end, let's ask how we can nurture compassion in ourselves. How can we become more spiritual, more prolific bearers of this fruit of the

Spirit of our Lord Jesus Christ? The answers, it seems to me, divide into three groups: first, we must do those things that create in us a passion for the kingdom of God; second, we must act compassionately; and third, we must set our minds daily on the things of the Spirit.

All of the peculiarly Christian emotions are founded on a passionate interest in the kingdom of God. We have seen this in Chapters 7–11. The relation of compassion to this fundamental Christian enthusiasm is somewhat less direct. When I give thanks in the most centrally Christian manner, I give thanks for the kingdom of God or for my inclusion in it. When I hope in the most centrally Christian manner, I hope for the kingdom of God. But when I am compassionate in the most centrally Christian manner, I am not compassionate toward the kingdom of God. Instead, I am compassionate toward a "neighbor," some individual or group of individuals with whom I have to do. I model my compassion on that act by which God established his kingdom (the incarnation); I am moved to compassion partly by my gratitude to God who has spared me for his kingdom; and in compassion I see my neighbor by the light of the kingdom, seeing him as one with whom Christ has compassionately identified himself. So compassion is tied in tightly with the gospel manner of construing the world, and takes root in the individual heart in ultimately the same way that the gospel does: by infusing the individual with a passionate concern for God's kingdom and for his or her participation in it. Thus a fundamental, though somewhat indirect, way of nurturing compassion is to undertake the disciplines described in Chapters 4 through 6.

The second kind of discipline for deepening compassion is action. Even if I do not feel very compassionate at a given moment, I may still be in a position to say a kind word, lend a hand, or make some gesture of solidarity. And if I do, it's a good chance that felt compassion will not be long in coming. First, my action tends to influence my construal of the other; in performing a gesture of solidarity with another I am likely to begin to see myself as in solidarity with him (especially if I am aware that he sees me as in solidarity with him). Second, such an action tends to draw me into practical fellowship with the other, and so to introduce me more intimately to his humanity and his troubles, thus giving me more vivid grounds for empathy. And third, if he in turn welcomes my action, this is likely to lure me into the fellowship (after all, being a love among equals, compassion is ultimately and ideally a form of friendship) and thus to deepen my present compassion — not to mention the positive reinforcement it gives me for compassionate acts in general.

Finally, St. Paul says that "those who live according to the sinful nature have their *minds* set on what that nature desires; but those who live in accordance with the Spirit have their *minds* set on what the Spirit desires" (Romans 8:5), and he says to the Philippians, "Finally, brothers, whatever is true, whatever is noble, whatever is right, whatever is pure, whatever is lovely, whatever is admirable — if anything is excellent or praiseworthy — *think* about such things" (Philippians 4:8; my italics). Having the Christian virtues is at least partly a matter of what occupies a person's thoughts. Salacious thoughts make one salacious; covetous thoughts make one covetous; generous thoughts make one generous; and God-loving thoughts make one a lover of God. I have argued throughout this book that Christian spirituality is a way of construing or attending to or thinking about ourselves, our world, and God. If that is true, it is natural that one kind of spiritual discipline that has always had a place in Christianity is meditation: setting one's mind on the things of the Spirit.

But what are the things of the Spirit, and what does it mean to set one's mind on them? I do not think Paul is recommending that we dwell on the doctrine of the third person of the Trinity. He is not urging us to become experts on pneumatology! The things of the Spirit are the things that belong to the Spirit of God, that evince his Spirit, things that God loves and that are fruit of his Spirit. The most central "thing of the Spirit" is Jesus Christ himself. One who wishes to become more compassionate will do well to turn his thoughts very definitely for a time each day to the compassion of God in Jesus Christ. As meditation on God's grace begins to take root in him, his way of looking at things will be gradually transformed. Another kind of thing of the Spirit is the lives and actions and words of spiritual Christians. To read or hear about Mother Teresa or Francis of Assisi can contribute powerfully to the formation of compassion in a Christian's heart. And even books like the present one (I like to believe), in which we think a bit analytically and methodically about the Christian virtues, can perhaps turn a person's mind to the things of the Spirit — for humility, gratitude, hope, compassion, peace, and longing for the kingdom of God are surely also things of the Spirit.

This is meditation that one does in a quiet hour alone with the Bible or some other book or sitting in church. But there is another kind, without which meditation in this more usual sense would be of little avail, a meditation that occurs in the midst of the activities and interactions of life. It is done not in the closet but in the street, the office, the factory, at the dinner table, the beach, the football game. I am driving to work in heavy traffic and make a blunder, infuriating the driver behind me. When he gets a chance, he screeches around me, honking his horn and making an obscene gesture. This circumstance does not lend itself to compassionate seeing, but it is an opportunity for such. And so I remind myself that Christ died for that man as he did for me, that he and I are fellows in our vulnerability and sin. Perhaps I think of the times I have been irritated in traffic, and speculate about what might be eating him. The Christian, unless he is a perfect saint, will find that compassionate seeing requires vigilance and continued effort. It requires concerted acts of compassionate attention throughout the day, a stretching of one's self-conceptions, active searching for hints of commonality with other persons, and intentional use of the gospel as a visualizing framework.

Works Cited

Anscombe, Elizabeth. "Modern Moral Philosophy" in *Philosophy* 33 (1958): 1-19.

Aristotle. *Nicomachean Ethics,* translated with an Introduction by David Ross, revised by J. L. Ackrill and J. O. Urmson (Oxford: Oxford University Press, 1980).

Augustine. *Confessions,* translated by E. B. Pusey (New York: Dutton, 1962).

Aurelius, Marcus. *Meditations,* translated by G. M. A. Grube (Indianapolis: Hackett Publishing Company, 1983).

Barfoot, Edith. *The Witness of Edith Barfoot,* edited by Sir Basil Blackwell (Oxford: Basil Blackwell, 1977).

Becker, Ernest. *The Denial of Death* (New York: The Free Press, 1973).

Boswell, James. *The Life of Johnson,* edited by Christopher Hibbert (New York: Penguin Books, 1979).

Corrigan, John. *Business of the Heart* (Berkeley: University of California Press, 2002).

Damasio, Antonio. *Descartes' Error: Emotion, Reason, and the Human Brain* (New York: Avon Books, 1994).

Dickens, Charles. *David Copperfield* (New York: Modern Library, 1900).

Dixon, Thomas. *From Passions to Emotions: The Creation of a Secular Psychological Category* (Cambridge: Cambridge University Press, 2003).

Dostoevsky, Fyodor. *Crime and Punishment,* translated by Constance Garnett (New York: Everyman's Library, 1993).

Edwards, Jonathan. *Religious Affections,* edited by John E. Smith (New Haven: Yale University Press, 1959).

Epictetus. *Enchiridion,* translated by Thomas W. Higginson (Indianapolis: Bobbs-Merrill, 1948).

Freud, Sigmund. *The Future of an Illusion,* translated by W. D. Robson-Scott, revised and edited by James Strachey (Garden City, NY: Doubleday Anchor, 1964).

Frijda, Nico. *The Emotions* (Cambridge: Cambridge University Press, 1986).

Griffiths, Paul E. *What Emotions Really Are* (Chicago: University of Chicago Press, 1997).

Griffiths, Paul J. *On Being Mindless: Buddhist Meditation and the Mind-Body Problem* (La Salle, Illinois: Open Court, 1986).

Herbert, R. T. *Paradox and Identity in Theology* (Ithaca: Cornell University Press, 1979).

Hilton, Walter. *The Stairway of Perfection,* translated by M. L. Del Mastro (Garden City: Doubleday, 1979).

James, William. *The Principles of Psychology,* 2 volumes (New York: Dover Publications, 1950).

Johnson, Samuel. *Life of Savage* (Oxford: Clarendon Press, 1971).

Kant, Immanuel. *Foundations of the Metaphysics of Morals,* translated by Lewis White Beck (Indianapolis: Bobbs-Merrill, 1959).

Kierkegaard, Søren. *Concluding Unscientific Postscript,* translated by Howard V. Hong and Edna H. Hong (Princeton: Princeton University Press, 1992).

Kierkegaard, Søren. *The Sickness unto Death,* translated by Howard and Edna Hong (Princeton: Princeton University Press, 1980).

Lazarus, Richard. *Emotion and Adaptation* (New York: Oxford University Press, 1991).

LeDoux, Joseph. *The Emotional Brain: The Mysterious Underpinnings of Emotional Life* (New York: Touchstone, 1998).

Lewis, C. S. *Miracles* (New York: The Macmillan Company, 1947).

Lewis, C. S. *The Abolition of Man* (New York: The Macmillan Company, 1947).

Lewis, C. S. *The Great Divorce* (New York: The Macmillan Company, 1946).

Liddy, G. Gordon. *Will: The Autobiography of G. Gordon Liddy* (New York: St. Martin's Press, 1980).

Lutz, Catherine. *Unnatural Emotions: Everyday Sentiments on a Micro-*

nesian Atoll and Their Challenge to Western Theory (Chicago: University of Chicago Press, 1988).

MacDougall, William. *Character and the Conduct of Life* (London: Methuen Publishers, 1927).

Moltmann, Jürgen. *Theology of Hope,* translated by James Leitch (New York: Harper and Row, 1967).

Muggeridge, Malcolm. *Something Beautiful for God* (Garden City: Doubleday, 1977).

Murdoch, Iris. *The Sovereignty of Good* (New York: Schocken Books, 1971).

Newberg, Andrew, and Eugene D'Aquili. *Why God Won't Go Away* (New York: Ballantine Books, 2001).

Nussbaum, Martha. *Upheavals of Thought* (Cambridge: Cambridge University Press, 2001).

Oatley, Keith. *Best Laid Schemes: The Psychology of the Emotions* (Cambridge: Cambridge University Press, 1992).

Phillips, D. Z. *Death and Immortality* (London: Macmillan, 1970).

Pinch, Adela. *Strange Fits of Passion: Epistemologies of Emotion, Hume to Austen* (Stanford: Stanford University Press, 1996).

Plato. *Great Dialogues of Plato,* translated by W. H. D. Rouse (New York: New American Library, 1956).

Prinz, Jesse. *Gut Reactions: A Perceptual Theory of Emotion* (Oxford: Oxford University Press, 2004).

Roberts, Robert C. *Emotions: An Essay in Aid of Moral Psychology* (Cambridge: Cambridge University Press, 2003).

Roberts, Robert C. *Taking the Word to Heart: Self and Other in an Age of Therapies* (Grand Rapids: Wm. B. Eerdmans Publishing Company, 1993).

Rosaldo, Michelle. *Knowledge and Passion: Ilongot Notions of Self and Social Life* (Cambridge: Cambridge University Press, 1980).

Russell, Bertrand. "A Free Man's Worship" in *Mysticism and Logic* (Harmondsworth, Middlesex: Penguin Books, 1953).

Seligman, Martin (with Christopher Peterson). *Character Strengths and Virtues: A Handbook and Classification* (Oxford: Oxford University Press, 2004).

Seneca, *On Favors.* In John M. Cooper and J. F. Procopé, editors and translators, *Moral and Political Essays* (Cambridge: Cambridge University Press, 1995).

Singer, Isaac Bashevis. *The Penitent* (New York: Farrar, Straus, Giroux, 1983).

Solomon, Robert C., *The Passions* (Garden City, New York: Doubleday, 1976; currently in print from Hackett Publishing Company).

Spacks, Patricia Meyer. *Boredom: The Literary History of a State of Mind* (Chicago: University of Chicago Press, 1995).

Steinbeck, John. *The Grapes of Wrath* (New York: Viking Press, 1940).

Steindl-Rast, Brother David. "Gratitude as Thankfulness and as Gratefulness" in Robert Emmons and Michael McCullough, editors, *The Psychology of Gratitude* (New York: Oxford University Press, 2004).

The Book of Common Prayer (New York: Oxford University Press, 1990).

The Book of Common Prayer (New York: The Church Pension Fund, 1945).

Tolstoy, Leo. *A Confession* and *What I Believe,* translated by Aylmer Maude (London: Oxford University Press, 1940).

Tolstoy, Leo. *The Death of Ivan Ilych and Other Stories,* with an afterword by David Magarshack, "The Death of Ivan Ilych," translated by Aylmer Maude (New York: New American Library, 1960).

Vitz, Paul. *Sigmund Freud's Christian Unconscious* (New York: Guilford Press, 1988).

Whitman, Walt. *Leaves of Grass* (New York: Modern Library, 1940).

Wittgenstein, Ludwig. *Tractatus Logico-Philosophicus,* translated by D. F. Pears and B. F. McGuinness (London: Routlege and Kegan Paul, 1961).

Index